Praise for *Smoking in Bed: Conversations with Bruce Robinson*, edited by Alistair Owen

e most purely likeable book about cinema I have ever read.
ɔinson talks about his profession in a way that is astonishingly
ɪr-headed, funny and wise'

David Hare, *Guardian*, Books of the Year

are and fulsome entertainment'

Select

nsistently enthralling, exhibiting impressive political and artistic
sciousness and the famed razor wit'

Observer

e recollections of Robinson are a treat'

Independent

binson's fiery intelligence blazes through, every sentence testa-
ɪt to his brilliant way with language'

Nova

ious and lyrical'

Sunday Times

ellent accounts of Robinson's work and an acute sense of the
enwriter's lot'

Total Film

goldmine of wit, wisdom and plain old bitchiness'

Empire

veals Robinson to be as lavishly down-at-heel, inspired and
dpan subversive as Withnail, his creation'

Daily Mail

cracking book of interviews'

Loaded

ith his spontaneous remarks reading like polished prose, these
ɪversations are a reminder of how entertaining the man can be'

Independent on Sunday

e next best thing to a one-to-one'

Time Out

ve with Robinson's voice, his turn of phrase, his passionate
essions. It's as if it has sneaked up on literature by not ever
sidering itself as such. His conversation is a work of art'

Nicholas

STORY AND CHARACTER

STORY AND CHARACTER

INTERVIEWS WITH BRITISH SCREENWRITERS

EDITED BY ALISTAIR OWEN

BLOOMSBURY

First published in Great Britain 2003

Introduction and commentary copyright © 2003 by Alistair Owen .
Copyright in the individual interviews remains with the respective interviewees

Photograph credits:
Rupert Walters © Johnny Haddock; Lee Hall © Simon Annand; Richard Curtis ©
Rex Features; Frank Cottrell Boyce © Liverpool Daily Post & Echo; Neal Purvis &
Robert Wade © Danjaq, LLC and United Artists Corporation; Shawn Slovo ©
Nigel Sutton; William Boyd © Jerry Bauer; Hossein Anini © Alex Jefford; Simon
Beaufoy © Sharon Thomas

The moral right of the authors has been asserted

Bloomsbury Publishing Plc, 38 Soho Square, London W1D 3HB

A CIP catalogue record for this book
is available from the British Library

ISBN 0 7475 5930 9

10 9 8 7 6 5 4 3 2 1

Typeset by Hewer Text Ltd, Edinburgh
Printed in Great Britain by Clays Ltd, St Ives plc

Contents

Introduction

This is the first ever anthology of interviews with British screenwriters. That gives you some idea of how the British regard screenwriting.

The real question is: why? Why do the press and the public ignore screenwriters while lionising stars and directors? Is it because stars are glamorous and directors are powerful and screenwriters are rarely either – even though they may provide the three ingredients in Alfred Hitchcock's famous recipe for making a great movie: 'a great script, a great script and a great script'? Is it because most films have just one director but many have more than one screenwriter, some of whom receive a credit for drafts long-since abandoned while others remain uncredited despite contributing nearly half the shooting script, reinforcing the old adage 'Film is a director's medium'? Is it because scripts are often changed to accommodate the requirements of the latest star or director attached to the project, rather than stars and directors accommodating themselves to the requirements of the script, reinforcing a newer adage, 'Film is a collaborative business – bend over'? Is it because a large proportion of films are adaptations of one sort or another, casting screenwriters as handmaidens or hatchet men beside the 'proper' writers whose books or plays they are adapting? Or is it because a good book or a good play is likely to be published or performed in the way its author intended, instead of being rewritten again and again and again and then written off entirely, as fine screenplays often are?

The answer, I think, is: all of the above – none of which diminishes the central role of screenwriting in popular cinema, a role which this book sets out to explore through thematic and technical discussions of the produced and unproduced work of leading British screenwriters. The book is not, however, a comprehensive survey of British screenwriting: among the anthologies waiting to be compiled are interviews with older screenwriters (all of the chosen interviewees were born between 1950 and 1966, but the thirties and forties produced many acclaimed dramatists), interviews with television writers (several of the interviewees talk about their work for TV, but the main focus is the big screen) and interviews with writer-directors (two of the interviewees have directed one feature apiece, but both are primarily writers). Nor is it a forensic study of the British film industry; nevertheless, much can be inferred from the fact that the interviewees all write or have written for American companies, or for British companies financed by America (FilmFour for example, a bastion of British film production for two decades, which is being wound up as I proof read these pages, Warner Bros co-production deal notwithstanding). It is, then, a broadly mainstream selection of British screenwriters, which happens to reflect my own interests and ambitions, although the final line-up would have been a little more eclectic if time and space had allowed me to include every screenwriter who generously agreed to be interviewed.

Each interview is preceded by a chronology of the interviewee's work at the time the book goes to press, with projects listed in up to four main categories. 'Film' covers theatrical features either released or in production; specified are the director, the year of first release and the country or countries of origin. 'Television' covers serials, dramas and sitcoms aired on British terrestrial TV; specified here are the director, the year the work was first broadcast and the channel which first broadcast it. 'Uncredited' covers theatrical features for which the interviewees either wrote an entire screenplay or were employed to 'polish' an existing draft; specified again are the director, the year of first release and the country or countries of origin. 'Screenplays' covers scripts either unproduced or in development; specified in this case is the studio or production company initially or currently involved, or else entries are simply marked 'spec' to indicate that the interviewees control the rights personally. By the time the book is published, some scripts which were in development may have gone into production, possibly under different titles and credited to different screenwriters; and, since certain interviewees requested that particular scripts should not be included among their work – despite, in one or two instances, discussing them in the actual interviews – these lists should be treated as a useful guide rather than taken as absolute gospel.

Finally, a big thank you is in order: to my family, to my friends (particularly Greg Owens), to my girlfriend, to my publishers (specifically Mike Jones), to the agents and PAs of all the interviewees, and, of course, to the interviewees themselves – last, but definitely *not* least.

Alistair Owen, July 2002

Rupert Walters was born in 1960, in Cardiff, and educated at St Edward's School, Oxford, and Oriel College, Oxford. He is married with three children and lives in London.

FILM

Privileged (Michael Hoffman, 1982, UK)
Sisters (Michael Hoffman, 1988, US)

Restoration (Michael Hoffman, 1996, US)
True Blue (Ferdinand Fairfax, 1996, UK)

SCREENPLAYS

Blue Moon (spec)
The Day of Two Suns (Wildwood Enterprises)
Pride and Prejudice (Warner Bros)
Quasimodo (Disney)

The Realm (DreamWorks)
The Devil Soldier (Paramount)
The Eve of St Agnes (spec)
untitled Michael Mann project (Disney)

The first film you received a credit for, *Privileged*, was one of the only student films ever to get a cinema release; it also spawned the careers of director Michael Hoffman, composer Rachel Portman and cinematographer Ueli Steiger, not to mention Hugh Grant. Pretty good for your début script.

I wasn't solely responsible for it; I just came up with some of the ideas. It may have looked like a script, but I'm sure it didn't feel like one. The problem with making films is that the learning process is a very public one and your mistakes are up there for everybody to see. If you did a little play with your friends no one would be asking you about it twenty years later. It started life as a little film we were going to make in the college, but this was at the time of *Chariots of Fire*, and an extremely good American producer called Rick Stevenson, who was there on a scholarship, said, 'Why don't we make a film with that sort of ambition?' He managed to raise £30,000, and got people like John Schlesinger and David Puttnam involved, and the film made its money back within two years. In Britain that year there were literally five films being made – of which that was one.

Was it your ambition to be a screenwriter?

Not really. It's such an alien process. I'd done a bit of writing at Oxford, a few sketches for revue shows, but before I got involved in *Privileged* it had never occurred to me that films were actually written. I went to school in Oxford as well, and there's a terrific repertory cinema in the town, the Penultimate Picture Palace, where the main fare was Bertolucci, Pasolini, Truffaut, Rohmer and Bergman, but I didn't know how these films got on to the screen. I came from a classic middle-class professional family – my parents hadn't been to the cinema since *Birth of a Nation* – and although I never came under any pressure to be a lawyer or a doctor, who knew what film involved?

Privileged must have led to a few offers, though.

I don't think any of us were flooded with offers. It didn't lead to anything for me. There wasn't anything going on in the film industry in this country. I went to university again. I got a scholarship from the Rhodes foundation to go to Canada and lived there for a couple of years. I did do some film work when I was out there. You could sit in on other people's courses, so I did a theatre-directing course and a Super-8 film-making course. I still wanted to convince myself that this was what I wanted to do. The phone wasn't ringing, saying, 'Come and write a series for the BBC', and there was this little story which I wanted to write, *Sisters*, so I decided to write it as a film. I didn't even know if it would work as a film, but I found that more interesting than tackling the story as a play or a novel – neither of which I ever began to write. There aren't many people who are good at writing for more than one medium and I think the reason for that is it's difficult to move between them. Some people are good at both playwriting and screenwriting, say, but they tend to be outstanding at one and OK at the other. Film is quite a technical way of writing and it takes a long time before you start using the form to its best advantage, but you get better not just at telling stories in that way but also at thinking about them in that way.

You spent some time at the Sundance Institute, together with Michael Hoffman and Rick Stevenson. How did that come about?

Mike and Rick did another film, called *Promised Land*, which Robert Redford executive produced and I had nothing to do with. When I say I had nothing to do with it, I mean I would read it and talk about it but didn't actually do any work on it. Mike and I always tend to do that if we're working on a script with someone else. Then I took a draft of *Sisters* to Sundance and actually got turned down, but Redford wanted it to go up so I was a slight pariah there. I remember everyone from New York wearing black, and I was wearing my Marks & Spencer tweed jacket – in Utah in June. I wasn't really part of the in-crowd, although I did share a house with a great editor, Jim Clark, and some really fascinating people read my script, like the great blacklisted screenwriter Abe Polonsky. Sundance at that time was just a radical idea of Redford's to discover and develop new writing talent, but it was run by a very interesting Czech guy called Frank Danielle, who also ran the film school at the University of Southern California, and the conversations that went on in the evening were as intriguing as someone giving you their suggestions about your script.

What was the reaction to your script?

Very generous. You get that in the States. Of course, there's two ways of looking at it – one of which is that it's effusive bullshit – but I think there's a generosity of approach: 'This is what you're trying to do and we'll try to help you.' That's why Sundance works: people don't have an agenda. They're not trying to make the script into something for themselves; they're just trying to help you work out how to do it better. It was a packed couple of weeks, and people took you incredibly seriously, which was really reassuring.

It must have been even more reassuring when Michael Hoffman wanted to direct *Sisters*.

One of the reasons I was interested in writing films was that I liked the collaborative aspect of the business, and it turned out that Mike and I spoke the same language. He thought that *Sisters* was something he'd direct well, Redford stayed on as executive producer, MGM ended up paying for it and we shot it later that year or early the next. A lot of people do good work in a partnership of some kind, particularly a writer and a director, and we have a number of things on the boil. It gets harder, because directors tend to have a lot of projects in the pipeline and I might be one of five writers working for him at any one time. Just because you know him doesn't mean you go higher up the pecking order.

Presumably by now you knew that screenwriting was what you wanted to do, so how did you set about learning the craft?

I began to read the scripts of my favourite films and I discovered that sometimes the scripts are even better than the finished product. I often go back and read something I really admire before I start to write something of my own. Everyone talks about the script being a blueprint – and it is, in the sense that it gets turned into something else – but it also has to be a piece of writing which stands up on its own, because the producer who's deciding whether to pay for it and the actor who's deciding whether to be in it want to be transported by the experience of reading it. Novelists are famously sniffy about the place of screenwriters in the order of things, but it seems to me to be as hard and as important a writing form. If you read a script by Steven Zaillian you realise how well written it is, even though if it doesn't get made only about forty people will ever see it. These guys are really good writers and they've chosen to write films.

When did you get an agent?

Around the time of Sundance; a great agent called Jim Crabbe who's now a producer. A powerful agent with a big list can get you in the door to a lot of places because they say, 'In exchange for seeing so-and-so will you see this person?' but on the other hand you wonder how much time they plan to spend on you. Jim hadn't been doing it for that long and I got the sense that we grew up together, as opposed to being with someone who looked after William Goldman. I was really happy to be with him so I didn't have a lot of other meetings. I remember having

9

lunch with him and a few other people at the Beverly Hills Hotel, and I thought, 'This doesn't happen every day.' So I ordered veal and a beer, and he looked at me and said, 'Guess who doesn't live in California.' Now, of course, I order chicken salad and iced tea like everybody else – and hold the sesame oil.

Sisters is a very offbeat romantic comedy set in Canada, where you were living when you wrote it. Was it based on experiences you had while you were there?

Everything is autobiographical and at the same time everything is fiction. I knew somebody there who provided the basis for a story, and events which had happened to other people were laid on top, but your perception of anything is so different from someone else's that they wouldn't necessarily recognise themselves in it. Experience is a potent source of material for some writers, in terms of relationships with family or friends or girlfriends – 'Write what you know', as everybody says – but I just took what was concerning me at the time and thought, 'Maybe I could write a story about this.'

The critics perceived it as a romantic comedy and complained about the farce and fantasy elements. Did you have a particular genre in mind?

No, I didn't. I wasn't thinking, 'I want to do a romance', or, 'I want to do a comedy'. I do think serious points can be made really well with comedy and I don't think you undermine the dramatic content of a piece by allowing the audience to have a laugh. In one of his books about the theatre, Simon Gray was talking about how you approach character, and he said that a friend of his got a call telling him that his father was dying and his reaction was, 'Damn, that means I'm going to miss the football.' This man was fond of his father and fond of football and that was just his human reaction, instead of, 'Oh, how sad.' In a general sense, people fall in love, and other people die, and those things happen together rather than one set of things in your life being funny and another set of things being tragic. I don't know whether that works in relation to a movie, but that's what I was interested in writing about and that's probably what confused the critics. It was during the act of writing it that I discovered what the script was about, the nature of the experience the hero has. I roughly knew what the story was but films also need to be about something, to have an idea. It's unpitchable but you can do really interesting work which is unpitchable.

And what *was* the film about – what *was* its idea?

I suppose it was about serendipity. You arrive in a situation expecting one thing and leave it realising that you wanted something else. The hero thinks that he wants the girl, but he actually has a more profound emotional need that her grandmother fulfils. It's not about him trying to find a family because he hasn't got one himself; it's about the mysterious nature of things and the fact that you don't quite know what it is that you want. That idea somehow informed every scene, but for most of the time I was writing the script I wasn't aware of that.

Was the hero an American for commercial reasons?

I didn't initially write him as an American, but it was quite fortunate for me that we cast an American because it meant that I was viewed as being able to write for Americans. It doesn't really matter whether he's English or American as long as he's an outsider. That's the defining narrative need: finding yourself in the middle of a strange world, unable to understand its rules and secrets and traditions. Don DeLillo wrote a piece about families creating their own myths in order to survive, and when you go into one it's always fascinating and baffling how they work.

A father who writes academic books in the nude, for example, and says almost nothing until a scene where he explains . . .

What the film is about, yeah. There's sometimes a point in a piece of dramatic writing – particularly a piece like that, in which everything is so unpredictable – where someone reminds you roughly what the piece is about. That isn't a bad idea. It was also useful to remind *myself* what it was about.

I've never seen a more visually sumptuous comedy. The sisters live in a house designed like a Gothic castle, for example. Did you envisage that in the script?

I suppose there were fairytale qualities in the story, but I didn't sit down and read my Joseph Campbell. You'd be mad to deny that the reason stories work in certain ways is that they have those mythical structures, but I think you're in trouble if you try to do that consciously. That's what directors and designers bring to a story and you hope that the script is robust enough to withstand that sort of attention. I didn't feel there was any element of the story which suffered from that, and in fact those contributions gave it a certain scale – which is never a bad thing for a movie to have.

The script does feature a rather passive leading man; the proactive characters are the sisters. Was that a drawback in critical and commercial terms?

That's an interesting point and an interesting problem. There's a real temptation as a first-time writer to write observant leading characters, because somehow they're you watching what's going on. That's a technical thing which you have to learn to overcome, so you make your protagonist do some of the running instead of just standing around. It works fine in a novel, because the characters have an interior life, but film requires that the interior life is seen, and generally it works better if your protagonist is acting rather than reacting. The danger is that you take it too far and the leading character ends up doing everything. I wrote a script for a well-known American actor – I won't tell you who, because I'd like to work with him again – and it was effectively a three-hander but in the final draft he wanted all the best moments. If you look at those big American movies, you have 150 scenes and the lead actor is in 148 of them.

Your latest spec script, *The Eve of St Agnes*, shares some of the same characteristics. The combination of romance, comedy, farce and fantasy. The mythical overtones. Even the passive hero, knocked from pillar to post.

Maybe I haven't learned that lesson yet. By now I'm probably reacting against it, trying to unlearn it. I wrote *The Eve of St Agnes* as I was writing *The Devil Soldier* for Tom Cruise and John Woo. That project had seven producers, of whom Cruise and Woo were two, and to put it mildly that creates problems about who is running the show. So I thought, 'Let's write something which has no producers on it', and returned to some of the concerns of *Sisters*. I clearly had unfinished business of a sort, not in terms of how that picture was received but because I wanted to write another little thing which interested me regardless of who bought it.

Why do you think that *Sisters* was a commercial failure?

It tested pretty well but it needed sensitive handling, and I don't think anybody knew what to do with it – and anyway, at $3 million what was the point? Rick McCallum, the producer of *Star Wars Episode I*, has pointed out that the budget of *Sisters* was smaller than the salary of the head of MGM. MGM contractually had to put the film on in a handful of cinemas, but they were on the point of being sold and were really interested in realising as many of their assets as they could. It played in the Beverly Center in Los Angeles for about twelve weeks, and all sorts of extraordinary people like Steven Spielberg and Dennis Hopper went to see it and thought it was wonderful, and then it closed because it came out on video. That was a real lesson. The studios always claim they can look after little pictures, but they very rarely can. You're not going to get much coverage because you haven't got big stars, and it's very difficult to get the studio to spend on advertising. It's easy for the publicity department to set up a press junket with Bruce Willis compared to rustling up interest in a small film which cost nothing and would only make a bit more. That's why the appearance of Channel Four here and Miramax in America was a revelation, because you could actually take a small picture like that and make a real go of it. But at that stage, MGM was the only studio who wanted to make that script. People have this notion of bidding wars. I wish. Unless you come up with a high-concept comic idea, like *Twins*, and then there will be five people who want to do it and you can say, 'We may get more money from that lot but are they the right people for the project?'

Why was the film greenlit in the first place?

I suppose they really liked the script. They were really generous with the cast list and that's when you know that someone likes the script. If they say, 'We'll do it if you get Tom Cruise', that's meaningless because they'd do anything with Tom Cruise. They'd make a film of him walking his dog around the block. With this they pretty much said, 'Cast whoever you like.' Then, when it's made, you realise that the world isn't waiting for it and you've even got to force the people who paid for it to distribute it properly. It's baffling.

You also had to change the title in the US, from *Sisters* to *Some Girls*.

Brian De Palma owned that title and wanted to sell it to us for $50,000, which on a $3 million budget is a big chunk.

Have you written any other spec scripts?

After *Sisters*, I turned down everything I was offered because I wanted to do my own stuff. Instead, I wrote another romance, *Blue Moon*, which I ended up doing nothing with. That was a salutary lesson. I did write an epic story with Mike Hoffman about the First World War, but if I'm doing something for myself I tend to take the opportunity to write small things, the sort of things I'm not writing for other people. Someone else is going to be involved in them sooner or later, but you can choose not to make it sooner and allow yourself a greater element of discovery in the writing process. You can do whatever you like with spec scripts, but if you've been commissioned people want to know what you're going to write. They like adaptations because they can see what they are, and you've got to be careful not to change the book too much because that isn't what they want.

Your first adaptation was also your first unproduced script, about Greenpeace founder David McTaggart. Can you tell me a little bit about that?

That was a wonderful project. I had a fantastic time researching and writing it. I've tended to focus on intense domestic drama within the context of period stories, but political things like *Defence of the Realm* and *Edge of Darkness* carry a lot of my preoccupations. It was based on a couple of books that this guy wrote, *Voyage into the Bomb* and *Outrage*, and it was about a midlife crisis and the radicalising of an individual. He was a construction millionaire who owned several ski resorts, but there was a disaster in one of them and somebody got hurt, so he ran away from it all and went to the South Pacific, where he accidentally got involved in the nuclear protests at Murarowa. It was called *The Day of Two Suns*, which was an expression used by the local islanders, and Robert Redford was interested in starring in it. David

McTaggart actually died a couple of months ago, but the project is still around and there are other writers working on it. The action stuff with the bomb going off was all fine but I never really cracked the beginning, and although it's quite a heroic piece it's also quite a tricky sell: a big, expensive, environmental film – on water.

Restoration, again directed by Michael Hoffman, proved an equally tricky sell. Why were you attracted to that adaptation?

Because it's a great book. I haven't been able to read any of Rose Tremain's other books because I want them all to be *Restoration*. I probably wouldn't have thought of making it into a movie – I probably wouldn't have even picked it up off the shelf – but sometimes you do your best work on things which you wouldn't immediately choose if you were left to your own devices. I think one of the things producers and directors and agents are good at is helping you work out what you can do and what you find interesting and what you should spend your time on, and it was great to be given the opportunity of writing something so different and ambitious and unpredictable. Merivel is a great character – an active character, to go back to that earlier point – a character full of ideas and schemes. He's also a man in denial of a great gift, which will come back to him once he's been through this epic journey.

Because of that epic journey, it's not a straightforward novel to adapt.

I agreed to adapt it after reading the first hundred pages, and I didn't realise it was going to be quite so picaresque. The stuff in the court suggested itself so obviously for film, but the hoops that Merivel has to jump through, which work terrifically well as a story, proved more difficult, because audiences want to see the same characters throughout, not meet a whole load of new ones all the time. European audiences don't mind so much but

American audiences aren't particularly used to it, and the fact that we stuck to that made it harder for them than if we'd given it a greater circularity of place and theme. The demands of a script are entirely different from the demands of a novel, and it's difficult to stay true to a novel and make it function as a movie. I think the main requirement is not to make it look like it came from a book, because you can always tell if parts of the story feel unnaturalistic in a literary way. There's a scene in *Howard's End*, the E. M. Forster adaptation, where a guy is crushed by a bookcase. This is a man striving for knowledge, so it's a literary device, but they filmed it like that, and it's an idiotic moment: Man Crushed by Bookcase. You have to reinvent those sort of novelistic devices and not betray their literary roots – in any sense.

In this case you reinvented the interior monologue as voiceover, but voiceover is often used to paper over narrative cracks. Did you always intend to use it?

The film always started with a little bit of voiceover, to set the scene, but we did use it more and more as the cutting went on, to guide the audience through. It can't be an excuse for not creating dramatic scenes, but if you've already done that and you still need some voiceover to help it along, that's fine. Terrence Malick uses it brilliantly in *Days of Heaven*, although someone told me that the reason for that was he edited it for too long and got bored with all the dialogue – and if you watch it closely you realise that each scene finishes just as they were about to start talking. I suppose ideally you wouldn't use voiceover because you'd be able to find pictures that said everything, but when it works well it's brilliant and doesn't feel uncinematic. At the same time, a movie that's in real trouble may also have it, because at the test screenings nobody could make out what's going on. On the other hand, voiceover is used highly successfully in *Apocalypse Now*, and that was added afterwards. It always works particularly well in French with subtitles, so maybe that's what we should have done!

I notice that you stuck quite closely to the language in the book.

The language in the book is really good. You don't write period dialogue in the way that people would have spoken then, but you do make the vocabulary as consistent as possible and try to bring a slight formality to the structure of sentences – which is what Tom Stoppard did with *Shakespeare in Love*, so that it sounded accessible without being anachronistic. The thing about dialogue is that people sometimes say, 'The dialogue in that film was terrible', and normally it's terrible because there's no drama. If you've got a great scene with great characters I don't think it matters what the hell they say. The dialogue is only carrying the weight of a moment, so someone can say, 'Pass the cornflakes', and that can be a knockout line for that situation. But if the story is half-baked, people won't care about the characters and certainly won't care about what the characters are saying. I tend to write a lot of dialogue to begin with because I'm trying to find out who the characters are. Even with an adaptation you have to sit them down in a room and let them talk to each other so that you can understand their behaviour. And when you know them you can find better ways of dealing with them than writing lots of dialogue.

How did you set about reconciling the comic tone in the first half of the novel with the tragic tone in the second?

I tried to balance the two things, to bring in shadows at the beginning so you know that Merivel is living in a false paradise – like that wonderful scene with the exposed heart – then to keep some lightness going in the character amid all the darker stuff. I felt that his character would lead us through the tonal shift, but you weren't going to get away from that tonal shift, and it may have been exacerbated by the huge and colourful settings in the first act. The wedding scene was like a Leonardo design for the Medicis, but it isn't like that in the novel and it wasn't like that in the original version of my screenplay. I remember going to the

London Film Festival screening of *The Insider*, which has an opening sequence in Palestine but then goes on to deal with the tobacco industry, and someone stood up at the end and said to Michael Mann, 'I thought this was going to be a film about terrorism.' Audiences do find it difficult if they're not told exactly what to expect, but you can't really second-guess these things – you can only tell the story as best as you can and hope that it works.

Was it a long script?

I guess it was about 120 pages. Mike Hoffman has a theory that 114 is a lucky number and said that a lot of 114-page scripts get made. I've done things which are considerably longer than that, but I think there's a tendency for films to be far too long. A light film really doesn't need to be above two hours, but you have no idea when you're writing the script. It just ends at some point, be it at 110 or 120 or 150. You have to get it to a length that's conceivable, but it doesn't matter as long as it's between 90 and 130.

It spent a long time in post-production, though. What was the problem?

It wasn't getting the high figures at test screenings which Miramax were after, so they reshot some scenes and added a couple of new ones. They were trying to confront the fact that preview audiences had a problem with Meg Ryan's character, and they also wanted to bump up the whole business of Robert Downey Jr curing people of the plague to give it a bigger feel and get audiences to stay with it longer. I didn't know what else to write, because it seemed to me that we'd done what we set out to do, so instead they hired Tom Stoppard – who probably got paid more for the two scenes he wrote than I got paid for writing the whole thing. I think the figures went up a little bit, but test screenings really work best for genre pieces like *Fatal Attraction*.

Audiences want her to die at the end, so you make her die at the end. Great. You can probably change the figures by twenty points. This was what it was, and there was a limit to what you could do to change that. It's a difficult story, not the sort of easy piece which tends to get those big numbers. It isn't good enough for a film to be as good as *you* think it can be, though, because a lot of people will have to work very hard to get it into the cinemas and *they* need to feel part of it too. Harvey Weinstein is very good at distribution, and if he says he wants to do some more shooting you'd have to be pretty headstrong to say the film should stay the way it is.

Why do you think audiences had a problem with Meg Ryan? Because she was cast against type? Because she was playing a supporting part? Because she only appeared halfway through the film?

I think you've got to be very careful of selling a film on the strength of an actor who's playing a character different from their usual roles. Meg Ryan is a good actress, and that was a very good performance, but it was hard for people to see it as anything but her. If the part had been played by someone who wasn't her but looked like her there wouldn't have been a squeak about it.

Rose Tremain made no bones about her dislike for the finished film. What kind of working relationship did you have before that?

It was a good relationship for quite a long time, in terms of talking about the novel with her and showing her drafts of the script, discussing it with her and getting her input. I didn't feel there was a lot to criticise, because I thought we were pretty truthful to the spirit of the book. It's a great book, and we wanted to adapt that book and not change it into something else. It was pretty unforgivable to go public when she didn't have to option the book in the first place. It's like building a house, selling it, then complaining about the furniture which the new owners put in. If you're that attached to it, hang on to it and furnish the thing yourself. To take the money and then put the boot in is unhelpful and unnecessary. But if a picture makes $100 million, you tend not to get that kind of criticism. When it seems to be a bit of a free-for-all, everyone jumps in.

True Blue, a dramatisation of events surrounding the Oxford Boat Race mutiny, directed by Ferdinand Fairfax, was your first collaboration with a director other than Michael Hoffman, and the first time you hadn't been involved in a project from the start. How did it come about?

I don't exactly know what its history was – I think it was at the BBC, and then it was somewhere else – but there had certainly been more than one writer on it before me. Ferdinand Fairfax asked me once before if I wanted to get involved, but the people who owned it at that point went down a different route. It had always been a story I was really interested in, because it was set in a milieu I was very familiar with. I didn't row myself, but I played a lot of sport and went to a great rowing college, and shared a house with a guy who rowed in the Olympics and was president of the Oxford Boat Club. Of course, a sports film doesn't work simply because it's about teams and how they perform; it has to be about something bigger, like friendship and the choices you make. The Boat Race itself is not a particularly interesting event, just two boats which never overtake each other, but this approach to that event was highly unusual and dramatically charged – about the price that you pay for trying to buy a victory and the realisation of your true potential to do well.

Did you refer to the previous drafts of the script?

I did work from an existing draft which I suspect was quite close to the book. I can't remember whether I was brought in to do some rewriting and ended up doing more and more, or whether I was asked to do what they call a 'page one' rewrite. Some people are really good at coming in and tidying up a few bits and pieces, but there are normally profound reasons why something's not working or can't get finance, and if you just do a bit of fiddling with it, the person reading it again who turned it down six months ago isn't even going to notice that you've changed it. I learned that from writing *Sisters*. You're in a state of utter devastation after tweaking a couple of lines on one page and dropping a scene from another, then you hand it to the director and he isn't aware that anything has happened. It took me years to realise that when a piece of writing isn't working you need to take a deep breath and confront its weaknesses. It's difficult to do. It's much easier to drop a line at the end of a scene than to put in a new idea of some kind.

What qualities do you appreciate in a director?

The main thing I need a director to do – which Michael Hoffman and Ferdinand Fairfax did – is to focus on the narrative through-line. You're banging away at some chatty scene and they're saying, 'What's the point of this? Do we need it? Get me in sooner. Get me out quicker. Get on with it.' Directors can be useful to writers in the same way that editors can be useful to directors. No story editor is as good as a director. Story editors work on a few things, but directors take responsibility for the whole thing. That's why you always lose the argument if the director says on the night before you start shooting, 'I'm going to be on set at six tomorrow morning with a hundred people waiting for me to decide what to do, so the scene is going to be this way.' Having had experiences of working for studios where no one was directly responsible for a project, I decided that one of the essential requirements of the jobs that I was going to do would be a partnership with a director. I haven't always done that, but the ones that I have done in the past few years have been extremely productive –

like the one for Michael Mann. A director who wasn't terribly interested in the script – and surprisingly, there *are* a few – would be a hard relationship for a writer.

The film may have been based on true events, but all the characters were given fictional names except for Donald Mac-donald, the president of the Boat Club, and coach Dan Topolski, the co-author of the original non-fiction book. Did you meet any of the real protagonists apart from those two?

I met one or two, and Ferdy met with a few others. The research process can be very useful, but you have to be careful not to confuse your dramatic premise. Let's say you have a new story to write, a Western. You travel around and meet a couple of cowboys and begin to find your story there. But, once that's locked in, the next lot of research is about filling in the gaps, not finding a new story. The realities of life – that the bad guy is actually rather nice, or whatever – can give colour to a story and make it more complex, but film is essentially a pretty simple way of telling stories, and you do research to fit in with whatever you decide the essence of the piece is.

Topolski was not only the author of the source book and a character in the film, he was also the technical adviser and played a cameo role. Were you put under any pressure to dramatise the mutiny from his point of view?

No. He's a fascinating man, but the film wasn't a eulogy to him. It was hard enough to get the story right anyway, and that sort of pressure would have made it intolerable.

To put it another way, newspaper reports initially suggested that the film would be going easy on the American mutineers, but the reviews eventually asserted that it was too anti-American. What did you make of all that?

23

I didn't have any particular axe to grind. I work in America all the time. It just seemed to me a genuine reflection of what happened, although the nature of the relationship between Macdonald and Topolski, and how their flaws were in large part responsible for the mess that they found themselves in, never came out quite as I intended it to.

The film was promoted as a sort of watery *Chariots of Fire*, but that was about two men instead of ten, competing for their country rather than their university, driven by Jewishness and a faith in Jesus not by a desire to thrash Cambridge. With hindsight, do you think that this story was just too diffuse, too elitist and too ephemeral to make good popular drama?

The way in which ego leads people do to things that they shouldn't seems to me an extremely interesting basis for a piece of writing, but there is a danger of writing stuff that's only understood by the people you know well. I remember reading a review of *Privileged* which said, 'This is exactly the sort of film that people called Rupert and Fiona would make', and I do take the point. As much as you're wrapped up in the postage stamp of territory you're dealing with – to quote Faulkner – it might help to be conscious of how it will play. I don't know how you do that, because in terms of finding and shaping material I tend to think that the biggest mistake a writer can make is to try and second-guess what an audience wants. People who have been working in the industry for fifty years don't know what an audience wants. So, if you've been truthful to the reasons you were interested in telling the story, then you're in with a chance that someone will like it. I clearly thought that this story would work, and in many ways I'm very pleased with it, but it may be difficult for some audiences to understand. I didn't try to avoid the class thing, I just didn't deal with it. The story isn't about that. I think once you get into class you end up writing satire, and satire on film is very hard to do in this country. Trying to write about ten people is a tall order, too, and a complex task in terms of knowing where to focus.

Between *True Blue* and the current untitled Michael Mann project, you worked on a number of period rewrites and adaptations. Presumably you were offered those on the back of *Restoration*, in spite of the way that film was received?

Unless you've got a huge hit on your hands, I don't think studios are terribly interested in how a film played – they just judge the script. That can work in your favour, because everyone appreciates that there are plenty of good scripts around that have not been made. I've also seen it happen the other way around: a film has made a lot of money and a studio has asked to see the script, then the writer wasn't given the job because they didn't think the script was any good.

What was the first of those rewrites and adaptations?

I wrote an adaptation of *Pride and Prejudice* for Warner and Paula Weinstein, who now runs Baltimore Spring Creek with Barry Levinson. That was another one I did with Mike Hoffman, and the project has just come back to life because Nicole Kidman is apparently interested in doing it. It actually turned out that the studio had hired another writer to work on it at the same time: a woman called Susan Shilliday, who wrote *Legends of the Fall*. I know her now so I don't care, but at the time I did care. There are three names on it at the moment, because Mike's been doing some writing on it as well, but I read it again and it seems to be mostly my stuff – or Jane Austen's stuff. There aren't a huge number of period films being made now, but at the time I was writing it there was a lot of interest in everything by Jane Austen and Edith Wharton and Henry James. It's impossible to predict the *zeitgeist*. The way that the studios predict it is by having something of everything on the books, so that if there's a hit 25

Western they can rush the Western into production. You're dependent on that level of fashion. They may not have wanted to make *Pride and Prejudice* then, but they may want to make it next year. I remember when people with Second World War scripts were laughed out of the studio, and now you can't move for khaki and Lee Enfields.

What's your attitude to rewriting the work of other writers, having experienced the process from both sides?

I haven't done a production rewrite, but I have been brought in to do quick rewrites and ended up starting again. If it was a very personal piece of writing I imagine you'd be particularly offended by that, but if someone wants to adapt a book in a different way I think they're welcome to it. I suppose it can be a bit frustrating. I felt that about *Pride and Prejudice*. I don't think it got any worse, but I thought it was pretty good to start with so I couldn't quite see the point. There is a tendency to hire a new writer because no one can think of anything else to do. I met with Istvàn Szabò to discuss *Sunshine*, the film he made with Ralph Fiennes, and I couldn't see what I could bring to it as a writer. He wanted to tell that story that way, and if I was going to tell it I'd tell it in a different way – and there was no point in my doing that. I do have to make a script my own. I find it difficult to sit and look at a scene which I would have done differently. *Quasimodo* actually had an existing script, but again I started from scratch. Ron Bass had written a version from Quasimodo's point of view, which was possibly problematic given that the character is a deaf mute. The novel is pure melodrama, and melodrama works rather well in cinema, but part of my job was to bring it down a bit.

How close did Disney come to making *Quasimodo*?

There has been renewed interest in *Quasimodo*, although not from Disney. There's probably nobody working at Disney

26

now who was working there then except for the guy in the car park – and maybe he's been fired as well. The executives have all gone to other places and some of these other places are interested in it. You only hope that the costs attached to it are not so substantial that they get someone else to write it, given that the book is out of copyright. Disney actually bought another version off the market when I was writing mine because they didn't want any competition out there, which shows how close they got to making it. Terry Gilliam said he wanted to direct it, we worked together on the script, Gérard Depardieu had said yes to Quasimodo and we were thinking of Penélope Cruz for Esmeralda. This was just after the Bigas Luna picture she did, *Jamón, Jamón*, and she would have been perfect. I probably thought of Depardieu quite early on but didn't dare hope anything would come of it, American casting being American casting. We even had people out looking for locations, but then there were political difficulties within the studio, and when Terry saw the animated version he dropped out anyway. Disney had cornered the Quasimodo market and he thought, 'They've used all the shots I wanted to do.' Pictures that almost get made are deeply frustrating, because when they don't happen you might as well have been sitting in the garden all that time. I was really pleased with it, I got paid for it and I got a lot of work out of it, but in some ways it might as well not have been that close.

You then wrote another historical script, this time for Steven Spielberg, called *The Realm*. What was that about?

That was an epic drama about the conflict between Elizabeth I and Mary Queen of Scots. It was based on an existing script – I don't know who by – and again I started over. I read it once and thought, 'We need to do some stuff here', but what I thought was great was the idea of calling it *The Realm*. Because, in the end, that's what it's about. It gives the story a sort of stature. If you're dealing with history it's best to deal with what an old teacher of mine described as the 'Victorian view of history'. Modern history is all about movements and economic trends, whereas Victorian history is all about the individual who changes the course of their world. That's what you need in cinema. So what I did was go back and read the Victorian stories where Elizabeth is solely responsible for everything that goes on within her realm during that time. I'm really pleased with it as a piece of writing, but Spielberg has an enormous number of things in development and is committed up to the hilt. Surprisingly, he seems to *have* to do certain things. There's nothing wrong with doing *The Lost World*, but if he was going to make one film you wouldn't think that a director with his power would choose to do another version of *Jurassic Park*. Clearly, I don't understand it.

What distinguished it from the historical pageants of the sixties and seventies?

I read a comment by Michael Mann about *The Last of the Mohicans*: 'period story, contemporary psychology'. In those historical films of the sixties and seventies, people behave in what appear to be period ways. I understand that manners were different, but the psychology should be the same. Who knows how upset Elizabeth really was about having to kill Mary, but in my script it occurs to her that their families have been slaughtering each other for hundreds of years and she sits down and says, 'This has got to stop.' That's a sort of post-Freudian notion of behaviour, but if you look at a great Shakespearean production it seems to me that the psychology is absolutely modern. Not many of us have been Queen of Scotland – or will be – but you can empathise with her dilemma. Mary is born in a beautiful house in the Loire and given a very privileged upbringing, then her husband, the King of France, suddenly dies, and the Medicis show up asking for the crown jewels back. Two months later, she's in

Edinburgh Castle and has virtually travelled back 200 years in time. That's what you start with. It's a tremendously rich story, and was very exciting to write, but this was around the time of *Elizabeth*, and the guys at Working Title just got on with theirs – so ours was stuck out there on a limb.

Another tremendously rich story was an adaptation of Caleb Carr's non-fiction book *The Devil Soldier*, about an American soldier of fortune in mid-nineteenth century China, which you mentioned writing for Tom Cruise and John Woo.

That was about a war called the Taiping Rebellion, which twenty million people died in and no one has ever heard of. I pushed it for dramatic purposes, but this guy, Ward, was one of the main instruments in putting down this uprising and, again, preventing the continuation of this slaughter. He married the daughter of the guy who employed him, and when he was killed she literally died of a broken heart, which is the sort of thing you leap on in writing a story. This woman had been engaged before, but her fiancé had died of typhoid or something, and under Chinese religious law she was held responsible. So, rather like the adulteress in *The Scarlet Letter*, she had to wear a ribbon on her sleeve indicating that she was unclean in some way. Then you get this American outsider coming in, the modern figure with the contemporary psychology, who has also been rejected by his own country, and he effectively says to her, 'I don't care about their rules. You're just fine for me.' That's all there is about their romance in the book, but I thought, 'God, I can really make something out of this!'

Why wasn't it produced?

At that point, Cruise and Woo were devoted to each other and were desperate to find something to do together – and this seemed to be it. I haven't really dealt with actors very much, so I would get notes from Tom Cruise but I worked primarily

with John Woo. John had come across this story and described it in interviews as his dream project, and he told me
that he would come back and direct it if everything went well
on *Mission: Impossible 2*. But who knows what happened on
that. The great thing about working with John was that when
you wrote a sequence, particularly an action sequence, you
really knew that he would elevate it into something fantastic. I
was tempted just to put 'Battle Sequence – directed by John
Woo', but even if you have John Woo directing your script,
action requires characterisation. The character points are
what you can write, however the action is going to be handled.
John probably wouldn't have handled the action at all like I
wrote it, but I would have hoped to get the dramatic focus of
each scene right.

**Tell me about the screenplay for Michael Mann. He's a very
American director; you're a very English writer. How do you
come to be working together?**

I know some other English writers who have worked with
him: Shawn Slovo and Troy Kennedy Martin. He was actually
interested in directing *Quasimodo*, but he didn't feel that
Disney really wanted to do it. We talked about a couple of
other projects, neither of which I got involved with, then two
or three years later this thriller came up.

**He always writes or co-writes his films. Has he done that on this
one?**

Not yet, but I imagine he will. He hasn't actually written any
words on the page, but he's hugely involved in the writing
process. He always does a lot of research: he and Eric Roth
read thousands of pages of testimony for *The Insider* to get the
rich detail of story and character and place that he loves.
Every meeting is just with him – there are never any producers
30 or executives in on those discussions – so you really know

where you stand. As you can imagine, it's been long and fascinating.

Apart from anything else, it's a contemporary thriller instead of a period drama.

I hadn't really thought about that until you went through them. I do some work for a Sundance offshoot called Moonstone, which was started by John McGrath, where you read other people's writing and help them with it, and one of the writers speaking at one of those sessions had an interesting notion about character and behaviour. She said that most of the people she knows are pretending to be someone else, despite the fact that everyone can see who they really are. That's probably true of writers. You believe you're one thing, but, actually, look at what you've done and see what you are. You're a B-list period writer, not some fancy thriller writer. On the other hand, I did some work on an adaptation of Barry Unsworth's novel *Morality Play* for Sam Mendes – which has just been shot by Paul McGuigan as *The Reckoning* – and the experience of writing something set in England in 1340 was so different from the experience of writing something set in China in 1860 that they might almost not be period. Period is everything that didn't happen here and now. A film set in Tibet or in the White House would seem equally period. They're completely different worlds.

Do you think that Hollywood considers British writers to be good at period?

Those sorts of jobs do tend to be offered to British writers, for some unknown reason. I certainly think that British writers can avoid some of the traps which period brings, but would a British writer have been able to write *Braveheart*? Probably not. They'd have done it in a different way which wouldn't have taken a fraction of the money. It would have been *Rob Roy* –

which is a good film, really well written, but not what they want. Ten Oscars and a hundred million dollars later, you can hardly go into the studio and say, 'You made a mistake. You should have used me. I'd have written you a nice little picture.' It's like an American writer coming up with the title *The Realm*: calling the film *Braveheart*, and thinking about that character in terms of Scottish independence, made it into something completely untrue but completely unapologetic. That's a useful thing to understand about cinema: it's not about truth, it's about drama. I think it's fine if you criticise something for being undramatic, and maybe the true story of William Wallace *is* actually more dramatic than the one that they did – sometimes that turns out to be the case, which is particularly ironic – but the instincts that lead you to put D-Day in the first twenty-five minutes of *Saving Private Ryan* seem to me to be good instincts, an inspired way of approaching historical material. British writers sometimes think too small. *Reds* wasn't small, though. It was huge and swirling. Trevor Griffiths approached it in a big way, and if you can do that perhaps you can be true as well.

The majority of your work – indeed, the majority of work by most screenwriters – takes the form of adaptations. Do you prefer them to originals, or vice versa?

Having spent a year and a half doing the original for Michael Mann, I wouldn't mind doing an adaptation now. I'm reading masses of books at the moment, not necessarily to adapt but because I've run a bit dry and need to take a lot of stuff in. An adaptation would obviously give me something concrete to hang on to, but the original came at a very good time as well because I'd done a whole run of adaptations and was slightly fed up with them. I sometimes feel that adaptations can hold you back. I'm obviously not likely to write a better nineteenth-century love story than *Pride and Prejudice*, but with con- temporary films I find myself thinking, 'What is this book really bringing to the table? If we've got to write a thriller, couldn't we come up with a better one?' At best, the novel is only part of an adaptation. It's the main one, in that it's giving you time, place and character, but your own preoccupations are another, and your own research is another. The novel is like a safety cushion, which is why production companies feel safe with adaptations – because it gives them something that everyone can agree on and keep coming back to, a physical asset as opposed to a pitch told to you by some guy who happened to walk in that morning.

How do you usually approach an adaptation?

You quickly get a sense of the scenes that are useful in telling the story – the greatest hits, as it were – and, indeed, a sense of how much of the story you want to tell. Then you try to abandon the book, which can take some doing. I write out pieces that seem particularly useful, a bit of dialogue or a description of something, to help remind me what the whole piece is about. With a novel, you can convert a piece of dialogue into action or a piece of monologue into dialogue; it's just a case of knowing the novel well enough to see how you can best use those pieces. The one major requirement is to try to express as much as you can in action rather than in chat. Take the beginning of *Pride and Prejudice*. I can't remember now what I wrote and what's in the novel, but essentially you have four or five daughters sitting in a house, and you see that one's impatient and one's placid and one's happy, and you emphasise the smallness of the room and the ticking of the clock, and you don't need to say much because you know that they're waiting for a man to arrive. That's a pretty good opening: it tells you that something has got to happen pretty sharpish and it's a lot better than having a bunch of women sitting in a room saying, 'God, I can't wait for a man to arrive!'

Do you write outlines and treatments before writing an original?

Yes, I do. For the Michael Mann story, I had to write a sixty-page outline. That was just for him. If you're raising money for something, you'll either have to pitch it or submit an outline – and if you're going to pitch it, you might as well write an outline because that's effectively what a pitch is. The fact that you didn't write it out doesn't mean that you didn't work out the story in some detail. Even if you're not raising money on an outline, I think it's an extremely thorough way of working out what the piece is really about. I didn't really outline *Sisters*, I just wrote it, but it's useful to know where you're going – without overdoing it, otherwise the process of actually writing the script will be boring. I fiddle around with an idea until I figure out who the characters are and what the ending is, then at some point I say, 'Right. Off we go.' Then, if I've written a draft and I'm stuck, I'll go back and summarise each scene in just one word so I've got the whole story on a single piece of paper. Often, by looking at that, I can go, 'Why is this boring? Why is this not working? Why do we feel bad here?' and, 'What if we shifted this bit much earlier?' I know what happens in each scene; I just need to move whole blocks around on paper. This sounds rather academic, but each scene needs to reflect the central thesis of your drama, so sometimes you can lose a scene and not notice it's gone even though it was a really good scene.

Having attended screenwriting courses as both student and teacher, what do you make of tools like character arc and three-act structure?

I think you can use those things to help solve problems, but I don't think you should start a script like that. You've got to have interesting characters and a good story to tell. I do sometimes look at something and think, 'We're not really getting into the story fast enough here', but the language of 'inciting incidents' is difficult to understand. It's difficult not to use it, because it's the language of development meetings, but it's much more important to understand what the story is and what the point of telling it is. If it's a good story, *why* is it a good story? Three acts is roughly how most stories work, as it turns out, but you can break a joke down in the same way. It works because you think it's going one way and then it goes another, or it doesn't work because it didn't begin well and the punchline's weak. You need to have a feel for telling a story and a feel for originality of character, and I don't know any tool that can help you do that. I don't think people should be put off going to lectures if they find them inspiring, but there's no comparison between listening to someone tell you how to write a script and actually reading one. I find reading the script as inspirational as seeing the film. It's all very well seeing Harrison Ford appear in a cowboy hat as Indiana Jones, but what did they do on the page? How did they show that? How did they create that figure? Basically, learning to write is all about being braver. Safe suggestions are normally not good suggestions. Good suggestions often sound absurd, and you have to teach yourself to trust your imagination. I remember something Mike Hoffman said to me: 'Make the strong choice. If there's a girl and a guy, and she hasn't told him about her boyfriend, don't make it her boyfriend, make it her fiancé instead. I don't think the process bears thinking about, though. I had a script note from Michael Mann which said, 'I'm not in love with the female lead.' So how do you solve that problem? What's the process? There's some analytical stuff you can do. There's some nicking from other people's stuff you can do. But in the end you've just got to come up with an original character. That's what it's all about, isn't it?

Let's talk about your routine. For example, why do you rent an office to write in rather than writing at home?

Because I don't want to come home to it. It reminds me too much of being a student, coming back to your desk next to your bed. I enjoy the process of going to work. My hours are office hours. I work late if I'm behind on something, but when I'm not in a great rush I like to cycle to my office and do a normal day. I like to have a good stretch at it. I can't just do a couple of hours. I may not end up doing more than that, but I need to know that I could. I also write better in the morning than I do in the afternoon, so I prefer not to have lunch with anybody because I find that disruptive. I might just sit on my own and read the newspaper, but that's different from having a conversation with someone. The first thing I do is go over what I did the previous day, which sometimes means I don't get any further than I did the previous day. I need to know what territory I've got to cover. I don't mean the number of pages, but what emotional situation the characters are in and how I'm going to deal with that. At one stage I would always start at the beginning again when I sat down, so of course the beginning was brilliant and the rest was massively under-written. You need to have the confidence to plunge into the middle of a script, which is why this 'Final Draft' computer program is quite good: it always goes back in where you left it, so you can just read that bit and then get on with it. I find fresh starts very helpful. I can go on for an extra three hours and only come up with one idea, but I may have a much more interesting take on it by the next morning. I don't think it through logically the night before, or even as I'm coming to work, but when you come back to the machine you've advanced. When I'm sitting on a train I always say to myself, 'I'll spend this time usefully and think about that problem in the script.' And I never ever solve it. But between the time you leave it and the time you come back to it, something happens.

For every script of yours that has been produced you've written two unproduced ones, the majority of those commissions from Hollywood. How do you deal with the fact that the script you're working on may never get made?

The easy choice is: don't work there. Of course, lots of things don't get made here. But, if you look at how many things a studio has in development and how many things they make, the strike rate is much worse there. If you *are* going to work there you always have to think, 'If this pans out, I'm on a roll' – because if you go in saying, 'Fuck it, this probably won't get made', you'll write nonsense and you'll never be employed again. To be honest, you just move on and write the next one. Somehow, you know that a corner will be turned. If one or two of those big ones had been done in the last few years, that would have been absolutely terrific; but it hasn't happened, and you're constantly reminded that it hasn't happened – so deal with it. I sat down with my agent at CAA the other day and he reminded me. I said to him, 'I wasn't unaware of that.' So people judge you for that, but if the writing's good they'll read the writing. Like I say, I got a lot of work on the basis of *Restoration* before the film was even made. There are intensely frustrating periods where a piece of work you're really pleased with seems to be stuck in a mire, although you can try and unstick things by changing agencies or doing a bit of producing yourself. There's this rule that after five years something can come back into your domain – the studio owns it outright until then – and it's about five years since *Quasimodo* so that's recently been sent to a couple of people. It sounds like pipedreams, but if you get a good agency things do move around. Sometimes, though, the relationship with a director can be the saving grace of working there.

Have you ever been tempted to direct?

At the moment, my feeling is that if you can get Michael Mann or John Woo why on earth would you do it yourself? If I did direct, it would only be on something small of my own; I'd never be available for hire, because there's no way I'd be better than a lot of other people. The thing that prevents me is not the responsibility but the enormous difficulty in writing good work. To be a half-decent writer is a tall order without being a half-decent director on top. A lot of directors end up doing writing on projects, but most of them come a cropper because they're really not as good at the one as they are at the other. Besides, I like the collaboration, and I don't know who I'd collaborate with.

So are you pleased with the way your scripts have been filmed?

It's extremely difficult to be objective about your work, let alone the process of going from script to film. There's always a shadow which falls between your ideal of how a script will turn out and the reality. Sitting through a première or a test screening is extremely hard, however well it goes down, and to begin with I was acutely aware of what I disliked about them. I don't think you sit there and say, 'I'd have done this differently', but you're incredibly conscious of the choices which have been made in terms of sets and casting – and also the choices that you made in terms of dialogue and so on. I'm finally getting better at watching my films again. I've started keeping copies because I could never find any of them, and occasionally something is on television again and I watch a snippet and think, 'This isn't bad.' My only regret about being a screenwriter is that it's much harder to see a film and just enjoy it for what it is.

Lee Hall was born in 1966, in Newcastle upon Tyne, and was educated there and at Fitzwilliam College, Cambridge. He lives in London.

FILM

Billy Elliot (Stephen Daldry, 2000, UK)   **Gabriel & Me** (Udayan Prasad, 2001, UK)

TELEVISION

The Student Prince (Simon Curtis, 1997, BBC)

Spoonface Steinberg (Betsan Morris Evans, 1998, BBC)

RADIO

I Luv You, Jimmy Spud (1995, BBC)
The Love Letters of Ragie Patel (1997, BBC)

The Sorrows of Sandra Saint (1997, BBC)
Spoonface Steinberg (1997, BBC)
Blood Sugar (1997, BBC)

SCREENPLAYS

Solomon Grundy (Miramax)
Peter Sellers (Maverick Films)
Yuri Gagarin (FilmFour)

Tulip Fever (DreamWorks)
Burying Ben (Warner Bros)

THEATRE

Leonce and Lena (1997)
Mr Puntila and His Man Matti (1998)
Cooking with Elvis (1998)
Spoonface Steinberg (1999)

A Servant to Two Masters (1999)
Mother Courage and Her Children (2000)
The Good Hope (2001)

You appear to have achieved overnight success twice, first in the theatre and again in films. How did you come to do so much work in such a short period?

I seemed to have found writing very late, so I was trying to make up for lost time. I was being asked to do films and asked to do theatre, and because I thought, 'I could have been doing this for years', I wouldn't say no if I could help it. By the time *Billy Elliot* came out I must have written six or seven screenplays, so I had quite a healthy body of work but rather a poor track record of getting it made.

Why did you find writing very late?

I did a lot of drama at school and directed a lot of stuff at university, and I thought that was what I wanted to do. But after two or three years of doing that, I adapted a version of Aristophanes's *The Birds* and discovered that I preferred writing to dealing with actors. That threw me, so after college I felt a bit lost. I did various things in the theatre for four or five years and then, when I was about twenty-six, I had the urge to do something more creative and thought, 'I'll try being a writer.' And luckily someone I'd met through my theatre connections, Kate Rowland, who later became Head of Radio Drama at the BBC, commissioned a radio play almost on spec. I hadn't actually written very much until *I Luv You, Jimmy Spud*, but even before it was done on the radio, my agent, Rod Hall, sent it out as a sample of my work, and a guy called Chris Bould really liked it and said, 'This should be a film.' Chris had a deal with Chrysalis Films and they commissioned a script, so I literally had to learn what to do. I'd never thought of being a screenwriter. I'd certainly never read a film script. I'd hardly even been to the cinema. I was living in New York at that point, and they have the most amazing video shops in the world there. I spent about six months watching eight to ten movies a day, reading all of those 'How to Write a Screenplay' books at the same time.

Did you find the books useful?

They're both useful and complete rubbish. All they actually say is that a screenplay should have a beginning, a middle and an end – in that order. The rest is filler, really. But, although this was the only screenplay I'd done and I had no aspirations at all to work in film, I really felt like I'd found a voice. I prefer screenwriting to other types of writing, which is probably unusual for people who work across different media, and the piece of work I'm most proud of is the film script of *Jimmy Spud*. It was a real breakthrough for me, and I think it's quite a successful piece of work. However, the making of it is another story.

How did you get an agent when you hadn't actually written very much?

Rod knew what I was up to and what I might be able to do, so he accepted me on trust. I also got an American agent called Bob Bookman, at CAA, who has quite a few clients here and decided to take me on when he read the film script of *Jimmy Spud*. You're so alone as a writer that the relationship with an agent can be very important. I've been very lucky with Rod and Bob, because agents normally just get you a good deal but both of them have actually got me work as well.

Why do you think it's unusual to prefer screenwriting to, in your case, writing for the theatre or the radio?

It seems like there are two cultures here. Screenwriting is not perceived to be proper work, but at the same time people are envious because they think that you make huge amounts of money off it – which you don't, necessarily. In fact, I've made more money off theatre than I have off screenwriting, but I'm drawn to the freedom of screenwriting. You can do anything you want in a screenplay, whereas in theatre or radio you have such limitations. In the theatre you tend to put a group of actors in one place over the course of an evening, whereas in a screenplay you can bring in a character just to do one scene before you zip off to Venezuela. And on the radio you obviously only have one thing, the sound, whereas in film you've got everything, and I'm very interested in juxtaposing sound and images.

In that case, you presumably didn't find it hard to open out *Jimmy Spud* from a radio play into a screenplay?

It's literally set around the corner from where I grew up, which means I could imagine those places very readily. I used to be able to see the cranes in the shipyards from my window, and gradually, through the seventies and eighties, there were less and less of them. The decline of heavy industry, and the impact that had on the northern identity, fuels most of my work, but I wanted to take an oblique angle rather than address that directly. *Jimmy Spud* and *Billy Elliot* are both veiled autobiography, a sort of fantasy version of that time.

In your introduction to the published script of *Billy Elliot*, you mention that social-realist pictures like *Kes* and the kitchen-sink dramas of Woodfall Films made a big impression on you. Was that tradition also part of your inspiration for *Jimmy Spud*?

I grew up watching those sort of movies on television, and a lot of television drama was like that too: representations of working-class life. I obviously knew that world very well and wanted to write about it, but social realism seemed to have been exhaustively mined so I set out to do a magic-realist version of those things. *Kes* isn't strictly a social-realist film at all. It's much more playful than it's often given credit for. I think a lot of that work was pushing against the boundaries of that tradition, and I probably spotted that subconsciously and wanted to take it a bit further.

It seemed to me that striking images like the Angel Gabriel sitting on the arm of a crane could be taken from Wim Wenders's *Wings of Desire*.

I still haven't seen *Wings of Desire*. I knew about it, though. I was actually trying, with both *Jimmy Spud* and *Billy Elliot*, to do Terence Davies with plot. I think his films are fantastic, but I'm attracted by narrative and he doesn't always organise his material in that way. *Jimmy Spud* is a sort of rites-of-passage narrative about a kid trying to come to terms with the death of his dad; normally that story would finish with him recognising his limitations and becoming a man, but I didn't really want to do that so I had him resurrect his dad as a sort of anti-rites-of-passage story. Hopefully, because it's ironic and funny, you can have your cake and eat it.

The question with magic realism is: how seriously are you meant to take it?

That was the most difficult thing. I wanted the screenplay to be simultaneously very realistic and very unrealistic. You know the kid can't actually resurrect his dad, but you kind of see it happen – so what you're watching is very ambiguous. It's incredibly arty in that sense.

Billy Elliot, Jimmy Spud, the opening of your *Yuri Gagarin* script, and all your radio plays, are written from the point of view of children. What are the benefits of seeing things through their eyes?

They're in the process of making their mind up about things, which makes them really good representatives of the audience. They're like an Everyman character going on a picaresque adventure, innocent outsiders absolutely in the midst of every situation. I can see why the Everyman character has been a useful one in literature. I was also looking at my own childhood and using that as source material.

43

Jimmy Spud shares a number of themes and concerns with *Billy Elliot*. The role of parents and grandparents, for example.

It's about the father-and-son relationship. He's rejecting his dad on one side and idolising him on the other. There's also that thing which sometimes happens where, if you jump a generation, the kid gets on better with the grandfather than with the father.

There's also an echo of Billy's relationship with his friend Michael in Jimmy's relationship with his friend Ragie, particularly in the scene where Jimmy seems to flap his wings on Ragie's chest — which carries a hint of homosexuality.

I suppose they're innocently exploring their sexuality, but that's not a big theme of the piece at all. I just thought it was an enjoyable scene. I also wanted to upset people a little. It was originally broadcast on Radio 4 at two o'clock in the afternoon, and Radio 4 afternoon plays are usually fairly staid, so I thought the idea of having this cheeky metaphor for masturbation was fantastically funny.

The thing which distinguishes *Jimmy Spud* from *Billy Elliot* is its preoccupation with faith. In fact, it has more in common with your radio, stage and television play *Spoonface Steinberg*, about an autistic Jewish girl dying of cancer.

I like writing about death. It's something that we can't avoid, and I'm surprised that people don't write about it more. *Spoonface* and *Jimmy Spud* are part of a little quartet of radio plays, and they're linked on another level by loss — death being the ultimate loss. They're sad comedies, really.

Like the *Yuri Gagarin* script, *Jimmy Spud* opens with a big chunk of voiceover. Why are you so fond of that technique?

I stumbled across voiceover by accident, because the story was originally written for the radio, but I found that by juxtaposing it with something visual, you very often create dramatic irony. People say you can't have voiceover – and I'm unhappy about using it just for exposition – but if it's used against an image then it can be an interesting anti-naturalistic device. *Yuri Gagarin* has got its tongue firmly in its cheek even though it's attempting to be serious about a lot of things.

Unlike the radio play, your screenplay avoids couching the dialogue in dialect. Why did you decide to change it?

I don't know why I did that. The radio play was the first thing I wrote, so I probably tried to over-explain and actually found that it didn't make much difference.

Why did it have a troubled path to the screen?

It was going to be directed by Chris Bould, and we worked on it for about four years. Then Chrysalis collapsed. The screenplay was bought by Simon Channing-Williams and he was going to do it with Chris, but they had problems raising the money. Then it was sold on for a third time. Marc Samuelson got hold of it, Chris stepped aside and John Roberts came on board. Then John left to do another film which didn't happen – *Busby's Babes*, about Matt Busby and the Munich air disaster – and Udayan Prasad came on board. So I worked on a draft for him, and the day I delivered it he delivered his own draft. At which point we all had a row and I left the project, because he insisted on using his version – which I didn't think was as good as mine.

The title was changed, for a start.

Yeah. It's called *Gabriel & Me* now.

What were the other differences?

The bulk of the story was still there, but he was trying to tie things up too much by making the characters talk too much. I think he panicked because he had to start filming and he didn't understand how the different elements were put together. I felt that the screenplay was more elegant before and was already doing everything that he was explicitly stating. Some of the writing he inserted I wouldn't put my name to, but it was also clear I couldn't take my name off it. It was terribly acrimonious and a real low point, since I'd worked on it for six years and it was a very personal piece. I couldn't understand why he was so high-handed. I enjoy screenwriting because it's such a collaborative thing. Working with a director on the draft that they're actually going to film is one of the pleasures of the industry. Since then, I've not seen it or been involved in it, and I've not spoken to the producer or the director.

Gabriel & Me might end up being perceived as a less commercial version of *Billy Elliot*, but, bearing in mind the order in which they were written, *Billy Elliot* was actually a more commercial version of *Jimmy Spud*.

I wrote *The Student Prince*, then I wanted to go back and re-explore growing up, so I used the same dramatic model as *Jimmy Spud*. But I never saw *Billy Elliot* as being commercial. I think it gradually became that because of Stephen Daldry's temperament and the elements he was interested in bringing out.

What elements *did* he want to bring out?

Basically, he was always saying, 'Can we take this further?' We pushed the emotional side and did a lot of character work. The tough love of the dance teacher emerged through that process. Originally she was a much gentler character, but I rewrote the role quite late in the day to give it more bite. I've known Stephen for years, which meant we had a kind of shorthand to talk about it. I took him the script to get some friendly advice but he really liked it, so it was two friends bouncing ideas off each other rather than a professional working relationship.

How long did you work on it?

As soon as I had the idea that it would be about the kid and the strike, it almost wrote itself. It was a very obvious plot, in that the kid had auditions and stuff, and the strike was almost a year long, which helped structure the whole thing. You could work all that out in a morning, and I wrote the first draft in about ten days, but then came several years of rewriting.

Do you tend to write an outline or a treatment before you start?

I tend to draw little maps, then write a card for each scene. I don't start until I know where I'm going to finish, whereas with theatre I tend to meander a bit more. I always work to commission, so I know the script has got to be 110 pages and I've only got three months to do it. I work through the thing quite methodically, because the time you get really isn't very long.

I notice that your stage directions are quite spare.

I agree with David Mamet on screenwriting: what you write either has a function or it doesn't. That's where good writing differs from not-so-good writing. If the scene is doing what it should be, then you don't need to put in a big blurb. There's also a practical thing about your 110 pages. If you put in all your purple prose, then you can't have as many scenes. The obsession now is for British screenplays to be under 100 pages because of budgetary constraints. I just try to cut down on the stage directions, but I know people in America who use 'Final Draft' to get an extra line on each page.

You said there was an element of fantasy autobiography in _Billy Elliot_, with ballet rather than drama as the bone of contention. In what respect?

My family were very supportive, but being interested in the arts I was always the odd one out among the other kids, and I wanted to write about that. Most of my work is about class and the limitations of class. The working class has evolved to think that this stuff is arty-farty crap and that the people who like it are poofs, but there are also fantastic elements of working-class culture: the emotion and the frankness and the pragmatism. That tension is what these screenplays are all about. The strike makes you feel sympathy for these people who are being oppressed, but they in turn are oppressing this kid – which is what makes the story interesting. It was very important that it wasn't black and white, that underneath it was quite murky and complicated. If they'd just been bigoted working-class people it would be much less interesting.

Why did you decide on dance rather than drama – or even writing?

I knew the story was about a kid who's the odd one out, so I was trying to find the most visual way of dramatising that. Dance seemed to be the most obvious because it was very cinematic and you could use it to do an awful lot of work emotionally. It's actually an important part of the working-class tradition: working-class people probably go out dancing much more than middle-class people do.

It's ironic that you should be telling this story in this medium, though, given that ballet is considered to be high art and film low art.

I was very interested in using the cinema form to investigate that thematic concern. It's actually a theme I'm constantly working out, because I'm fascinated by high art but feel so at home with low art. Somebody in America said, 'That's why we get you Brits over, because that's what you Brits do: slap high and low together.' I think that's probably right. There is an impulse in British writing to be populist. Ealing films were made by very proper middle-class people but they deal with the warp and weave of real life, so I see myself as part of a grand tradition rather than trying to do something anomalous.

It's not only a very visual film but also a very musical one, encapsulated by the opening shot of Billy bouncing in and out of frame to the sound of Marc Bolan.

The first image that came into my mind when I had the idea was Billy jumping up and down on the bed to that song. Marc Bolan was the right feel for that film, so I structured it around the places where I wanted those tracks to be. Music is one of the colours on the palette. I used a lot of Handel in the radio play of *Jimmy Spud*, because it linked in thematically as well as sounding nice. It's a really useful element in screenwriting, too.

In spite of the music and the dancing, Billy Elliot doesn't use magic realism to the same extent as Jimmy Spud, does it?

I suppose in that way *Billy Elliot* was a regression from *Jimmy Spud*. But I still wanted to ironise this social-realist world, and 49

I do think the film is very tongue-in-cheek about where the strings are being pulled.

You mean, the audience knows they're being manipulated?

I'm not trying to manipulate anybody – because I'm not trying to hide anything. I try to push the emotion because films are all about emotion, but I also try to undercut things which could be seen as being sentimental. I'm not vigilant against emotion but I am vigilant against sentimentality, and if there is something sentimental in a scene then a joke is generally close behind it. I don't set out to write jokes – I only realise it's funny when I read it – but some people would say that's where the manipulation happens.

Billy is accused of being a 'poof', and may or may not be, but his friend Michael certainly is. What was your thinking behind that?

I thought that it would be difficult to write *Billy Elliot* without addressing the issue of his sexuality, but I also thought that if you made Billy gay the whole thing would become unpalatably cute – and very over-determined. A few of the critics in the gay magazines said, 'Of course you should have made him gay', but it seemed a lot more elegant to explore that through another character. But part of the fun of writing it was addressing that issue, because sexuality is another reason why people become outsiders in that environment. Again, it's analogous to me feeling different, because I was interested in the arts and nobody else was.

In fact, if you *had* made him gay, it would simply have reinforced the notion that an interest in the arts is synonymous with homosexuality.

That's what I meant by over-determined: it looks like you're drawing conclusions which you're certainly not drawing.

Presumably that same reasoning explains why the strike largely functions as the background to the story rather than actually being the focus of the drama, as exemplified by kids trailing sticks along a brick wall and then across a barrier of riot shields without so much as a second glance at the army of police?

The thing with the stick was something they improvised on the day, but that image of them walking past the riot shields was the second image I had after him jumping up and down on the bed – and putting the two images together, the story just clicked. We knew that the strike was one of the more controversial elements, and the producers wouldn't want violence and stuff, but we were determined that the police would always be in the background so they couldn't be cut out.

You did cut out some scenes relating to the strike, though.

It was originally the story of the two brothers, but in the editing room we dropped a lot of that and chopped the structure around. It was never going to be an examination of the strike, but we did cut out a whole subplot about the brother's relationship with his best friend who was a scab.

The guy he now meets in the supermarket?

They had four or five scenes together in the original script. He'd been working, so he was the one with the money to pay for Billy to go down to the ballet school. We lost the irony of the situation and the detail about the wider community, but it would have been a longer movie and I don't think it could sustain being much longer than it is.

Billy Elliot is one of three recent high-profile social-realist northern comedies, after _Brassed Off_ and _The Full Monty_. Were you influenced by either of those?

I'd just finished writing the first draft when *The Full Monty* came out, and I was just starting to plan it when I read in the trades that Mark Herman was writing his thing. I was horrified and thought, 'I'll have to abandon this', but when my story got around to being produced enough time had passed.

Why do you think films like this strike a chord?

My pet theory – and I don't think the industry has really figured this out yet – is that things about working-class people are more likely to get a big audience than things about middle-class people, simply because there *are* more working-class people than middle-class people. It's less to do with the fact that they're comedies than the fact that they're about working-class life. That's not to say *Four Weddings* won't be successful, but there are so few films made in the popular style about working-class people – and, in fact, arthouse movies tend not to be about working-class people either. *East is East* found an audience despite its ethnicity because it's as much about working-class life as anything else. I don't understand why class is seen as an unfashionable subject, because I don't think things are any different than they were pre-Blair. These films are so successful because audiences recognise themselves in them and want to see this subject represented.

Perhaps another reason why you prefer screenwriting to other types of writing is that film is a more democratic medium in which to tell this sort of story?

I think you're right. Film *is* a more democratic form. A lot of working-class people have an issue about going to the theatre – should they be there? – whereas you can watch a film in your home or watch it close to your home. It's much easier to access.

When did you realise that you had a potential hit on your hands?

I don't know what other people thought, but Stephen and I thought it was a complete dog's dinner. Then we held a preview in Reading, where the test audience gave it the same marks as *The Full Monty*. We couldn't believe it, because at that point we were tearing our hair out and thinking, 'It'll probably go straight to video now.'

In fact, you got an Oscar nomination.

Billy Elliot, and then the Oscar thing, changed my life dramatically. If you've got a play in the West End, even quite a successful play, most people don't know about it – but everybody knows about *Billy Elliot*. That doesn't really affect the work – you're always several years ahead of what other people think about you, because everything takes so long to do – but it does thrust you into the limelight. Every studio wants one or two of its films to be nominated each year, whether they win or not, so they literally hire a company to run your campaign. You're given an Oscar manager, and you go and talk to the Writers Guild and so on. I was more flattered to be nominated for the Writers Guild award than for the Oscar, because the Writers Guild is actually your peers.

Jumping backwards for a moment: *The Student Prince*, which you wrote for the BBC between *Jimmy Spud* and *Billy Elliot*, also deals with the subject of class – and being the odd one out.

Again, it's a sort of fantasy autobiography. If you don't move out of your own cultural environment you take everything for granted, but I've been forced to move between two worlds and I found that the limitations of each are very stark. You're 53 considered to be arty-farty in one place and a pleb in another. I was fascinated by that as a subject because I think it must be part of my identity, and I'm sure that's why I want to write popular stuff with a certain artistic aspiration.

It's your one and only romantic comedy, which can be a very popular genre.

I thought it was a marvellously fun way of dealing with those issues, but I would have been happier if it had explored them more fully. In the earlier drafts the relationship between master and servant was more quirky, but in the process of development and filming it was ironed out and became a lighter piece. I'm always struggling to make things as accessible as possible without diluting my personal concerns. *The Student Prince* is on the wrong side of that, I think, whereas something like *Spoonface* is a philosophical tract, really, but hopefully a very funny one. I'm quite successful in some things and not successful in others.

And jumping ahead a couple of years, the master–servant relationship crops up again in your unproduced adaptation of Deborah Moggach's novel *Tulip Fever* – not to mention your translation of the Goldoni play *A Servant to Two Masters*.

There was a lot of *A Servant to Two Masters* in *Tulip Fever*, I thought. It's important for me to be writing about that subject, because I understand the people who are the servants rather than the masters, if you like. I like to do at least one project a year with a group called Live Theatre, in Newcastle, who set out to put on new writing about the people of the north, because growing up watching plays in that sort of Fabian socialist tradition probably influenced my entire outlook. A lot of writers write for themselves, but I'm very concerned about who watches my work. I try to address political issues – with a small 'p' – in a populist way, so it's

entertaining and hopefully isn't didactic.

Who actually hired you – and fired you – on this project?

Alison Owen, who produced *Elizabeth*, had the rights to the book. I'd been talking to her about a Sylvia Plath project that I ended up not doing, so she gave it to me and I saw some themes in it that suited my preoccupations. Steven Spielberg also liked it, so they cut some sort of co-production deal, but of course he was busy, so I dealt with his development people. They were all very rigorous and terribly civil, but my version was not what they wanted and they got somebody else. You're hired by the draft, so you know it's likely that you won't be staying with it after you've done your bit of work. The screenplay is often just the hook to get an actor, and the actor is often the film in the eyes of the director, which is why some of these American actors come with their own writers.

Your voice as a writer emerges most clearly through dialogue, even in a script like *Yuri Gagarin*, which is set in Soviet Russia, so how did you mould a period piece like *Tulip Fever* to suit your preoccupations?

I think one of the reasons I was interested in it was because it was a period piece, and one of the reasons they were interested in me was because my take on it was to work against the grain of it. Some literary adaptations work hard to create the mystique of the period, but I was trying to make it very modern in feel, and in the end maybe they thought that was the wrong way to go. I don't know. I don't really want to know. But it was different, and it was a challenge.

What's your main concern when you're approaching an adaptation?

Half of it is deciding what to choose, as you're increasingly offered more things. If the story has a good structure that can be the making of a good film, so my main concern is to map out the architecture of the screenplay. I then piece together the narrative like a jigsaw, putting in bits to see how they fit, and my second pass tends to be about character and motivation. The approach to adaptations is really very similar to working out original stuff – because it's impossible simply to translate a novel into a film, so there are always some things that you have to re-imagine. With a play, it's much less work adapting something than writing something new. With a screenplay, there's not much difference because there are so many technical demands.

The dialogue in *Yuri Gagarin* is not just in English, it's in a northern working-class idiom – and the British and the Americans speak in subtitled Russian to distinguish them from the Soviets. That's working against the grain, too.

You could quite easily do a straightforward biopic of Gagarin, a *Thirteen Days* thing, but I was much more interested in doing something playful and satirical, like a Soviet *Forrest Gump*. If it was shown in America everybody would be rooting for, as it were, the wrong side – those awful Reds – and that irony was one of the main attractions of the subject matter.

The biopic is a notoriously difficult genre. How did you set about condensing thirty-odd years of Gagarin's life into 120 pages or so?

I decided early on to make it very upfront. The opening monologue starts with the Big Bang, because I thought, 'If we're going do to a biopic, let's send up the whole thing about chronology.' I think anybody would be fascinated by the story of the first guy who went into outer space, but I was also very conscious that the background detail might seem rather arid, so I worked quite hard to make it entertaining.

It's highly reminiscent of the opening monologue in Powell and Pressburger's *A Matter of Life and Death*: 'This is the universe. Big, isn't it?'

Powell and Pressburger were in the back of my mind when I was thinking about how to do *Gagarin*. I don't know their films too well, but everything I've seen has confirmed that I'm very much in that tradition. They're not scared of emotion, but it's done with supreme wit and intelligence – which is something I would aspire to.

Did you do a lot of research?

I did six months of solid reading before I started, because the subject is so fascinating. There are so many strands that the first draft I did for myself was about 250 pages. I just thought, 'I'm going to write about whatever is most interesting', and then started cutting it down. There was originally much more of the political background, but it was impossible to get it into a sensible timeframe – and equally difficult to throw it all out.

It must be your biggest canvas to date.

Paul Webster at FilmFour commissioned the development of the script, and I was encouraged to be bold and not scale the thing down. I appreciated being pushed in that way. The scale of the thing *is* enormous: it would certainly cost more than the standard three million quid.

We've mentioned that the script opens with Gagarin as a child, but he's actually quite childlike throughout.

I was drawn to the story because I saw that element and found it really funny. I'm sure he wasn't as childlike as I've made him, but he's the ultimate Everyman character and I want people to identify with him. I consciously used *Candide* as a

57

model, because *Gagarin* was clearly an innocence-to-experience narrative. He goes on a complicated journey of hope and disappointment, and ultimately finds some small bits of pleasure in a Tolstoyan – or Woody Allen – way.

The narrative peaks with his trip into space, where he looks down at a world which seems beautiful and peaceful, but on his return to earth he sees nothing but barbarity and poverty. It's very much a story of our time, isn't it?

I hadn't really looked at it like that, but I suppose you're right, in a sad way. I think his naivety made him believe that things were really great, and then his success forced him to see things as they actually were. The institutional problems of the Soviet Union are represented in capitalist society, too, and I was trying to use the one as a metaphor for its negative opposite.

The theme of class is important again, and the feeling of being the odd one out: Gagarin finds that he is simultaneously of the people and above the people.

It's similar to the central concern of *Billy Elliot*: the sense of separation and disjuncture when you leave your roots and follow an individual path. Yuri Gagarin became the first working-class hero in the Soviet Union, the first celebrity in a country whose whole *raison d'être* had been that individuals were not important. He was Khrushchev's boy, basically, an emblem of the thaw. The Khrushchev period was a real reaction against Stalin, and the writing of the time is full of hope that Russia could undo some of the damage of those years and actually achieve the utopia of Communism. But when Brezhnev got rid of Khrushchev, Russia went back to the dark days and it was the beginning of the end for Communism. It seemed to me that Gagarin's story was about the change from Khrushchev to Brezhnev and that utopian urge not being fulfilled.

Your satirical approach has a lot in common with the films of Stanley Kubrick, and there are humorous references in the script to Lolita and Dr Strangelove.

Immediately before this I wrote another biopic, about Peter Sellers, and I'm sure those references came directly from working on that story. *Dr Strangelove* obviously deals very explicitly with the Cold War, so that deep irony seemed really useful, and when Gagarin first goes to the military base there's a sergeant-major figure who I pinched from *Full Metal Jacket*. Most of my scripts are full of nods to other films, but *Gagarin* was also drawing on my theatre work in a way that my other screenplays hadn't – the sardonic humour and political satire of Brecht, for instance.

I read an interview where you said that you like Brecht because a laugh is often followed by a punch in the gut. Is that what you were attempting to emulate?

I think so. I hope so. I'm much happier when you get that heterogeneous mix. I'm also very aware of how humour works, because in the theatre the laugh is a tangible thing: you're sitting in the stalls biting your nails, and the laugh either happens or it doesn't.

Presumably one of the reasons you were attracted to the Peter Sellers project was the presence of the same element you saw in Gagarin: a childlike adult?

The two screenplays were thematically twinned, I think. Hal Ashby's *Being There* was a big influence in my approach to *Peter Sellers*, because he saw himself as the lead character in that film, Chauncey Gardener, a sort of blank page, and that feeling also seemed to fit *Gagarin*. There were a lot of subconscious parallels.

How did you come to be involved in that project?

Freddy De Mann, who used to be Madonna's manager, wanted to be a film producer, and he bought the rights to this dark, crazy biography of Peter Sellers by a guy called Roger Lewis. I think Freddy De Mann wanted a Brit to tackle it, although I'm not sure why he picked me. I wasn't a Sellers freak, but I'm very interested in popular culture, and he seemed to have taken part in the most interesting bits of it – from *The Goon Show* to *The Ladykillers* to *Dr Strangelove*. His film career was meteoric from *I'm All Right Jack* onwards, and by the time he did *Dr Strangelove* he was the highest-paid British actor: a million dollars a film, and that was in 1963. But after that, because of his personal failings, he became drunk on his own power and made some terrible choices. He optioned the book *Being There* in about 1969 or 1970, but it wasn't made until 1979 because he was unfundable for so long – and he died soon after making it. Like Gagarin, he achieved everything and then threw it all away.

I think he said that when he wasn't playing a part he didn't know who he was.

Exactly. The biography was all about that, about this man who saw himself not acting. It was fascinating material. The problem was trying to find a structure, because it was incredibly unwieldy – and deeply upsetting. His relationship with his kids was parlous. The producer was shocked that my take was so dark. The book is also very dark, but I think he expected [*American accent*], 'A funny film about a funny guy.'

How much research did you do beyond the biography?

The biography is exhaustive, about 900 pages. It's an amazing piece of research, a history of popular culture since the war, really. I talked to Roger Lewis, who spent ten years writing it and interviewed everybody there was to interview, so I got a lot of it second-hand. I decided not to talk to anybody else, because I thought I might have to represent them in the film and I was worried about compromising myself. The only person I did try to see was Spike Milligan, just because he's a hero of mine, but he wasn't having any of it.

Were you worried about compromising them, too?

Well, I was going to write that film about Sylvia Plath and Ted Hughes, and I was very attracted to the subject matter, but I had trouble reconciling myself to writing about real people who were still alive. I felt OK about that with *Peter Sellers* because he was such a monster, and everybody was so candid about him, that nothing could be as egregious as his terrible deeds. I was more cagey about representing his wives or his kids, because there's an ethical responsibility not to intrude on people's lives, so my aim was never to show them in a bad light. *Gagarin* is different because most of the people are dead. Or Russian!

Most of your work is life-affirming to one degree or another. This seems to be the exception which proves the rule.

I don't start with a moral or aesthetic principle that everything should be life-affirming; that's just how they come out. In fact, that's why they felt this script was unsuccessful: because I hadn't worked out how to achieve redemption among all that wife-beating. American producers have this problem about characters not being sympathetic, and because I have sympathetic characters in my other work they probably thought that I would make Sellers sympathetic – but I actually found him deeply *un*sympathetic. I was still a bit disappointed that I was unable to continue with it, because I think it had some of my best writing in it and I knew what to do on the next pass, but with both that and the *Solomon Grundy* adaptation for Miramax there was a real problem about my use of humour.

What happened to the project?

It was bought by HBO. The producers sold the rights to the book but didn't pass on my script because they thought it would put people off, and then I got a call from HBO asking if I wanted to write a movie about Peter Sellers. I thought that was very funny and hugely ironic. I actually tried to wangle it so that I could just pretend to do it, but that didn't work because I was busy on something else – so in the end they got it rewritten by a couple of American writers, who had a completely different take.

What was *Solomon Grundy* about?

Solomon Grundy was adapted from a novel written by a friend of mine, Dan Gooch, which was based on that rhyme about a person who has his whole life in one week: 'Solomon Grundy, born on Monday, raised on Tuesday, married on Wednesday . . .' It's a fantastic conceit, but a logistical nightmare: each day is a decade, so how do you show that accelerated growth on screen? And, because American producers came on after British producers, I don't think they understood what I was trying to achieve with the humour. I worked on it for Paul Webster after writing *Billy Elliot*, and when he left Miramax it was rewritten by the screenwriter of *Chocolat* who basically dumped what I did and set it in America.

What *were* you trying to achieve with the humour?

The humour was there to make a serious point – everybody is after this guy because he's a complete freak of nature – but they thought it was far too Carry On. The tradition of using humour to make serious points is very British. So much of our popular culture is like that and so little of theirs is. American films which use humour in that way tend to have been made by people who aren't American. I think there's a certain European or non-American sensibility. It's no surprise that Capra and Lubitsch, who are the kind of people I admire as geniuses of comic film-making, were foreigners.

Do you prefer writing for British producers to working in America?

The two worlds are so different that it's very difficult to compare them. I certainly have no problem about working in America. This crass caricature of the studio system is not entirely accurate. I also discovered film over there, so it feels natural to write in that idiom. It's amazing how many British writers do write for America – and write prime projects. I think the film industry in Britain is like the village cricket team, whereas the Americans are the New York Yankees: they're playing a proper ball game, and we're just messing around on the green. The worry is that producers in Britain may feel that they've got to try and ape the American model when they haven't got the resources to do it. People have told me that the problem with British films is that they need to be rewritten more, and hiring and firing the creatives in an American way docs seem to have started here now. But if you're getting a million bucks for your screenplay and you're treated worse than the janitor, at least there are some compensations. When you're doing it for your standard five-figure contract and you're still fired, there are no compensations at all.

I take it you disagree that British films need to be rewritten more?

I think it's ridiculous. If a producer tells you that something is wrong with a screenplay then there's probably a good reason for it, but never listen to their suggestions about how to fix it because that's probably the worst way to go. You've got to find your own way. The problem is that film producers aren't creative people on the whole. In radio, the producer is generally your director. In the theatre, the artistic director is often your creative partner. But in a film, the director is your partner and the producer is a businessperson corralling the creatives. That's why film producers get very impatient: because they speak a different language and have different concerns. They call the film rights to a book or a play a 'property', which is indicative of how they think: it's something they've got, something tangible. This is the frustrating thing about dealing with less good producers – that everything has to be concrete. If anything, my work is too simplistic; yet again and again they say, 'We don't understand the motivation for this.' What they don't understand is the subtle and complex contract of give and take which you have with an audience, so you've almost got to say, 'Go away and trust me.' Films which explain everything are inevitably disappointing, because they exclude you from the process of watching them.

How do you get excited about a project when you know it may be rewritten – or never made at all?

I think you have to suspend your disbelief and do the job as best you can, because if you considered all the possibilities for failure beforehand you would probably never even start. I'm so excited by the craft that I can live with nine out of ten screenplays ending up in the bin, but it must be a horrible job if you don't actually like the act of writing. Some people are much more cynical and see screenwriting as a way to fund their other artistic pursuits, but screenplays are at the heart of my work as a writer so those sorts of compromises cost an awful lot. I write for the theatre simply because most of my life is spent waiting five years for the next film to get made, and I need to balance that with the fantastic immediacy of seeing my work put on. I've also found that if I only do one thing at a time I tend to get stuck, whereas if I do two or three things I get distracted – which stops me becoming obsessed.

Will you continue to write popular films, or are you tempted to try your hand at an arthouse movie?

I haven't got a prejudice against arthouse movies. I'm just about to start two projects, one for Working Title and one for Warner; the one for Working Title is about Boadicea and the resistance to the Roman invasion of Britain, with elements of those revisionist Westerns seen from the point of view of the Indians, but the one for Warner is basically an arthouse movie, a proper adult drama with real emotional subject matter about a father coming to terms with the suicide of his son. I'm sure I will write some impenetrable pieces of work which no one goes to see, but I think popular films could and should be meaty and difficult and I'm always trying to find ways of dealing accessibly with abstract concerns. My aspiration is to write things which can be read in various ways, so you could go and see a good yarn but at the same time if you're alert to certain preoccupations you will have them addressed.

Richard Curtis was born in 1956, in New Zealand, to Australian parents, and educated at Harrow and Oxford. He lives in London with Emma Freud and their two children.

FILM

The Tall Guy (Mel Smith, 1989, UK)
Four Weddings and a Funeral (Mike Newell, 1994, UK)
Bean (Mel Smith, 1997, UK)

Notting Hill (Roger Michell, 1999, US/UK)
Bridget Jones's Diary (Sharon Maguire, 2001, US/Fr/UK)

TELEVISION

Not the Nine O'Clock News (1979–82, BBC)
Blackadder (1983, BBC)
Blackadder II (1985, BBC)

Blackadder the Third (1987, BBC)
Mr Bean (1990–95, ITV)
Blackadder Goes Forth (1989, BBC)
The Vicar of Dibley (1994–9, BBC)

Your first film reached the big screen in 1982, a short support-ing-feature with Rowan Atkinson called *Dead on Time*. Did you learn anything from that?

It was about a guy who had twenty-five minutes to live, and when it was shot it was about forty minutes long and it was very hard to cut. Each thing was contingent upon the thing that had happened before, and cutting it down to the right length made it less good. Perhaps the one thing I learned was that editing was going to be an absolutely crucial part of my film career.

And the next film you wrote didn't even get produced.

That was called *Four Eyes and Fat Thighs* – not a good title, I think – and it was about a man who comes home one day and discovers that his wife, the only girlfriend he's ever had, is having an affair with his best friend. His wife is a rather powerful person, and for some reason or other it's him who has to leave the house and move into a hotel. At the same time his eighteen-year-old son, with whom he doesn't have a very good relationship, has exactly the same experience with his girlfriend. So these two sad acts are stuck together for the first time in their lives, and the second half or the last two thirds of the film was about them finding girlfriends and becoming friends.

Who commissioned the script?

It was written for an absolutely delightful producer called Michael Gruskoff, who had just finished making *Young Frankenstein*. It was an educational experience for lots of reasons. Firstly, I made up the idea on the afternoon that Michael and I had been organised to meet, and that did leave me, a year later, with absolutely no idea why I was writing the film. So I learned my first screenwriting rule: don't set pen to paper on anything which you haven't had in the back of your mind for a year or two. It may not work for other people, but that's the way it works for me. I need to know that a story has haunted me to be able to put up with all the complexity of writing it later. The only other time I tried to write like that, I had an idea at a petrol station for a complete film, spent two months writing it, starting that day, then gave it to my then girlfriend, who read it and said I should put it in a drawer – which I did.

Was the father–son script set in England or America?

It was set in America, and I suppose that was when I learned rule number two. I had a meeting with some incredibly nice executives at MGM, who said they loved the script. Then, when they went into it in more detail, they said they didn't like the leading character, or indeed the second-leading character, because they were too wimpy and both failures; and they didn't think the dialogue was right, because it was too English; and they thought the supporting characters were a bit shallow; and they weren't sure the plot worked. I said, 'That leaves nothing except the title', and a rather embarrassed person in the corner of the room said, 'We're not crazy about the title either.' So that didn't leave anything at all. And because it was set in America, when people said, 'An American wouldn't behave like that in the face of his wife doing this', they had one up on me by being American, even though I didn't necessarily believe them. So I resolved, if ever I wrote another film, only to write something I was a hundred per cent sure of and no one in the world knew more about than me. I knew what it was like in Camden Town and Shaftesbury Avenue, so I next wrote a film about someone who was in love with a nurse in Camden Town and performing as a comedian in Shaftesbury Avenue, which was exactly what I was doing at the time.

In fact, *The Tall Guy*, *Four Weddings and a Funeral* and *Notting Hill* form a loose trilogy of comedies – and the last two tell very similar stories.

It came as a great surprise to me when I realised that *Notting Hill* was rather like *Four Weddings*. Apart from the fact that Hugh was in it again, there was an American who came and went away, there was a group of friends who had stories of their own and there was someone wacky he lived with. I was deeply disappointed in myself when I realised that something inside me had wanted to tell the same tale twice, because I definitely didn't set out to write similar films. I've clearly been haunted by this idea of true love and how to find it and how to recognise it – and it's very ironic that someone in America should now be suing us who feels he wrote a similar story years before. If anyone should be suing me for the unoriginality of *Notting Hill*, it's me.

It's also ironic that your first script was criticised for its wimpy leading men, since the huge success of both *Four Weddings* and *Notting Hill* was built on having a diffident leading man.

It's just one of those things that people say. The movie that I had in mind then, even though it's a unique movie so you can't strictly use it in evidence, was *The Graduate*. Dustin Hoffman plays the least heroic hero of all time, a loser in almost every way, yet he's fantastic. Also, I was very keen on Woody Allen movies when I was young, and he isn't at all heroic. I think the feeling that heroes must be heroic is probably not right.

The Tall Guy was originally called *Camden Town Boy* . . .

I wish we hadn't changed that title. It was about the only serious advice we got from America: 1) Jeff Goldblum wasn't a boy; and 2) Camden Town had no reverberation anywhere.

The problem is that the title we came up with wasn't distinctive, and the fact that Jeff was tall wasn't mentioned anywhere in the film. A few people now know what it's called, but for years I was endlessly answering questions about *The Tall Man* and *The Big Guy*.

Did you have to alter the script to accommodate Jeff Goldblum?

We hardly changed it when Jeff came in apart from cutting the word 'arse' and one or two other things which Americans find hard to say. It was written for someone English, but we wanted Jeff because we needed an extraordinary and idiosyncratic figure. It didn't matter that he was American but the film wasn't meant to be about an American, which may be one of the reasons why it's not completely right. If you're writing about an American in the UK, you should address the fact that they're American.

Was he cast for commercial reasons, or because he seemed right for the role?

Because he seemed right for the role. This is something I should probably say here: I'm very happy with almost all criticism of my flimsy little movies, but the idea that they're written for an American audience is completely wrong. If you want to write things which are good or funny you've got to write for yourself and your friends. When I was writing radio comedy, I went to a meeting and someone said, 'British Rail sandwiches are funny.' I didn't find them funny, and if you don't think something is funny then you mustn't write it. I would never write anything thinking, 'This will appeal to that market.' It must always be, 'This will appeal to me.' The only concession we ever really make to America is when we test the film and see if there are things we want to change, but in the case of the last three films the reaction was exactly the same as in the UK so there wasn't much reason to change things.

Surely you have some sort of audience in mind when you write a script?

That's a complicated area. I was talking to Anthony Minghella, who genuinely swears that he doesn't think of an audience. He tries to think what the characters would do in any given situation that's most true to them, and he doesn't consider the audience reaction to the behaviour of the characters at that moment. I definitely do. I definitely think, 'What will the audience make of the way this person is behaving? Will they be amused by it, shocked by it, sympathise with it?' I hope I'm neither condescending, thinking the audience is dumber than me, or aspirational, trying to please people who are more emotionally complex than me. I just write what I'd like to see. I've learned that the process of writing is a tug of war where you're pulling in the audience from quite far away until you're face to face at the end of the movie. A lot of film-making seems to me to be trying not to cut the rope so that they fall backwards and you have to pick it up again and drag them out of the mud. All sorts of mistakes can make the audience, whether they know it or not, lose faith in you and lose interest in the film.

In your introduction to the published script of *Four Weddings*, you list the twenty-odd times you rewrote it. Did you rewrite *The Tall Guy* equally often?

I can't remember. I took a lot of advice from my best friend, Helen Fielding, who read it a few times – in a more general way, the detailed job that Emma now does. I seem to remember that when Jeff gets sacked from his theatre show and eventually gets a new job, I originally had him becoming the presenter of a kids' TV programme, so his whole life had shrunk to having to worry about what Big Teddy thought of Little Teddy. I definitely handed in a draft which had that in it and was strongly advised, I think by Helen but it may have been by Working Title, that something grander might be better, which is why he now gets a job in a musical. So it obviously did go through quite a lot of drafts with one or two substantial changes.

In a diary for *Time Out* about the making of *The Tall Guy*, you wrote about being away the day they shot a key scene, and dismayed by the rushes until you saw them edited, when you realised your presence on set was not crucial after all.

It's very interesting that I wrote that. In fact, the opposite is true. It's completely crucial to me that I'm there. There was one moment in the movie which I missed, and I still think the movie misses that moment. In all the rehearsals there was a crack in Emma Thompson's voice when she faced Jeff with the fact that he's been unfaithful – and it said in the script, 'with a crack in her voice' – so you were meant to know that this had broken her heart and she was leaving him very unwillingly. When they did it, since there were jokes in the scene, Emma got into the swing of being in control of the situation, and you think that she doesn't mind splitting up because she didn't do the crack in her voice that day. If she had done it, you might have thought it was a better resolution when they got back together at the end than you do when you see it now.

Judging by the screenplay of *Four Weddings*, you tend to avoid directions like 'with a crack in her voice'.

If ever you say, 'quietly' or 'with anger', it always turns out that it's better to do it noisily and without anger. If I'd been there that day I would have been pretty happy with what they did, but I would have said, 'Let's have a stab at doing it the other way just in case it was right.' I do tend to put in the scripts, 'This is a very important moment', or 'This is the moment he realises', just to remind myself what the key moments in the film are, but I think it's best not to advise the actors too much.

I also read that some of the film was reshot because LWT, who co-financed it, objected to the bad language in a couple of scenes.

I doubt that. Unless we were very irresponsible. You always have to take into account the TV showing, so if you're shooting a 'fuck' or a 'shit' you do a tame version. I would very much like to see the tame version of *Four Weddings*, because Mike Newell was hilariously intolerant whenever we had to remind him that it was time to redo the whole scene changing one word. He just would not do two takes of the 'blast' and 'bugger' version, so I'm sure there are huge mistakes and truck sounds all over the TV version of that film.

It might be crucial, but the level of involvement in a film which you demand is the exception rather than the rule for most screenwriters.

I am the luckiest man in movies. I got very used very early to being involved in films from beginning to end. Tim Bevan – I don't exclude Eric Fellner, but he wasn't at Working Title then – decided that *The Tall Guy* was an inexpensive movie and I was an experienced TV writer and therefore let me pick who I wanted to direct it. And Mel, being a fantastically accessible and confident person, was happy that I should be there when it was shot and when it was edited. Whether or not you can tell other people that this is what they should aim for, my experience is that being there the whole time is what writing a film is actually about. You're there when it's being cast, so you hear the words coming out and realise where the faults are. You have a read-through once it is cast – or even before it's cast, in the case of *Notting Hill* – and make massive changes as a result of that. You're there during the rehearsals and change things because of that. You're there every day of the filming and, because the director is concentrating on something else or you notice something else you want to change, there are little contributions you can make. I don't know how much that adds up to, but it adds up to something. Then, when the film is over, I'm always there at the editing. In many cases the film is radically changed, and to consult the person who wrote it seems to me extremely helpful on the whole. The cuts are a kind of writing, a way of seeing what is necessary and not necessary. Then, when you start to test it, you're useful there. We added a new ending in *Four Weddings* – all those photos at the end – which had to be written. If my screenplays had just been made when I handed them in, I'm not sure any of them would have been good films – so I don't know that they're good screenplays. What is good is the process whereby I've been able to contribute from the very beginning to the very end. It's something that people should think about allowing to happen a bit more often. I don't know whose fault it is that it doesn't, but it certainly seems to me to be very important.

The Tall Guy is less polished than your subsequent films, more like a series of satirical sketches. Have you deliberately moved away from that?

Perhaps to some extent I have learned to hide the sketchy nature of what I write better, but I do think that oddly enough the sketches are absolutely key to the movies working well. One of the things that I learned on television, and with Rowan on stage, was writing bits of material that are three minutes long but quite funny. I'm probably still trying to do that. I've got a feeling that these carefully crafted comic set-pieces are a strength of the films.

The concept of *Four Weddings* is brilliantly simple. Where did it come from?

It was a very lucky break. Two things must have collided. A period in my life had just finished where I was going to lots of weddings, and the sense of reflection on the fact that I was single was probably more intense at weddings than at other times. That, and weddings were very funny. I was also keen – I don't know why – on writing a film where you saw just about everything that happened between the leading characters. I was particularly annoyed by films where the couple start going out with each other, then you cut to six months on and they're starting to fight with each other, and you wonder what has happened during the six months in between. I was trying to find a context where you might be able to see pretty well every word that the leading characters say to each other, without it being a film which just covers a two-hour conversation between two people. That's why the girl had to be an American, because she had to have somewhere to bugger off to between every single wedding.

Why not European?

We did consider French, but I had a doubt in my mind whether a French actress would be able to get the comic nuance behind the lines in the way that I wanted. It could have been Australian, too, and we did think about one Australian actress but didn't like her as much as the American ones.

I know that the first draft of *Notting Hill* was a very different script, but did you make any false starts on *Four Weddings*?

A lot of core things were there from the beginning, but my original title was *Four Weddings and a Honeymoon*, and I had a dreadful sequence, like the Dudley Moore film *10*, where Charles followed Carrie on her honeymoon and jumped around in the sand. Helen suggested that it might be better to have a stab at something brave, so I never wrote that version. Then I spent a lot of time with Emma trying to get the dynamics of the end right, and I wrote endless versions with different people marrying Charles. I eventually picked the girl he should be marrying because she was just about nice enough and a bit complex emotionally but obviously not right.

The photos at the end help overcome the problem that Charles has to treat the character played by Anna Chancellor very badly in order to pair off with Carrie.

I think we could have got away with that because of the way she went 'Yes!' when she looked at herself in the mirror on her wedding day. She was suddenly a character who deserved to be punished. I think the audience would have been all right with that, but it was great that we were able to be nice to her at the end anyway. The most difficult thing in *Four Weddings*, without which the movie might easily have collapsed, was the scene where Hugh talks to the James Fleet character after the funeral and before he marries Anna Chancellor. That was the toughest scene to write, because there was a severe logical problem. The funeral established that there is such a thing as true love, that there is such a thing as two people who are meant for each other, and everyone who watches the movie knows that. So to have your hero, two minutes later, marrying someone he's not right for, would have meant you didn't sympathise with what was going on. We went on holiday, Emma and I, and wrote eight versions of that scene: where he talked to Andie; where he talked to Kristin and she told him she loved him – which now happens somewhere else in the movie; where he talked to everyone. I couldn't make it work and I couldn't make it true. In the end it's sleight of hand: the nicest but stupidest person in the film offers him some bad advice. You completely sympathise with what's happened at the funeral, about the one person you love, then James says, 'I don't expect that to happen. I'll probably just find someone and hope for the best', which is absolutely the right reaction for him. And because he's so sweet, it's perfectly apt for Hugh to behave accordingly, so that when you see him marry the wrong girl you think, 'He shouldn't have done that but I know why he has.' The lesson I learned from that is it's worth spending a month writing one scene if that scene is crucial.

Was the scene tough to write simply because it was structurally crucial, or also because it was one of the most serious in the film?

I think it was just the structural thing. As a writer, you probably learn very early on that there aren't plots made in heaven, that whatever you pick will turn out to be flawed somehow. You stomp around Hampstead Heath for three hours thinking, 'There must be a way, there must be a way . . .' and actually there may not be a way. I'd gone all the way through *Four Weddings* when I found out that was the flaw in the structure, so I had to put all that work into papering over that flaw. It was a very funny scene to film because Hugh, who was always very disrespectful towards his own acting, said that he only had three techniques: normal; then, when he was trying to be sexy, his voice would drop an octave; and, when he was trying to be serious, his voice would rise an octave. We were all really aware when it came to that scene that he was going to do it falsetto – and sure enough he did do it falsetto the first few times.

By limiting yourself more or less to events surrounding five social occasions, did you have a problem fitting in all the necessary character development?

I probably squeezed most of what I wanted to say about the characters into those limits, and sometimes if you create restraints for yourself it makes you free. Instead of thinking,

'Where does Scarlett work?' I had to say, 'Where can I show how she stands emotionally?' and devise something to do that job: talking to a little girl under a table.

Some of the critics complained that you don't know where the characters work, or why someone like Scarlett would be living with Charles.

I don't believe that is a problem. I don't think it's a problem for most people who watch the movie. My argument was that when you're hanging around with your friends, who are often more miscellaneous than you might think, you don't explain who you are. You don't say, 'Hello, Charles Bennett. How's life at the bank since your father died?' You exist in a world which doesn't reveal what you do and what your surname is. I wanted to reproduce real life in that way, not to have endless reference to extraneous things but for friendship to be the key. We did shoot a scene that explained all of that, but we didn't put it in. It came in the cab ride back to Carrie's flat after the second wedding. Charles explained that Scarlett had come to a party at his house, and when he woke up the next morning she was asleep on the floor having been abandoned by her boyfriend and he never had the heart to throw her out; and that Simon Callow's character had been a brilliant young teacher who befriended him at university, and was then sacked for some disgraceful act and came down to London and became friends with them. I knew all that, I just didn't want to include it.

The industrial backdrop of the funeral contrasts sharply with the monied luxury of the weddings. Did you choose that setting as another way of showing where at least one of the characters came from?

That was the combined brilliance of everyone in the production except me. I imagined that Simon Callow's character came from up north, and it was going to be a rather bleak chapel in a small town on the moors, which would show something interesting about his background. But somewhere along the way the decision was made that it should be industrial, and the location person found this brilliant church with this huge factory behind it. Also, in terms of realism, all the people in the church – including his mum and dad – were actually extras who lived around there, marvellous found faces who came on the day. I do think the idea of monied luxury is slightly overstating the social context of *Four Weddings*, but there you go.

The producer this time around was Duncan Kenworthy. How important is your creative partnership with him?

I do like to keep things intimate; I do like to work with people I know. There's less chance of it going wrong later on, when you discover they're child-murdering sadists – which wasn't clear when you first met them. I've since found a million other reasons why Duncan was a good choice, but originally I was impressed by the aesthetic quality of his work and I thought it would be great to have a guy with a good eye – because that wasn't something I had. I thought, 'If I ask Duncan to do *Four Weddings*, he'll make sure it looks lovely and sounds lovely.' The producer of *The Tall Guy* was a guy called Paul Webster, who later ran FilmFour, and I loved the way he did the job and would have asked him again but he was a thousand miles away in the States.

And presumably you learned a lot from collaborating with Mike Newell?

Both Mike and Roger Michell added a maturity and depth which I'm not sure were there in the scripts. I learned a lot from Mike, so maybe there was more balance in *Notting Hill* when we started it, but I remember handing the script of *Four*

Weddings to a few people, and reading it myself, and thinking there was the possibility of it looking like a light-entertainment-sketch film. I specifically picked Mike because he was a serious director who gave it that third dimension. I really did my homework. Emma and myself probably watched a hundred films to try and find who we wanted to do it. I even watched a three-part Australian TV thriller because there was a guy who I'd been told was quite interesting. We finally decided on Mike after watching something he did on television called *Ready When You Are, Mr McGill*, an extraordinarily good Jack Rosenthal film about an idiosyncratic group of people under a lot of pressure. Mike had the ability to make that funny yet humane. And watching his other films, I noticed a documentary edge, the sense of real life going on. To be able to go to Tim and Eric – as it was by that stage – and say, 'This is the guy, and this is the reason why this is the guy', lifted a tremendous burden off them. Otherwise they would have been thinking the same thing that most producers think when they get a script that they like: 'Who the hell should we get to do it?' Maybe one of the things that writers should do before they hand in their scripts is work out who would be able to direct it, because they might find that they get their way more often than they might think – though it might have been harder if Mike hadn't just done *Enchanted April*, which was a lovely and successful movie, and maybe it would have been harder if I'd gone for the director of the Australian TV thriller.

Did you work more rigorously with Mike Newell than Mel Smith?

I think that's probably true. Mel and I were new to it, but Mike had some extraordinary qualities. One was the detail with which he auditioned the movie. Mike will spend a day with ten actors, forty minutes each, for a part four lines long. He absolutely must find the right person, and every bit of the film got raked over during the hugely long time we set aside for casting it. You'd have a character called Third Gentleman; a lovely actor who was far too good for the part would walk in; Mike would say, 'This is a very complicated part. Richard, explain something about the background of this person'; and I'd have no idea – he was just Third Gentleman. I'd have to make something up, and then Mike would chip in, and by the time the audition was over we actually would know more about the character, and sometimes I would rewrite it to make it better. Mike also wanted to make sure that the drama was right and thought that the jokes could take care of themselves, whereas at that stage in our careers Mel and I would probably have been tempted to say, 'Let's make it funny and hope the drama survives.' Mike was quite firm with me about that. He was also very good on the 'arc' of every character. He said that you must give everyone a beginning, a middle and an end, no matter how small their part, and that was very apt in *Four Weddings* where there were all these characters. Sometimes I stuck in a middle and sometimes I stuck in an end, and I now do that on every film I write. I go through the long process of pretending that I'm the actor who's just got those lines, and only those lines, to see whether or not they make sense as a story outside the context of the film. So there was a lot of work done on the script.

How important is the role of script editor?

It's a hundred per cent important. When the director and Duncan come on board, they never quite believe that all this stuff went on beforehand, and think it's to do with the fact that Emma's my girlfriend that I insist on this credit, but it's absolutely crucial to the way that the films work. What I had with Helen and have with Emma is a person who wants well for you, shares your view of the world to a great extent and is therefore very critical of everything which is not as good as you can do. When I finish a script – or even long before – Emma will read it. It'll take her seven hours, which always makes me incredibly angry. I say, 'How are you meant to like the film if it takes you seven hours to read?' But that's the speed she goes, and she'll completely annotate it – and where she's most right I'll get most angry, because that'll be an area where I know there's a problem and I think I've been cunning, and she instantly spots that it's only cunning and it's not true. She puts these fateful letters – CDB (Could Do Better), or NG (No Good), or NF (Not Funny) – all the way through. I'll then rewrite according to those notes, many of which will chime with my own concerns, and sometimes she'll write stuff in. My favourite line in *Bridget Jones's Diary* is when Bridget says, 'He said you'd slept with his fiancée and left him broken-hearted', and Colin Firth says, 'No, it was my wife, my heart.' Emma wrote that line. And she wrote the speech that Bridget makes under the stairs. And she wrote a speech that James Fleet makes in *Four Weddings*. This is not her sitting down to write; it's her scribbling in the corner, 'Surely it should be more like this?' It's actually very demanding, because time and time again the script will go to her and come back – this sounds like we have the most boring relationship in the world! – and we will discuss over long meals who Hugh Grant should be marrying at the end of the movie.

Were you prepared for the success of *Four Weddings*?

No, we were amazed. The most exciting night of our lives was when we tested *Four Weddings* in Santa Barbara and got higher marks than we did in the UK, because at the same moment with *The Tall Guy* we got the most terrible reaction. We had no idea how it would do there and were absolutely delighted that it did well.

You've written three solo scripts: *The Tall Guy*, *Four Weddings* and *Notting Hill*. You've collaborated on two: *Bean*, with Robin Driscoll, and *Bridget Jones*, with Helen Fielding and

Andrew Davies. And, of course, you wrote *Blackadder* with Ben Elton. Do you find that both writing methods work equally well?

I think the answer to the question is concealed in the question: co-writing is easier when emotion isn't involved. The only time when the writing process didn't work in *Blackadder* was whenever emotion entered into it. There were a few times when Ben or I tried to make Blackadder softer or hurt – apart from the very end of the final episode – and the process never allowed that to happen because it's very hard to co-write with people when you come to matters of the heart. *Bean* was not a very heartfelt movie, even though we tried to make it a bit heartfelt, so it was apt that I wrote it with Robin. *Bridget Jones* stands out as being an exception to that, and in a way it is, but from when I got the script to when the film was made I worked with no one else. I simply took all the stuff done by Helen and Andrew, which was deep and good, and either left it or changed it a bit. I didn't have to go back to them and check whether or not they agreed this would be a more sensitive way of doing something. If that had been the case it would have been hard.

Bean was a complete change of pace between *Four Weddings* and *Notting Hill*. Why did you want to bring *Mr Bean* to the big screen?

I thought it would be my last chance to make a stupid movie with toilet jokes in it.

Had your working relationship with Mel Smith changed since *The Tall Guy*?

Bean was a bit different. The working relationship with Mel was completely delightful during all the sections I was there, but actually I wasn't there for the shoot because it was in

America. I didn't want to leave my family for that length of time, I was doing something else which was late and I thought that Mel, Robin and Rowan were quite enough cooks for that broth.

What was the main problem in expanding TV half-hours to feature-film length?

Finding a plot which could sustain it; a plot which was bigger, broader and had a bit more depth. In the end, we came up with a story where he was: 1) abroad, a fish out of water; 2) mistaken for someone else, which allowed the level of mis-understanding to grow; and 3) in a situation where there could be some kind of emotional change, so he would start out destroying someone's life and end up being friends with them. We were setting out to three-dimensionalise him, and the interesting thing is that implicit in all the TV stuff is a third dimension of sorrow and selfishness that comes from living alone – so actually there was quite a lot to work with.

Why did you choose America as the foreign location?

Having denied that we ever do anything for the sake of Americans, I suppose that might also have been in our minds – though we hadn't suffered on *Four Weddings* from setting it all in Surrey – but I thought that he would come across more strange things over there, and something about the emotional openness of Americans made it more plausible that he would be mistaken for an artistic genius. Thank heaven we did go abroad, because when we first screened *Bean* in the UK it had a much longer beginning, with jokes which were more similar to what was shown on the telly, and the audience couldn't have been more indifferent. They wanted something different to happen to him, on a different scale, so the instinct to go abroad was correct.

Were you worried that giving Bean an unfamiliar context, an emotional journey and actual dialogue might undermine the things that made the character work – not to mention the international appeal of pure visual comedy?

For the TV series, Rowan's catchphrase was, 'Will they get it in Egypt?' In the film, we tried to keep the key comic bits completely understandable, but by putting in a lot of dialogue it was automatically not going to be as extraordinarily international. But we were certainly aware of trying to keep his speech down to an absolute minimum. In fact, there was a draft where he said absolutely nothing, but it turned out that really did leave us up a creek. The whole film became about desperately striving to think of contexts where he could be silent. So even if we did lose something by having him speak, on balance it was better.

How long did it take to write?

A long time. *Bean* was a complicated process, one driven by there being no particular need to make it. We were busy doing other things, and we had lots of meetings where we asked, 'Shall we do it, and if we did it what kind of film would it be?' It went through various manifestations until we finally plumped for this very simple plot.

What role did Rowan Atkinson play in that process?

He was there before Robin and I got down to writing it, and he was as involved in the script as Mel or any other colla-borator, probably even more, because he started on it earlier – not writing it, but criticising it inch by inch. Then, having written a first draft of the film, Robin, Rowan, Mel and I went to a room off the King's Road – as we always did with *Mr Bean* – and spent two weeks improvising visually on about twelve scenarios which we thought were funny and then fitted into the script – and those remain the best bits of the film. Rowan's part in that creative process was equal to ours, because when we said, 'Now let's pretend the room is an airport. Now let's pretend the room is an art gallery,' he thought of as many funny things as we did. All four of us really came up with those key moments, but by the time it got to shooting every word and every movement was absolutely set in stone. Except what Rowan did in the two-way mirror, which he made much funnier on the day.

Was it a full-length script, 90 pages or so?

Probably 120. There was a great deal cut out of the film that you saw. It was probably about two hours ten originally, and the final movie was two thirds of that. That's turned out to be par for the course on my films, but the reason for cutting that one was very specific. Even though we were trying to tell a story and humanise the character – Bean making his first friend and the family coming to love him – when it was first shown to us it was very obvious where we had failed to be as funny as we wanted to be. On the whole the serious bits were intertwined with the bits where we were trying to be funny, and normally you would leave the bits that worked and take out the bits that didn't, but here it was so obvious that we were trying to be funny that if we failed the whole chunk had to go. We cut a great big twelve-minute section when Rowan arrives in Los Angeles. The family is waiting for him but don't know what he looks like and don't see the police show him out of the airport, so he goes to their house and breaks in, thinking they're asleep, then they come back and go to bed, not knowing he's there, followed by lots of farcical to-ing and fro-ing. But because the farce didn't ring true, or the percentage of jokes wasn't high enough, all that lovely stuff about a lonely man arriving and unpacking and his anal attitude to everything had to be cut wholesale.

The key to successful farce is meant to be good pacing, isn't it?

I don't know that it is to do with pacing, actually, because when we edited it we tried every pace! Anyone involved in a TV sketch show will tell you that at least a third of things just don't work – and you never know which third it's going to be. The reason we didn't pare the script down from the start, knowing the film would always be no longer than ninety minutes, was because we said, 'Some of this stuff won't work. Let's give ourselves some choice.'

You once denied that *Mr Bean* was pure slapstick. What's the difference?

I don't think I know what 'slapstick' really means. Pure slapstick probably depends on the fact that there is a plank, a bucket of water and some glass, and these things will inevitably collide. *Mr Bean* is built on Rowan's extraordinary characterisation of Bean, who has a certain intellectual attitude to everything which drives the way he behaves and what happens as a result. In a slapstick thing, Rowan, having wet his trousers, would probably get totally wet in a hundred ways, but in *Bean*, having wet his trousers, the interesting and complicated thing is how he attempts to hide it.

After the enthusiastic response to *Four Weddings*, the reviews of *Bean* were a throwback to *The Tall Guy*. Most critics simply didn't find it funny.

The Tall Guy got terrible reviews, but I'd seen it with audiences who thought it was a funny film, so I looked into it and found out, as happened when I was a film reviewer, that the definitive screening for the most important critics in this country had taken place one morning at a cinema in Wardour Street where there were thirty seats and ten people watching it.

And I'm sure they didn't laugh. Not once. And I'm sure when they wrote, 'This film has no jokes in it', they really meant it, because they hadn't laughed and neither had anybody else. Whereas if they'd come to Reading, where I saw it in front of 500 people, they would have realised there *were* some jokes in it. We protected ourselves by having critics see *Four Weddings* and *Notting Hill* with proper audiences, which creates a different mood, but *Bean* must have been shown to the ten guys in the subterranean cinema, because it was perfectly fine in front of a crowd.

Notting Hill was one of the most eagerly awaited and heavily promoted films of all time. Did you feel under pressure to repeat the success of Four Weddings?

No. I felt under no pressure at all. The process of writing the film was so long and so laborious that the idea of a final public or critical reaction was irrelevant. And no one gives a damn who writes films, so the fact that it was written by the same person was not going to create public hysteria. While I was writing it I didn't even know Hugh was going to be in it. It was obvious by the time I finished it that he should be in it, but I knew that the female lead had to be a very famous film star, and there was always this doubt in my mind whether it would be all right to cast another star opposite her.

You originally took the script in a different direction, didn't you?

Notting Hill was originally about choice, about choosing a girl. A man falls in love with a film star, and when she goes away he starts going out with an extraordinary local girl who works in the shop opposite – very like the character Emma Chambers played in the movie, Honey, who was eventually his sister. Then the film star comes back, and he has to make this choice, and he chooses the local girl, and the Julia Roberts character goes along to the wedding. I wrote that film and it was a different film, and in the end I couldn't bear it because I couldn't bring myself to make that choice.

Couldn't you have paired off the Julia Roberts character with someone else?

There was no one to pair her off with – and, since the central thesis of the movie at the very beginning had been, 'What would it be like to go out with someone famous?' and since I was finding it painful to reject someone the character had been in love with, I decided that I would just try and make it about one girl not two. The weakness of the film is probably that it doesn't have a subplot, so when she goes away there's not quite enough happening. That's partly explained by its genesis.

Notting Hill is almost the reverse of Four Weddings: what the characters do for a living is not only discussed but is the whole point of the story.

The jobs were crucial. I took a long time picking what he should do. I thought he might work in a photographer's gallery, but then I thought that would probably mean he had met famous people before. Actually, I now remember that until the very end there was a scene set in Hugh's place of work in *Four Weddings*. Not only was he late for his wedding, but he actually had to go to a business meeting on the way. He walked in, spent forty seconds apologising for being late, made one contribution and then said, 'I'm sorry. I have to leave.' But we cut that.

After the huge success of Four Weddings, though, did you consider writing a sequel rather than a follow-up?

It never occurred to me. I've never been very interested in the break-up of love; I'm much more interested in the finding of it.

Having established two people who love each other and are happy, I wouldn't have wanted to write a film about how that went wrong – which you would have had to do. I did have the idea of doing a sequel to *Notting Hill* in a completely different genre, which would have been quite fun, so that you meet these characters in a romantic comedy and they then get caught up in a thriller, but I never wrote it.

In interviews about the films, Hugh Grant more or less said that the characters he played were more or less you. What are your thoughts on that?

Well, I think you're very lucky if you find an actor who says your lines absolutely right. We auditioned at incredible length for *Four Weddings* and found one person who did it right. Hugh has found a way of making the slightly dull central character that I write funny and interesting and sympathetic. How the character relates to me, I don't know. To be honest, what constitutes a character is very confusing. He's probably a muddle of me and my four best friends and people I know and how I dream I might be, but I don't think, 'Secretly, this is what I'm like.'

Do you think William Thacker is a sadder, wiser version of Charles?

I think he is. We were very happy with the idea that Hugh was older and looked it, and he was perfectly happy to play someone who had been battered around a bit.

Did you write any of the other parts in your films with specific actors in mind?

Not really. Oddly enough, I'm writing a couple of parts in the new film with specific actors in mind, which is not necessarily a good thing. The actresses I had in mind when I was writing

Julia's part were Grace Kelly and Audrey Hepburn, but if I were writing it now I *would* write it for her, because what happens between Julia and the camera is astounding and makes what I wrote look so good. She did a fantastic thing of smiling all the way through that scene at the end where she comes to the bookshop and he rejects her. It certainly didn't say in the script, 'She smiles', and the power of that scene is infinitely greater because of her decision. But on the whole I don't write for specific actors. Two friends of mine, Emma Chambers and Tim McInnerny, were among the friends in *Notting Hill*, but they had to audition insultingly hard to get those roles.

Like *Bean*, a lot of material from *Notting Hill* hit the cutting-room floor. Why, and how did that compare to *Four Weddings* and *The Tall Guy*?

The Tall Guy would have been shot in thirty-four days or something, and I don't know that there was that much to cut. Not much was cut from *Four Weddings*. But you're right – a lot was cut from *Notting Hill*. It came out very long. The final read-through wasn't too long, so we probably got into a rhythm of doing stuff a little slowly while filming. We'd rehearsed it a lot, everyone knew what they wanted to get out of a scene and in getting that out of a scene on location you often go a bit slower. Also, the film was repetitive to a certain extent. There was a long wedding sequence at the end, and we realised that all you wanted to see was Julia looking gorgeous and Hugh looking happy, and that Spike being funny and Bernie being insecure was already there in the way they behaved at the press conference. The scene where Julia and Hugh were alone in the house for a whole evening was much longer, but ten seconds of them both reading was all it took for you to know that they're comfortable with each other, therefore you didn't need a conversation to establish it.

Perhaps it was slower than *Four Weddings* because it was more thoughtful.

Maybe. *Four Weddings* always had people buzzing around quite frantically, whereas *Notting Hill* had people interviewing each other or talking late at night or worrying about whether they were going to get a phone call. It was a more sedentary film. In fact, at one point Tim Bevan said to me, 'The film isn't funny enough', so I thought, 'Right. I'll go away and make it funnier.' It seemed to me that the best way of making it funnier was to extend the bits where it was quite funny already rather than saying, 'Oh, Christ. Let's introduce another new scenario or an entirely new character.' That stuff at the press junket where he comes out of her room and is guided in to interview other people was all added afterwards.

The supporting characters seem to have been the main casualties. The friend who runs the restaurant, for instance, is introduced in the opening voiceover then says almost nothing until the end.

We cut a lot of the friends' stuff. You did become very interested in Hugh and Julia very early in the movie, and it actually turned out to be counter-productive going too far in other directions. There used to be a big scene between the friends at the beginning, but we found the joy was meeting the characters at their most interesting moment. If you'd met them earlier in the movie, it would have been a guy with some friends, then a guy with some friends talking about stuff, and then Julia visiting those friends. But to meet those characters when she walks in on them, when they behave quintessentially to type under pressure, was such a gift that it made the other scenes unnecessary. I think what you end up cutting from movies, mainly, is stuff which the magic of movies renders unnecessary – when the director gets things absolutely right.

What made you choose Roger Michell?

I like all Roger's work. I went to see *My Night with Reg*, which I loved, and I liked *Persuasion* a lot. The piece which made me absolutely sure he was right was *The Buddha of Suburbia*. There were a lot of worlds portrayed in that, and it could have been horribly mismatched, but he managed to make all those worlds fit together. I thought that he'd do the same in this movie, which has one world meeting another world. It also had that thing I most need in my films: an interest in the truth of things, the realistic rather than the parodic.

What's your attitude to the so-called 'vanity credit' which directors often take, specifically 'A Mike Newell Film' and 'A Roger Michell Film'?

I don't feel strongly about it, although I once saw a film which came to the final frame and then cut very dramatically to something saying 'A so-and-so film', and I thought, 'That's weird. I definitely saw three actors on screen, so they must have been involved in the process somewhere, but apparently it's just this guy.'

You had a lot more money to spend second time around. What are the pros and cons of not having to be so frugal?

Nobody ever thinks they've got enough money. Ridley Scott was saying in something I read the other day, 'I battled the budget as much on *Gladiator* as on *The Duellists*.' In *Four Weddings*, we only had three days in the studio, I think, and the rest we had to do on location, sometimes in tiny rooms, squeezing up staircases with the sound man down two floors. In *Notting Hill*, we actually built Hugh's house, which would be a lot more expensive, but once you're at it you strangely don't feel the benefits. You're still filming. There's still a lot to do every day. The major benefit, I'm sure, was that we could afford Julia. And, of course, by that time, afford Hugh.

A widespread criticism was that Notting Hill itself looks less multicultural than it really is, partly because the film shares one of the features of *Four Weddings*: the absence of any major ethnic characters. How do you respond to that?

Well, it's not great, and I'd prefer it if I hadn't done that twice. It's not that we didn't see actors who might have fitted that bill, but we just happen not to have cast them. I hope I can rectify that. It was quite right that people should criticise the thing about Notting Hill, but they wouldn't have done if we'd called it *The Famous Girl*, as we very nearly did, so to some extent it's the title rather than the content. There was also some stuff in those big cuts which would have made people happier than they were.

And perhaps people are more ready to criticise a film which is heavily hyped.

That doesn't worry me particularly. Hype can hurt films if they don't work as well in front of an audience as you hope, but you can benefit from it if people expect they're going to have a good time and consequently laugh more than they would have.

Notting Hill changed shape several times between conception and completion. Were you pleased with it ultimately?

The problem with films is that by the time you've finished making them you can't bear watching them. When you're testing a movie you fly all the way to Los Angeles, where there are ten films on you'd like to see, and you have to sit down and watch your own film, twice, then fly back and recut it and watch it again – and again and again. After seeing a film 200 times it's hard to evaluate. You start to only love one thing – in *Notting Hill* it's Julia's face – so it might be better to ask me what I think of them in five years, when I can watch them properly again. The process of writing a film is much more than writing the screenplay. I think the movie is made at least four times. Once in the writing. Then in the shooting, which is the second film. Then in the editing, which is the third film. Then I think there might be this fourth film, which is stepping right back, being even more ruthless, losing bits that you love because they interfere with the flow and the energy of what has emerged, and because some scenes are funnier and some performances are better than you thought. The screenplay is only the beginning.

Which seems to have been reinforced by *Bridget Jones*. So who wrote what?

I wouldn't say I've got to the bottom of the complex sequence of events surrounding *Bridget Jones*. Helen did a draft. Then Andrew did a draft. Then I did a draft. And I'm sure all of us did more than one draft. And somewhere in there Sharon Maguire also did a draft, attempting to put together my early suggestions, stuff that Helen and Andrew had done and stuff from the book. I then worked on it for around two and a half months before it started shooting. And after all that, when we went to the read-through it was still only about sixty-seven per cent right. *Four Weddings* and *Notting Hill* were more right than that.

Were you always scheduled to work on the film?

No. It was a very personal and personable thing. The script didn't seem to be right, and Helen's godmother of my daughter, and Sharon's godmother of my son, and Tim and Eric are godfathers of my career, and I had a couple of months where
the choice was between writing *Bridget Jones* or starting

another film for Tim and Eric, so it seemed like a perfectly benign thing to do.

You seem to capture the spirit of the book without being faithful to the letter.

It's famously difficult adapting books, and the people involved in *Bridget Jones* have now got a sniff of why that is. It took a long time to get right because it took us a long time to realise how different the film was going to be, and how much effect it would have on the book to actually see Bridget. Everyone who reads *Bridget Jones* is critical of her and amused by her but also partly is her, looking at things through her eyes, yet when you first see Renée she is a specific person who you feel specific emotions for, and those emotions are rather different, I think, from the emotions you feel when you read the first page of the book. The most important thing in adapting *Bridget Jones* is that you should care for Bridget Jones, which Sharon and Renée achieved, and they probably achieved that more in making the film than we did in writing it. We created the context for Bridget to be human and lovely and touching, but it needed Sharon to direct it beautifully and Renée to act it beautifully, and the moment we got that a lot of what we'd written became slightly unnecessary and slightly wrong. Then, when we got to the edit, because the screenplay was flawed and the strength of material in the book was waiting behind it, there were lots of things wrong with the movie. It was long – about three hours, and the finished film is only ninety minutes – and the first forty minutes were not the slightest bit engaging. Bridget seemed like quite a nice girl who men kept making passes at, and it was only when we moved the turkey-curry scene right to the top and the song 'All By Myself' to second position that everyone started taking her problem seriously. Darcy treats her horribly at that party, and you see how painful it must be if you're a klutzy singleton with a dreadful mum – all the things *Bridget Jones* is about – then we went straight to her drinking on her own in her bedroom in her cosy pyjamas, and by the time that sequence was over everyone was rooting for her and the film really takes off. At first it absolutely didn't, because we hadn't put enough obstacles in the way.

Do you think the screenplay was less than 100 per cent because, in part, the project was something of a departure for you? First, it was an adaptation. Second, it was a rewrite . . .

And third, it had a girl in the lead. Well, I think the script was less than 100 per cent because we should have spent longer on it. Writing scripts is very difficult, and just because you're adapting a book doesn't mean it's any easier. You've still got to deal with problems in tremendous depth. The big plus of the whole process was that Helen had given us so many gifts. When I got quite near the end, I just went back to the book and stole lots of jokes. She'd cut out the whole fire-pole thing, but for Bridget to get another job seemed to me a good idea. When there was a problem it was lovely to be able to go not to your own imagination but to Helen's. That was a new pleasure.

You're now writing a film with multiple characters and inter-secting storylines. Judging by the ensemble casts of Notting Hill and particularly Four Weddings, that's a film which has been struggling to get out for quite a while.

Yes. I've obviously been very interested in this subject of a person finding true love, but the moment you start writing other characters you're interested in them as well. I wanted to try and write a movie with lots of stories because a lot of really enjoyable movies have done that recently, such as Smoke and Short Cuts, and because my favourite film throughout my adult life has been Nashville. Also, I can't bring myself to spend another three years just writing about two people. It might be quite nice to write about sixteen.

Have your own films always been inspired by other films?

Only in the most general sense. With *The Tall Guy*, my inspiration was that *Gregory's Girl* was such a good film and *Rita, Sue and Bob Too* was such a good film. Another particular favourite of mine is a bicycling film called *Breaking Away*. These movies gave me confidence that I could write about things which had happened to me or I'd like to happen to me and they might turn out to be good movies. With *Four Weddings*, I don't think I had any particular precedent in mind. With *Notting Hill*, I think I had in mind – without any presumption that either movie is of the same quality as these two movies – the progression from *Annie Hall* to *Manhattan*, two of my favourite movies, both on the same sort of subject but one of them less sketchy and more melancholy. I think I was hoping that *Notting Hill* would be that sort of progression from *Four Weddings*. But even though I love films, writing my own films is such a long process, and so involved with itself, that trying to be like another film, or in the genre of another film, would be too oblique, not something which would last all the way through the process.

Which comes back to what you said about the unproduced script. It must be . . .

A tale you want to tell, yes.

I read that you were also working on a script about old age.

There is a script about two old people, but it may end up as a play. Since, for ten years now, I've been in love with the same person, and because a happily married couple – as it were – is   99 a famously boring subject, I was trying to think, 'How can I write about that subject?' And I thought maybe the way to do it is to write about people at the end of their lives, where there is a danger that one of them might die and their love is all they have left. That's a way of writing about things that I'm most interested in now – but it's taken years of practice to do the comedy, and I don't want to be all cocky and think I know how to do drama not having practised it.

Do you have any ambitions to direct?

I'll probably give it a try soon. I think it would be an apt thing to do in my forties. And I fear for the films as a result. But the thing is, I'm very at ease on film sets now. I haven't got that fear of seventy people standing around expecting you to know what you're doing. I'm sure I'll still make a mess of it, but I won't be paralysed by it, as I was when I first tried to direct a commercial fifteen years ago.

You write in one of the offices here at Portobello Studios. How important is that daily routine to your writing?

The truth about writing is that you have to work at it long and hard. I've always thought that in order to write well you've got to work for eight hours a day – and since becoming a father it's a question of which eight hours. When I was writing *Blackadder*, I used to get up at eleven, make a couple of phone calls, go shopping, watch *Neighbours*, work from three until six, watch telly until eleven, then work until four in the morning. Now, I work from ten until six, because I want to walk my children to school and get home in time to spend the evening with them.

And, of course, you only write for half the year. The other half you're working on Comic Relief.

And on actually making the films. But when I do write I work pretty hard. My working life has three qualities. First, I'm still managing to ignore the fact that ninety-eight per cent of what I write will never reach the screen. I worked out that I wrote twenty pages' worth of script every day on *Notting Hill* and twelve seconds of that appeared in the final film – about a fifth of a page – but I still try to write with the optimism that what I write today is definitive. The second thing is that I never start with a blank page. I always leave myself a note or a thought at the end of the day, which means I'm always rewriting. The other thing is that I listen to music all the time, to create an artificial atmosphere of emotion or enthusiasm. The whole of *Notting Hill* was written listening to a version of the Tom Waits song 'Downtown Train' by Everything But The Girl. I actually had a tape with that on, forty minutes on one side and forty minutes on the other. There was something about that song which reminded me of the level of love and sorrow that I wanted.

Which part of the film-making process do you enjoy most?

'Is there *any* part I enjoy?' is a more relevant question. The best moments are when the right person turns up for an audition, when the read-through goes well and when the total despair with which one first screens a movie becomes elation if people like it. And being on set with Hugh is always fun.

Is it true that you're not a visual writer?

When I started in telly we had to portray Elizabethan England with three rooms, so my mind didn't get honed on pictures. I don't think of what my characters look like, much, and on the whole where they live is based on places I live, which other people can re-imagine. That might be a weakness when I get around to directing, or it might be a strength because I don't assume that pictures will do the job completely. There's a scene in *Notting Hill* where the paparazzi are waiting outside the door, and I thought, 'That'll be interesting: noisy and lots of people.' If I'd been more visual I might have thought, 'It'll be great when Spike comes out in his underpants,' but I'm not aware of the visual power of things so I tried to write more jokes in the corridor afterwards. Where other writers might stop, I simply bashed on – and if the director makes the visuals interesting you double your money.

What do you see as being your other strengths and weaknesses?

I suppose my strengths are that I write from instinct and, from time to time, I write things which are funny. My weaknesses are that I don't write visually, I don't know about three-act structure – and I'm scared to find out in case it affects the way that I write – and I'm not a master of the short scene. I was watching *You Can Count On Me* the other day, which has a fantastic screenplay, and there were some really beautiful scenes where people say three lines. Maybe if I was more concise, more visual and had more sense of structure, I would write much better, but learning from a film is a bit like saying, 'I've got a new girlfriend, but I'd like her to have the same teeth and hairstyle as my last girlfriend.' In any new context, the package is so different that you can't salvage much information from the last. When I try and think, 'What wisdom can I hand on, even to myself?' I don't know that there is much. You might find that one type of beginning is incredibly good for one movie and another type of beginning is incredibly good for another movie. It won't necessarily be the same. So it's hard to learn from films.

Frank Cottrell Boyce was born in 1960, in Liverpool, and was educated there and at Keble College, Oxford. He is married with six children and lives in Merseyside.

FILM

Butterfly Kiss (Michael Winterbottom, 1995, UK)

Welcome to Sarajevo (Michael Winterbottom, 1997, UK/US)

Hilary and Jackie (Anand Tucker, 1998, UK)

The Claim (Michael Winterbottom, 2001, UK/Can/Fr)

Pandaemonium (Julien Temple, 2000, UK/US)

24 Hour Party People (Michael Winterbottom, 2002, UK)

The Revenger's Tragedy (Alex Cox, 2002, UK)

SCREENPLAYS

Delirious (spec)

Millions (Mission Pictures)

The Golden Man (Archer Street)

Gambit (Universal)

The Railway Man (Archer Street)

Code 46 (Revolution Films)

The Tower (Working Title)

Milk (Archer Street)

When did you decide that you wanted to be a screenwriter?

That's what I always wanted to do, for as long as I can remember. As a kid I absolutely loved movies. I'm probably the last generation that went to Saturday-morning pictures regularly. I don't know how I knew that people wrote them. I meet grown-ups now, with degrees and families, who still don't know that people write them. I think it might have come from watching *Sunset Boulevard*. William Holden had this lovely overcoat, and I've always been a sucker for big overcoats, so I thought that in screenwriting a world of overcoats awaited me.

What was your first step towards a big overcoat?

Working on a soap opera here in Liverpool, the revolting *Brookside*. The programme was just starting up and they would literally take anyone on. They would also chuck anyone out, so the turnover was really rapid. You'd go to a story meeting one week and be introduced to twelve writers, then go the following week and meet a completely different twelve writers. I didn't stay very long. They were doing a link-up with schools programmes, and they put me on a sabbatical to Thames Television to write a one-off drama about some characters from this soap opera who take drugs and go to jail or take up smoking and die. Some cautionary tale or other. And at Thames Television I met Michael Winterbottom, who was a trainee editor. In those days the only way you could become an editor at Thames was if another editor died, and Michael was champing at the bit and desperate to direct. So we met in the canteen, swapped dreams and agreed to form an escape committee.

It was several years before you made your first feature to-gether, though.

Well, when I jacked *Brookside* in, it was 1980-something, and the idea of making movies in Britain was considered bizarre and quixotic. It was a bit like saying, 'I'm going to become a roof-thatcher', or, 'I'm going to go door to door mending fishing nets'. Making movies was a lost art. I realised very quickly that Michael having been to film school and having seen lots of films by Godard didn't mean we were going to be able to make our own films. I'd spec-written a film called *Delirious* which was always on the brink of being made, and when I left *Brookside* it was because someone with a chequebook was definitely going to make it. We still haven't made it, actually. This went on until my kids were starving and there was a repossession order on the house. So I started writing for *Coronation Street*, which was just delightful. It was nice being connected to an audience of fifteen or twenty million, and I was the youngest writer on the programme by about 190 years.

What did you learn from writing soap opera?

I learned some very bad things which I think infect a lot of British screenwriting. Soap opera has become the dominant narrative mode for many young people, and whereas American soap opera follows the story, British soap opera follows the day through, starting with breakfast at the Duckworth's and ending with last orders at the Rovers. I've no idea why. It's like a folk custom, the narrative equivalent of morris dancing. If you work on soaps for a while and then try to write your own stuff, you find that you're waking your characters up in the morning and putting them to bed at night – and if there's a car chase in between, you feel obliged to make them stop off for petrol. It's true. And it's a terrible habit. But the good thing I learned from soaps was the value of hiding set-up scenes by making them work on their own terms. As a young writer you tended to get the Monday episode, which was all set-up, but the pay-offs would come in the Friday episode.

You learned to write a very good scene about someone buying tea, so that no one at home would suspect there was going to be a tea party. Then, on Friday, they'd go, 'Look at that! That's the tea he bought on Monday!'

Did you bring any of these lessons to bear on *Butterfly Kiss*?

The official ideology of screenwriting has a puritanical approach to dialogue: less is more and cross it out and make it transparent. But *Coronation Street* had basically been going for forty years on the back of its fabulously rococo dialogue, and I really enjoyed writing it. I was still writing for *Coronation Street* when I wrote *Butterfly Kiss*, because again I was writing the film on spec, and *Butterfly Kiss* is really *Coronation Street Goes Psycho*. When we couldn't get *Delirious* off the ground, Michael and I had one conversation about what else might be possible and this was really the last shot. I went on holiday to Ireland and crashed the car in the back of beyond, so I wrote the script in about five days because I had nothing else to do. It was like a scream of pain against the lack of Volvo parts in the west of Ireland – and I don't think we changed a word of it.

Do you often write scripts that quickly?

I've probably written a couple more scripts like that, although that makes it sound as if it was easy to write it in five days. In fact, what happens is you're really in there, you're not trying to do other things and all your powers are working. It's a fantastic feeling, to write something really quickly, in one burst of energy, because you just know you're doing it right. If someone says that they've written a screenplay really quickly, they've probably given it their very best shot.

Were you concerned with things like character arcs and three-act structure?

I've only had to deal with that stuff in meetings with script editors, and when it comes up I give them a steely look. I'm nonplussed by it all. Have you ever met a real person with a character arc, a person who had an experience, learned from it and moved on? That's one thing about soap opera: at least you were writing about people who never changed, people who were resilient to the lessons of their own experience. Someone could be married to a bigamist or be shot by a bank robber and carry on being the most boring person on earth.

Where did the idea come from?

I don't know where the idea came from. The whole thing happened so quickly that I've never really had time to reflect on it. We went from script to shooting in a few months. I think the idea was simply to make a low-budget film with just two actors and no art director, and it seemed to me that if the film was going to have a low-budget look then it should have a really grand theme – like spiritual despair. Michael's always taking the piss out of my Catholicism, so my revenge on him was to write an intensely Catholic film which at the same time was very do-able. And there was really only one place you could set a film about spiritual despair, which was the M6, so I did relish the fact that Michael would have to shoot the Book of Job up there in Barrow-in-Furness.

It may have been very do-able but it wasn't exactly entertainment, was it?

Well, it entertained me. I liked the way they talked, and it seemed quite warm. It wasn't entertaining, I suppose, but I'm pleased that we did it. I'm pleased that we didn't try to make a comedy or a gangster movie. At least it was ambitious, even if it was small. Most British movies just want you to like them. I'd rather make something which a lot of people won't like but at least leaves a mark on them – either a black eye or a bleeding heart. If I want to go to the cinema I've got to get a babysitter, and I want to know that it's worth getting a babysitter *for*. I don't want to go to the cinema and think, 'That would have been perfectly good on the telly.' It's the same reason I'm attracted to extravagant characters and massive timescales. There's no point getting a babysitter so you can go and watch people who are like you. Telly is about people who are like you. Cinema is about people who you either wish you were like or are glad you're not. I was wrong about it being very do-able, though. It was meant to be shot in motorway service-areas, and we thought that since these places were cheap to eat in they would be cheap to film in. It's actually cheaper to hire the Albert Hall than it is to close down a Trusthouse Forte, because in five minutes they're out by a hundred grand and there aren't any quiet times.

Were you surprised when the critics called it nasty and nihilistic?

There was quite a firestorm around it, and I was thrown by that because it felt like a very private thing. I didn't expect it to be made, because we'd spent years not getting a film made. One of the weird things about screenwriting, even for someone like me who has a fairly good batting-average, is that you expect the audience for your work to be extraordinarily limited: just you, whoever commissioned it and two script editors.

It was the last in a run of lesbian killer films, after *Fun*, *Heavenly Creatures* and *Sister My Sister*. Do you ever have other movies in mind when you write yours?

When you start working with Michael, he'll always give you a movie to watch. I think in this case it was *Breathless* – and I can't see any connection there, because that's about two carefree people for whom life is a big laugh. And then they get shot. All the stuff that I remember in *Butterfly Kiss* came from me: the Book of Job, the M6, car trouble – and people who talk like *Coronation Street* characters. Originally it was about a man and a woman, and the man never stopped walking and never stopped talking and was obviously the embodiment of something. But I think that when Amanda Plummer read it she wanted the male part, and that adding the murders gave it more narrative momentum and a thrum of suspense. So it got its lesbian killer overtones quite late on.

What movies did you watch before sitting down to write *Welcome to Sarajevo*?

Things like *Salvador* and *Under Fire* and *The Killing Fields*. I thought I was being bold with *Welcome to Sarajevo*, but *The Killing Fields* had literally done it all before. The real pressure wasn't from other movies, though, it was from stuff which happened in Sarajevo which we wanted to get into the film. Michael and I had made several films for schools programmes about things like the fall of the Berlin Wall, so this was very much of a piece with those. It needed to be like a hand-grenade, as packed with stuff as possible. The war was still going on then, and it felt very cutting-edge. Michael has this foreign-correspondent side to him, so he went out there and got me all these films from a group of film-makers who were in the city during the siege.

Did you go to the city before you wrote the script?

No, I went during the Dayton Peace Accord, which was actually a kind of lull in the war. Now, I would probably insist on going first, but Michael kept saying, 'Just write the thing. This is real footage from people who were actually there. What good is it going to do you walking around after the siege has been lifted?' I wrote the first draft very quickly because the main point was to get the film made, but it changed a lot once I went out there and especially after Michael decided to shoot it there. Michael's devil-may-care, 'over my dead body will we shoot this anywhere else' attitude gave the film its authenticity. So the pre-production process was very hurried, but that put us in the driving seat and gave us a certain freedom.

Did the script specify all the shifts between fictional scenes and real footage?

We knew we were going to use real footage, and I saw the real footage while I was writing, but the alchemy happened in the editing. Michael loves mixing different styles of film-making, and if I can respond to that it gives me a chance to mix different styles of storytelling as well. I think in Michael's new film, *24 Hour Party People*, I've finally found a way of responding properly. It's a naturalistic script with bits of sitcom and bits of archive and bits of monologue dropped in, a collage in the same way that Michael's shooting becomes a collage. I love that: here's an idea, here's another idea, here's another idea. It's the opposite of most cinema, which is really starved of ideas. Most of the time the development process is: 'You've had an idea. Let's really stretch it out.' Michael was the one who emboldened me to make the story of the journalist and the girl just a thread to hang a lot of other stuff on.

Like the murders in *Butterfly Kiss*?

Exactly. Michael and I thought, 'This is a very simple story. We can tell this in twenty minutes. That gives us an hour and ten minutes to put other stuff in.' I suppose that's something I learned from soap opera: I can look at a storyline and immediately think, 'five scenes'. A conventional adaptation of the Michael Nicholson book, *Natasha's Story*, would have focused on the hard-bitten journalist who meets a young girl and realises there's more to life than getting the story through. It would have had a nice three-act structure – journalist meets girl, journalist gets girl out of city, journalist and girl live happily ever after – and he would have had a lovely character arc – he grows as a person and she responds to the love that he offers – and it would have been a TV Movie of the Week.

This was one instance where the facts actually fitted the fictional model.

Yeah, but that was kind of unimportant. The important thing was to look at the hell of Sarajevo, and finding a story which people could engage with gave us permission to do that. Michael and I fought really hard to keep the third act of *Welcome to Sarajevo*, which is that having got her out he goes back without her to get some papers signed. It goes completely against screenwriting wisdom, but it embodies an essential truth: the situation was not resolved by helping one person, and life is full of loose ends. I think that third act is what makes the film a good film, what lifts it above being a TV Movie of the Week.

The first act is also unorthodox. It has very little to do with the girl.

But there are two other girls it could be. I wrote other children into it partly because I wanted to say that war is about children getting hurt, but also to give people who knew that it was about a little girl the impression that something was happening when it wasn't. There's something similar going on in *24 Hour Party People*: characters disappear then reappear unexpectedly, or make a huge splash and never turn up again. I love films that float like that. They exist more in the present tense somehow, because you can't see where they're going.

You're watching what's happening for itself, not as a signpost to the next event. My favourite film is probably *My Darling Clementine*, for exactly that reason. What's going on? Nothing's going on. And everything's going on. Like Henry Fonda sitting on the porch with his feet on the rail, testing how far he can push his chair back. It's fantastically inconsequential but really tense. The scene goes on for ages and ages but you're completely fascinated as he bounces in this chair.

Had you stuck closer to the book, do you think the film would have been a bigger hit?

Yeah, and a less important movie. It's about the failure of journalism; it's not about a journalist's crisis of conscience. You're not that concerned about the journalist; you're more affected by the local characters. It was one of Bill Clinton's favourite films, and he organised a special screening of it when Congress didn't want to back the UN on this issue, so it had a direct political influence – which is great, and very unusual.

Why did you change all the names?

Michael had played fast and loose with certain aspects of the story and just wanted the licence to distance it even more from reality. He's not scared of real characters; everybody's got their own name in *24 Hour Party People*. But if we'd kept Michael Nicholson's name there would have been a knock-on about things like who found the Serbian concentration camps. ITN were very chuffed with having broken that story, so if you'd called him Michael Nicholson then you'd have had to call the ITN reporter Maggie O'Kane – and therefore who would the Woody Harrelson character have been? All the made-up characters would have had to become real, and all the real characters would have had to be credited for their scoops, and none of that would have had anything to do with the story. Letting ourselves be persuaded to cast Marisa

Tomei for box-office reasons was probably a mistake, because she was too American to play a celebrated French character who worked for an identifiably French charity, but I don't think we changed anything of substance.

Martin Bell wrote a newspaper article in which he said you did change things of substance.

That's the first wedding. It opens with someone being shot at a wedding, and in the script it's clearly a Serb wedding, but the art direction made it look more like a Croat wedding. I haven't got any control over that sort of thing. It was understandable, given the circumstances in which the film was shot, but we should have been more careful, because from a Serbian point of view that was a very big deal. It would have been more even-handed. But it was a movie, not a piece of war reporting. I don't want to be dismissive of Martin Bell, but it was wrong to get war reporters to review that film. John Sweeney, a foreign correspondent who writes stuff of real substance, did a great piece on it in the *Observer*, but most of the foreign correspondents just said, 'I was there and it wasn't like that', which was rather boring and very destructive. The whole point of the film was to tell people about this war which had passed them by because there was no coverage of it, and all these negative comments gave them an excuse not to see the film and to ignore the war all over again. The most annoying thing was reading 'think' pieces in the broadsheets which said, 'So what? The war is over.' Well, as it turned out, it wasn't over, and they couldn't have been more wrong.

What was the purpose of the character played by Woody Harrelson?

One of the things that interested me was this international community of war reporters living under siege. It's seen as quite a glamorous and dangerous job, carpet-bagging around the world as a war reporter, but mostly they just get a few good pictures then shack up in a hotel and phone stuff in from contacts. In Sarajevo, they were really in the thick of it. People are normally quite concerned not to shoot journalists, because both sides want them to tell their story to the world, but the Serbs didn't give a fuck. They were happy to turn journalists into targets and to shell their hotels. There were some real over-the-top characters who never made it into the movie, like the famous Italian journalist who went around in a big hat all the time and wouldn't wear a helmet. That's what Woody was for. He was there to say, 'Here's CNN', and to get a different take on things – and to have a go at personality journalism.

Welcome to Sarajevo was your second feature film with Michael Winterbottom, and Hilary and Jackie your first with Anand Tucker. How do your ongoing working relationships with those two directors compare?

They're very different people. Michael made me into a screen-writer, whereas I was already a screenwriter when I met Anand, who'd directed documentaries but hadn't directed a feature. So I guess I feel like a pupil to Michael, whereas with Anand it's more a relationship of equals. The first time I worked with Anand was actually on an *Arena* special about Antoine de Saint-Exupéry, who wrote *The Little Prince*. More to the point, he was an early aviator, and his best writing is about the danger of the first postal flights: flying over the Andes in the dark, with no radar and no wireless contact, in planes which weren't built to go that high. He ran a group of twenty-six, and twenty-four of them died before the age of thirty, just to get the post through. That's a public-service ethic, isn't it? That's what we need today. The whole thing was very cock-eyed, because we were sure we would get a big enough budget to make a massive epic and we never changed the script even when it became obvious that we were going to be shooting it all in the studio. But it was an utterly delightful experience, and Anand and I got on like a house on fire, which is why we wanted to carry on working together.

Having had the war reporters gunning for *Welcome to Sarajevo*, you then had the classical musicians shouting down *Hilary and Jackie*.

I stopped reading the papers around the time of *Hilary and Jackie*. Worldwide, the film got great reviews, did fantastic business and won a lot of awards, but the press coverage damaged it in Britain. The thing I found truly sickening was that with *Welcome to Sarajevo* we really fought for press coverage, but with *Hilary and Jackie* we had a piece on the front page of every national newspaper. I thought, 'Well, there you go. A war happening on your doorstep: can't get a column inch. Dead blonde: got 'em all.'

Did you stick closer to *A Genius in the Family*, the book by Hilary and Piers du Pré, than you did to *Natasha's Story*?

I stuck closely not so much to their book, because they were still working on it when we were working on the script, but very much to Hilary's take on things. Up to a point, because the film then gives you Jackie's take on things as well. I interviewed Hilary and Piers at length, I interviewed all their friends and I had access to Jackie's letters home – which of course none of those classical musicians did – and you couldn't have a more primary, more intimate, more unmediated source than that. I had her voice, really, which was a fantastic thing. It's obviously much simpler material than *Welcome to Sarajevo*, but it was much more directly based on that material.

Much of the criticism focused on the revelation that Jackie asked Hilary if she could sleep with her husband, which the press salaciously pounced on as if it was somehow the fulcrum of the book and the film.

I guess fulcrum is the right word, because it is the point at which the film turns around. But there isn't a sex scene, is there? There's a scene with two people in bed, but it's very fleeting. You couldn't say it was a film about sex. It's a film about sisters and the choices they make. I don't really know why people got so worked up about it. I think a lot of the time people get worked up because the papers pay them to get worked up. The papers all say what a hero she is now, but I've got some appalling reviews from towards the end of her career when nobody knew she had MS. There's a review of a concert at Carnegie Hall which would break your heart, saying how the strings of her cello were twanging like cats.

What attracted you to the story of Jacqueline du Pré?

I'm a big classical-music fan, and here was a great opportunity to make a film about classical music; and I'm an English romantic, and here was *the* great English-romantic interpreter of *the* great English-romantic composer – Elgar. Anand was attracted to the story first and dragged me down to meet Hilary, and the minute we met her I knew the film was sitting on a plate. Hilary's mother had just died and Hilary had nursed her through her final illness, and prior to that she had nursed her father, so she had sat on her feelings about Jackie for several years since Jackie's death. She dealt with them in the form of a thirty-page letter to her dead mother, which her brother Piers sent to a publisher, so she was publishing a book and selling the movie rights before she had really started to talk about these things. We were among the first people she talked to, and she told us two anecdotes, and as we left her house that night I said to Anand, 'We've got two sequences already written.' I wrote them the following morning and sent them to him, before we even had a backer, because it was easier to script them than it was to make notes on them. It came to about ten pages, and those ten pages eventually went into the movie.

Which were the two sequences?

She told us about winning the woodwind section at a music competition in Purley with the highest marks that any kid had ever got, coming onstage to collect her prize and getting a nice round of applause, then Jackie winning her section with similarly high marks, coming onstage and getting a completely disproportionate response from the audience. They stood up and applauded and the applause went on for ever and ever, and Hilary went and sat underneath the stage and listened to it, and when she came out Jackie was having her photograph taken and nobody had noticed that Hilary had gone. You could see that she was reliving this incident as she was telling us about it. It wasn't an anecdote which she had dined out on a lot; it was red raw even though it had happened forty years previously. She was actually crying and she's normally quite an emotionally restrained person. The other sequence was being very happy on the farm with her husband, and being very excited when a taxi turned up with her sister in, then realising that Jackie was in pieces and thinking, 'What are we going to do?' So we basically had the beginning and the middle of the movie.

The film contains three acts, but those three acts are rather unusual. Act One shows Hilary and Jackie as girls, Act Two shows Hilary's point of view and Act Three shows Jackie's point of view. Was that structure your idea?

Completely. I'm pleased about the structure. The structure is what really struck people about it. It was even more extravagant originally, because we were going to structure it in four movements, like a symphony, but it became obvious that you couldn't really do justice to both points of view – so why not tell a story with two different points of view? Although the film is based closely on Hilary's point of view, listening to her talk about her sister, who went away and became successful, I, as someone who has gone away and become quite successful, could feel how things were for Jackie: 'She doesn't call. She doesn't write.' I'm proud of the fact that her dirty washing plays such a big part in the movie – this parcel that her family think is something exciting from Russia – because the turning point comes when she gets it back and can smell home on it. That's why I like writing movies about real people and real things. Most films which are completely invented are based on a whole tradition of film-making, but if you turn your attention away from film-making to the real world there will always be stuff you could never have invented which will rejuvenate your technique. I think this is a classic example of that. Who could predict that a film would turn on the smell of newly washed socks?

Because you have to wait an entire act before she gets them back.

Exactly. It wouldn't work unless it had put you in the position of making a judgement about her. But when you go into script meetings with studios and backers, they want a sympathetic character and they want the character to be sympathetic all the way through – and their definition of sympathetic is very narrow. They never want the character to do anything that alienates the audience, and what I like about *Hilary and Jackie* is that it depends on you hating a character and then finding out you were wrong. It takes the audience on an emotional journey, and conventional film-making is all about not taking you on that journey. Instead you watch other people take it. This film-school ideology basically comes down to the fact that every movie should be like the Mr Men: 'Here's Mr Messy. Isn't he messy? He's far too messy! He'll never be messy again.'

They're cautionary tales, and your role is to sit there thinking, 'I'm not messy. And it's a good job I'm not messy. Because I'd end up like Mr Messy.' Whereas watching *Hilary and Jackie* you think, 'God, what a cow! Shit, I was wrong!'

How many drafts of the script did you write?

Quite a few. It was at the BBC for a long time. Anand and I work by sitting in a meeting, and talking and talking and talking and talking until we can talk the movie. It's a verbal performance, and probably the closest you get to seeing the movie until you make the movie. We did this for David Thompson at the BBC, and after an hour and a half he definitely wanted to make it. Then, as we were going, he said, 'There's just one thing. The BBC can't represent living people without their permission.' So I said, 'You can't make it then, can you? Because Daniel Barenboim's obviously not going to give his permission. He may not interfere with the film, but he's certainly not going to give his permission.' But David said, 'I'm sure we can work around it.' We spent a year trying to work around it, trying to make the script more sympathetic to Barenboim, and in the end I said to the BBC, 'This is silly. If I wrote a script in which Danny laid his hands on Jackie and cured her of MS through the force of his personality, he still wouldn't like it, because he's a great musician now and he doesn't want to be remembered as the spouse of a sixties icon.' The BBC were very gentlemanly about it and said, 'Take the script wherever you want to', so we took it to FilmFour, who snapped it up and put it more or less straight into production.

Your third feature with Michael Winterbottom, *The Claim*, spent even longer in development, didn't it?

Of all the scripts I've written, that's the one which spent longest in development. I must have written thirty drafts of it, and in the end it felt very arbitrary which one we went with. It wasn't like we had reached the end of a process; it was like some of the money was suddenly available so we shot whatever script we had that week. We were naive, basically. It was a given that a Western set in the snow, during the gold rush, was going to be fairly expensive – expensive for a Michael Winterbottom film, anyway. So instead of being an intimate conversation between me and Michael, it was developed with the money men looking over our shoulder all the time and script editors making suggestions which we had to take seriously. We were constantly rewriting it according to other people's agendas. Rewrite it to include a great part for Madonna, who was attached for a while. Rewrite it for a male lead like Clint Eastwood, or whoever was flavour of the month. Rewrite it with less snow in it. Rewrite it with more snow in it. The head of Pathé and the head of Pathé UK didn't have anything in common and didn't have any criteria that they could agree on. One was a sort of Gallic swinger and the other was this Scottish Presbyterian, and I just sat in the middle. It was a miserable experience and a rotten way to develop a script. I found myself having conversations with Michael where I'd say, 'What if we did this bit and then that bit?' and he'd say, 'That bit went two years ago', and I'd say, 'Oh, yeah.' I lost my bearings completely.

Whose idea was it to transpose *The Mayor of Casterbridge* to the gold rush?

Michael's not a big Western fan, but his producer, Andrew Eaton, is a big Western fan, and I'm a big Western fan, and Andrew said to me, 'I'd love to make a Western about Irish people.' It turned out that the year of the gold rush was the worst year of the potato famine, and it seemed fantastically interesting to connect these two events: the apex of foolish hope and the nadir of absolute poverty. I happened to meet Michael at Euston station as he was about to start shooting

Jude, and he said, 'Andrew wants to make this potato Western', and I said, 'You should do a Thomas Hardy story for that as well.' We laughed about that, and I came up with this thing which I called *The Mayor of Kingdom Come*. Then, while Michael was shooting *Jude*, Andrew and I had lots of other ideas for Irish Westerns. There was one which I really wanted to do about the funeral of T. P. McManus, the Fenian activist whose body was brought slowly back from San Francisco across the Midwest to raise funds for the Fenian Brotherhood. I loved that idea, but Michael said you couldn't make a movie in which the corpse was the most interesting character. Finally, when Michael finished shooting *Jude*, he rang me up and said, 'I've read all your ideas and I think it's much better to do *The Mayor of Casterbridge*.' Hardy actually based the story on a newspaper article about a man who sold his wife, and you could easily imagine something like that happening during the gold rush. The novel is all about money, so what setting could be better?

The finished film is cosmopolitan rather than Irish: Wes Bentley is American, Milla Jovovich is Russian, Nastassja Kinski is German, Peter Mullan is Scottish and Sarah Polley is Canadian. How did you manage to end up there?

We lost control over the casting. When you go over a certain budget, you become the plaything of the gods. There were only two Irish actors at that level: Liam Neeson, who turned it down, and Daniel Day-Lewis, who had given up movies to be a cobbler. So it just became cosmopolitan. A cosmopolitan cast is probably truer to life, but if I'd sat down to write a cosmopolitan film about the gold rush, I'd definitely have written a third of the characters as Chinese, because the Chinese ran the gold rush. To me, that's a gap in the movie. We didn't do justice to the coming of the railroad, either. The gold rush and the coming of the railroad were like the whole of European history in about ten years: vast tribal movement and enormous technological change. You went from 1840, when there were just 25,000 Europeans west of the Mississippi, to 1852, when San Francisco and the state of California were pretty much as they are now. If the film is still about anything, it's about the limitations of money: an infinite amount of wealth can't buy your daughter back. That's very Hardyesque, but I think there should be space in the development of a project for you to turn around and see whether the script has drifted too far from the movie you wanted to make – and to address things if it has. Even though this one took years, somehow there was no time for that.

It doesn't even open with the future mayor selling his wife and daughter. That sequence is split into several flashbacks.

That's the thing I feel most upset about, because I should have made a fuss. I can see how we ended up there, but I think it's a catastrophic mistake. The film starts in a very fuzzy way: you're not sure who the most important character is. There's a scene quite early on where he watches his daughter do a performance of a poem, and in the script he had quite a lot to say, but Peter Mullan was so brilliant that he literally did it all with a look. He looks at her, then looks away just before she looks at him, and if you know what's going on it's absolutely beautiful, but because you don't know it's completely meaningless. Pathé were obsessed with the possibility that this character might lose the audience's sympathy if he sold his wife and daughter at the start. I just thought, 'Your job as human beings is to try and sympathise with all kinds of people, and my job as a dramatist is to try and engage with the most unsympathetic characters.' And for God's sake, Thomas Hardy opened a novel with it. That's a pretty good guarantee that it works.

Is there anything you like about the film?

I'm very proud to have had a part in a film on that scale, because one of the things I truly dislike about the British film industry is its poverty of ambition, visually and emotionally and philosophically, but I don't think I did the job I should have done on it. It's incredibly beautiful, and there are some extraordinary performances, but the script doesn't have that extra level the way *Hilary and Jackie* does. The chemistry between Michael and I is that Michael is a very arm's-length person and I'm an unashamedly emotional person, and I think I stopped putting emotions into that script too early on. I stopped putting the Frankness in. Usually, Michael will put Michaelness in and I'll put Frankness in, but with *The Claim* I just started putting Pathé-ness in. Then the guard changed at Pathé, so when it came out it was no one's baby. That wouldn't happen at Miramax; they'd fight for it because it was their film. It wasn't so bad in the States, but here it did no business at all. I run a cinema, and *I* couldn't get hold of a print. It died because nobody loved it.

A third director you work with regularly is Julien Temple, for whom you wrote *Pandaemonium*, about the troubled friendship between Samuel Coleridge and William Wordsworth, another film which reflects your love of English romanticism.

I met Julien on the back of *Butterfly Kiss*, which he really liked when it came out. I was already a huge fan of his, because the movie that made me want to make movies was *The Great Rock 'n' Roll Swindle*. I was dead excited by that film, and went to see it even though I was underage, so it was very exciting to meet him. His family are from Somerset, where he now lives, and Coleridge was a local hero. Julien wanted to make a film about him, and saw him as a kind of early Sex Pistol, so *Pandaemonium* was a bit of a rock-and-roll take on things. Having said that, Julien is a very scholarly bloke. It's fantastic walking around London with him, because he's got anecdotes about every corner. He's like a human Radio 4: erudite and learned and really good company.

A film about the life and work of Coleridge can't have been an easy sell.

The film actually engages directly with the work and pushes the life to one side, which I'm very proud of although it's a mad thing to do commercially. When you walked into meetings with producers and commissioning editors saying, 'We've got this movie. It's about the second edition of the *Lyrical Ballads*. You're going to love it,' you knew that they were only listening out of politeness and were just being kind if they gave you the train fare. But of all the films I've made, that's the one which has had the most loyalty from its audience. They put it on in Ambleside the week it came out and they had to extend its run because people kept coming. Here at the Plaza we've had it back lots of times. People who like it, really, really like it – which is great.

How much research did you do before you wrote the script – and how accurate is the finished film?

The framing story contains an emotional truth but is completely made-up. The core of the film, about this great summer they spent writing the *Lyrical Ballads*, is incredibly accurate. It was a privilege to be *able* to be that accurate. It's easier to get hold of information about what Coleridge did during that summer than it was to get hold of information about Sarajevo or Jacqueline du Pré. Coleridge kept a notebook with him all the time, so it was as though someone from the 1830s had a video camera pointed at himself. Every jot and tittle of his life was available to us. Also his wife's letters, which were all written in childish gobbledygook. Also his lesser-known poems, which were often about very intimate things. There's a wonderful sequence in the film based around the poem 'Frost at Midnight', which is about waking up in the night, hearing the baby crying, going downstairs and trying to get the baby back to sleep. No one, even now, writes with that level of domestic intimacy. It's a wonderful thing to be able to reconstruct someone's feelings in that much detail from that long ago.

Why did you make up a framing story if the rest of the film was so accurate?

Basically, the film deals with a group of friends who start off with a set of ideals, and in some ways they betray them but in other ways they fulfil them. At the beginning of the film there's talk of forming a utopian community in America, and by the end of the film there's such chaos in their lives that half of them are sharing the same house. Robert Southey pays the rent, Coleridge's wife teaches their children and Coleridge rattles around being mad, so in a weird sense they do form a utopian community. It's about the way people bring out creativity in each other, and the way loyalty evolves and falls apart but, because these things play out over a long period, I made up a framing story that brings them all to a head quickly: a dinner at which Wordsworth expects to be made Poet Laureate and instead it goes to Southey, a lousy poet but a good man – and the character I most identify with. The framing story ends up being a bit melodramatic, but it's only fifteen minutes of the movie and there's still some fantastic film-making from Julien. And a film about poetry just seemed like a madly ambitious thing to do.

Are you reconciled to the fact that if you carry on working in Britain, your films will be seen by fewer people?

Yeah, but how many people do you *want* to see your films? A huge number of people saw *Hilary and Jackie*, say. If I'd written a massively successful novel, that would be one per cent of the audience for *Hilary and Jackie*. I love looking on the Internet Movie Database and seeing write-ups of *Hilary and Jackie* from people living in Brazil or Senegal. You can reach an enormous number of people without writing a blockbuster. *Pandaemonium* wouldn't have sold out Screen One at our cinema here, but we were getting eighty people a night for two weeks in Screen Three. It's like the money: how much money do you want? I'll never get a ludicrously big cheque, but this lifestyle far exceeds my expectations anyway. I have to say there's quite a vibe around *24 Hour Party People*, though. I think there's close to 300 prints, which is the biggest I've had.

24 Hour Party People, your fourth feature with Michael Winterbottom, is about a very different group of creative people. Do you think there are any similarities to *Pandaemonium*?

They're very alike, actually. *24 Hour Party People* is the story of Factory Records, an independent label in Manchester which had enormous resonance for people of my generation in the northwest, and the death of Ian Curtis, another English romantic, who hanged himself at the peak of his artistic achievements. When we started talking about it, I imagined a Michael Winterbottom misery-fest about a suicidal young rocker, but ten minutes into my first interview with Tony Wilson, who was the boss of Factory, I thought, 'We're sitting on a great comic movie here.' Michael came up for the next interview and we were just pissing ourselves laughing. I had this image of Factory as a glossy, eighties, money-orientated pioneer of designer goods, and talking to Tony I realised what a mad, chaotic, anarchic life he'd led, and how unlike that image many of the people around him were. They're like *Coronation Street* characters: rococo, larger than life, lost in their own world. Like Coleridge, Tony's documented his life in intense detail – he's kept tickets from every gig he's ever been to as well as things like press cuttings – and throughout the interviews I'd find myself saying to him, 'You did *what*?'

It's also similar to *Hilary and Jackie*, then: stuff you could never have invented.

Exactly. Tony, and Rob Gretton, and Alan Erasmus – the guy who really ran Factory – did things that no fictional character would ever do. I've sat in story conferences where script editors and commissioning editors will say, 'This character would never do that because it would be against their own interests', but in the real world people do things against their own interests all the time. They do them because they felt like it or because somebody told them to, which are much more legitimate expressions of the way life is. In the fictional world you're bound by these mad rules, derived from a half-assed understanding of psychology and some second-hand bits of Aristotle. Real life is multiform and complex, and unbelievable things just happen.

You said that with *24 Hour Party People*, you finally found a way of responding properly to Michael Winterbottom's style of film-making. How did that happen?

It was a very interesting process. The film stars Steve Coogan and many of the new generation of British comedians, and while Michael was shooting *The Claim*, I would come up with lots of ideas with Steve, then go away and write the script. So, when Michael finally came on board, there was already a creative ethos developing: the script was fairly loose – a few sections weren't written at all – but the structure was very tight. It may be invisible now, but it was every bit as formal as *Hilary and Jackie*. I think film structure is nothing to do with acts, it's to do with suspense. From the start of the film there should be something you're either hoping will happen or dreading will happen, and if you set that up nicely and discreetly then when the payoff comes it will give the story a satisfying retrospective structure. In practical terms, that means you can improvise as much as you like, but if you cut a note from the melody the whole thing will fall apart, so my job on *24 Hour Party People* was to guard the melody. I went backstop so that Michael could enjoy the chaos – and it was a very chaotic shoot. Comedians are prone to improvisation, and Michael took that a step further. So if I'd written a scene with two people in it, he would put four people in it, and if I'd written a scene with four, there'd be eight, which means it got looser and looser and looser. And now, in post-production, the structure has come through, and the character of Tony is presented in exactly the way I wanted him to be – which is a great feeling.

Were you on set that much during the shooting of your other films?

Not for *The Claim*. My wife had just had a baby. We had a baby at the beginning of *Welcome to Sarajevo* as well, so I didn't get there until about halfway through. But the logistics of shooting the film were so complicated – landmines, no water, intermittent electricity, hassle from gangsters – that the script was the one thing you could leave alone. With *Hilary and Jackie*, I was on set every day because the actors obviously had lots of questions. It meant that Anand was able to say, 'Let's ask Frank', instead of being on the back foot all the time. And *24 Hour Party People* was probably the most enjoyable shoot of any film in history, so it would have been stupid not to be there.

Until recently, you were due to write your first studio projects: a remake of the sixties heist-movie *Gambit*, and an adaptation of Eric Lomax's non-fiction book *The Railway Man*,

both with Anand Tucker as director. Are you still doing them?

They were originally going to be a package, but you really can't deal with the studios. We went over there and thought, 'Why do people moan about them? They're all so lovely and polite.' But actually they're terrible bastards. They just lie to you, basically. So we both walked off *Gambit*, but we've regained control of *The Railway Man*, and we're hoping to make it ourselves. It's structurally interesting, in that the first fifty pages are set in a Japanese PoW camp in Burma, and the second fifty pages are set half a century later in a terraced house in Berwick-on-Tweed. The linking thread is that Eric, who was forced to work on the Burma railroad and wrote the classic book about it, remained obsessed with railways. A lot of the prisoners who worked on the railway suffered traumas very late in life, and in Eric's case it destroyed his pleasure in everything else. It's such an important story and he's such an amazing person. The world would be a better place if there were more people like Eric, and I just think it would be fantastic to put him in a movie.

You also have further projects lined up with Julien Temple and Michael Winterbottom.

The Golden Man and *Code 46*. I'm a big science-fiction buff – I read a lot of sci-fi and I write sci-fi stories – and *Code 46* is my first sci-fi film. That's going to be quite interesting because there's no design budget, but actually the physical appearance of the world hasn't been changed that much by science. If you look at the history of aviation, from Kitty Hawk to Concorde was only about fifty years, and from Concorde to now is more or less fifty years – and Concorde is still the last word in aviation. I grew up thinking the world would look like Dan Dare and people would go on excursions to the moon. So this is set in the future but the scientific changes are genetic. The actors will be young but the characters will be hundreds of years old, with bizarre insurance policies which cover their stem cells so they can constantly regenerate themselves. It's based on the Orpheus legend: trying to bring someone back from the dead. *The Golden Man* is a thriller, a true story, about the Elizabethan secret service. That's another one we had to get back the rights to. For a long time it was with FilmFour, a bunch of indecisive idiots. Losing control of the material is a terrible mistake. It's a huge waste of time, apart from all the artistic heartache. I'm getting on a bit now; I've got better things to do than listen to idiots.

So working in this country is no guarantee that you won't encounter the same problems you had with *Gambit* and *The Railway Man*?

I think there are a lot of things catastrophically wrong with the development process in Britain. If Michael Winterbottom comes to you and says, 'I'm going to make a comedy with Steve Coogan about Factory Records', you should be able to say whether you're in or out. But if you send a script to one of the funding bodies in this country, they just go, 'It's really getting there. Let's see the next draft.' The script-editing process is used to cover up a poverty of decision-making ability. That's no disrespect to script editors; I've met some brilliant people who work in script editing. But the job of a script editor is basically to find fault with your script. If they walk in and say, 'This is brilliant. We should make it', they're not doing their job. The script editor will probably change two or three times in the period you're working on the script, because it's a point-of-entry job and sooner or later they all move on. At least if a director gives you notes and then changes his mind, it's because he changed his mind about the movie. That's easier to live with. You should rewrite as part of making the movie, not as a way of forcing some idiot to make up his mind.

Do you agree with the increasing tendency over here to hire different writers?

I don't think that's a bad thing. At least it's a decision: 'Good project. Wrong script.' I'm doing one at the moment for Working Title called *The Tower*, about Tower Colliery in South Wales where the miners bought their own pit. There were scripts by Alan Plater and Colin Welland, but it's basically a page-one rewrite. I did exactly what I'd normally do, which is talk to people and read lots of stuff. I even did a shift down the pit, which was amazing. It's the first time I've done anything with Working Title, and they cosset you quite a lot, but I've mainly been working with the director, Marc Evans, and we tend to be ahead of the script editors' notes. They'll come in and say, 'We think that in scene three . . .' and we'll say, 'Actually, the first ten scenes have been cut.' You want to make the movie, so you're very tough on yourself. I'm not saying the script editors are irrelevant: they've been really good at facilitating the conversation between me and Marc, which is the conversation which really matters. Marc directed *House of America* and he's very Welsh, so it's a great idea for him to be doing this. But it's quite a big movie, and the studio structure means that everyone is very nervous about getting the script perfect before it goes to Tim Bevan. We're not at that point yet, so I don't know if it will come off.

In the midst of all these adaptations and true stories, do you ever get the urge to write an original script – perhaps to recharge your batteries?

No, not at all. I'm doing a musical with Danny Boyle, *Millions*, which is completely my own idea, but that's my first original since *Butterfly Kiss*, and it's been knocking about for years. I find that interviewing people and going through letters and looking up stuff in libraries recharges my batteries. That's all input, whereas an original is coming out of *me*.

There's also the constant fear that you'll lapse into copying something else. I loathe movies which are like other movies. A lot of film buffs enjoy variations on genre, but I like stuff which makes you go, 'Where did that come from?' I like it when people play with genre, but I think that used to happen more than it does now. People used to be more genre-literate. Now, 'thriller' just means anything with guns in it.

You seem to be quite a prolific writer.

I don't see myself as prolific. I don't work especially hard. I probably just get more of my scripts made, and that's probably because I usually work with friends and tend to hang in there. My screenplays aren't very long, either. *Hilary and Jackie* is my longest film, because we had to leave room for the music, but it was quite a tight screenplay, 90 pages or something. I feel a physical revulsion for screenplays over 115 pages long. I'm quite a *fast* writer, but that's because I have a flaw which can play as an advantage if the right people are around me: I won't defend my scripts. If somebody says, 'That doesn't work', I'll never say, 'Yes it does', I'll just say, 'Oh, doesn't it?' and write something else. Anand will sit there and say, 'This is brilliant. I'm not changing a word', but if I'm in the meeting I'll already be thinking, 'I don't know. Maybe it *would* be better if she had a gun instead of a cello.' I'm very easily swayed.

What kind of relationship do you have with Andy Patterson and Andrew Eaton, the producers of *Hilary and Jackie* and *The Claim*?

Andy and Anand and I have just started a company together, Archer Street, so that's obviously a very friendly relationship. Andrew's a good friend too, but we each relate separately to Michael – in the same way that Andy will never be party to conversations between me and Anand. I'll find out months down the line that Andy was desperately wanting the fall of Singapore removed from the script but was patiently waiting until I reached that decision with Anand. I've never been in a relationship where a producer initiates a script and then goes looking for a director, which I think is a bizarre way to do things – although I know it's the norm in British films.

You work very closely with a small number of directors, yet the results of those collaborations are billed as 'A Film by' Michael Winterbottom or Anand Tucker or Julien Temple. What's your attitude to the invisibility of the screenwriter?

Delighted, to be honest with you, because it means someone else is receiving all the flack. I can get away with not being at the centre of things, because there are madly ambitious people somewhere else in the equation. I don't give a toss about my public profile. I care what my friends think of me, and what the people I work with think of me, but I don't care what anyone else thinks of me. I find that invisibility very enjoyable. *Welcome to Sarajevo* was in competition at Cannes, and I remember having the most fantastic time but now and then catching sight of Michael, looking glum, surrounded by journalists, trotting out the same old stories. I get interviewed about once a year. I think if you have any profile at all as an artist, it starts to cut you off from your material. Interviewing people who I'm going to write about, they're unlikely to know who I am even if they know Michael's films. I'm a blank as far as they're concerned, and I think that's great.

Do you have any ambitions to direct?

None whatsoever. I'm producing a couple of low-budget films, because Archer Street is going to make other people's movies as well as our own, but I have no desire to be a director. I'm grateful that there are people who do, but I've got no idea why anybody would want to. I can't imagine standing around in the cold all day dealing with electricians and actors. What a combination. One group going, 'Can't be done', and the other one going, 'Why, why, why?' That's real manual labour!

Neal Purvis & Robert Wade were born in 1961, in Hampton Court and Cardiff respectively. Purvis is married with three children and lives in Twickenham. Wade is married with two children and lives in London.

FILM

Let Him Have It (Peter Medak, 1991, UK)
Plunkett & Macleane (Jake Scott, 1999, UK)
The World is Not Enough (Michael Apted, 1999, UK/US)

Die Another Day (Lee Tamahori, 2002, UK/US)
Johnny English (Peter Howitt, 2003, UK/US)

SCREENPLAYS

Good News for Dreamers (spec)
Solid Gold Easy Action (spec)
Limelight Blues (Bevan/Fellner/Warr)
The Magnificent Eleven (Production Company Unknown)
Velvet Gun (Front Page Films)
Return to Sender (spec)
The Mabus (Oxford Film Company)

Killing Me (The Producers)
Lying Doggo (Impact Pictures)
The Wycked World of Brian Jones (Scala)
The Wasp Factory (Renaissance)
The Combination (spec)
The Grid (Working Title)
The Italian Job (Paramount)

UNCREDITED

The Puppet Masters (Stuart Orme, 1994, US)

An American Werewolf in Paris (Anthony Waller, 1997, US/Lux/Fr/UK)

Where did the two of you first get together?

RW: The University of Kent at Canterbury. We were sharing bunkbeds, but Neal left after one term.

NP: Unhappy with the sleeping arrangements.

RW: He went off to do a useful degree . . .

NP: Film and Photography, at the Polytechnic of Central London.

RW: . . . and I carried on learning about pre-1906 cinema. My original plan was to write a script while I was at Canterbury then go to the National Film School, but what the Film Studies teachers were trying to do was create more Film Studies teachers not help people become film-makers, so I was actively discouraged from writing anything.

When did you start writing as a team?

RW: Well, we wrote a few songs at university, and made some Super-8 stuff, then I had a stab at a script called *Good News for Dreamers*, about a boy pursuing a girl and trying to impress her.

NP: A very naive piece of work.

RW: But we knew a guy who had lots of money, and it was agreed that I would direct this film, Neal would edit it . . .

NP: I was qualified for that.

RW: . . . and we would rewrite the script together. This guy even went out and bought an Apricot computer for us to write it on . . .

NP: It was good, the Apricot.

RW: . . . and that was when they were really expensive. And because the boy in the story drove around in a fifties pink convertible, this guy bought us one of those as well – or, rather, he bought one for himself and let us use it. So we were off to a flying start. We had an office on the Strand, which we painted pink . . .

NP: . . . and we purchased a photocopier . . .

RW: . . . and we requested the books from all the modelling agencies so that we could select girls . . .

NP: . . . and then we just sat there and waited for the phone to ring.
RW: We spent all this time getting the office ready and we didn't really know what to do with the script. But there was an organisation called . . .
NP: . . . the Association of Independent Producers . . .
RW: . . . and they had these evenings where people would try to help each other, and a lady suggested that we send the script to Robert Bierman.

The director of *Vampire's Kiss*.

RW: Yeah. So we did, and he liked it, and the idea was that he would direct it as his second feature film. He put us in touch with his agent, Jenne Casarotto, who is now our agent, and she said, 'I can't represent you, but I can represent the project.'
NP: We knew in about a week that it wasn't going to get made, because all her major contacts said no very quickly. That's one of the good things about having a top agent.
RW: Someone who was in the year above me at university ended up writing an article about Neal and me in the *Face*, using us as a vehicle to explore the British film industry in 1986. They were truly dire times, with very few films being made, and we were only interested in films, so we were getting nowhere. We did this comedy stuff for a while, supported by the dole, occasionally getting a hundred quid for writing a pop promo, and our first commission was an adaptation of a novel by Tony Parsons.
NP: *Limelight Blues*.
RW: The people who paid for that adaptation were Tim Bevan and Eric Fellner. Tim was at Working Title and Eric was at Initial, and we were the first people they came together for. Unfortunately, it was a big waste of time. The aspiration was an eighties, British pop version of *Sweet Smell of Success*, but we weren't allowed to read the book because they liked the idea of the book but not the book itself.

NP: Tony Parsons did a treatment which was different to the book and we were allowed to see that, and then we did something different again.

RW: Eventually we pooled our resources to buy an answerphone – because they cost about £140 – and one day we got a message saying, 'Can you get to this hotel in half an hour?' So we went to the hotel, and there was this larger-than-life continental producer waiting for us. He looked very smart and we looked absolutely terrible, and he said, 'I hear you boys like football.' I'm not particularly *au fait* with the game, but Neal is.

NP: I talked to him about Bobby Charlton and that sort of thing, and before we knew it we were flown to Rome to meet a Libyan producer who lived in a converted television station. It was basically an enormous bungalow with an elevator in it, so we stepped into this, wondering where it might go, and found that there was the same-sized place underneath, a storage area with all these paintings stacked against the wall.

RW: Magrittes and Matisses – and photos of our host with Colonel Gadafi. We made several trips out there and it was very surreal. He didn't speak English and we didn't speak Libyan, so everything was done through an interpreter.

NP: He also had a young nurse from Birmingham.

RW: Who was giving him injections.

NP: This is what happens when you don't know what you're doing.

RW: It would have driven one person out of their mind, but when there's two of you it's rather interesting. And the film was a football movie. A Libyan-backed football movie.

NP: *The Magnificent Eleven.*

Did the film ever get made?

RW: It might have done, but I think we'd know if it had been. We did write a film for an Italian producer which we believe got made . . .

NP: . . . but which we didn't fully get paid for. We saw a

poster in *Screen International* – the Cannes edition – and it was all written in Italian but it had the same producer and director. We never heard from them again and never got paid our final money.

RW: That was actually very bad. Not getting paid is bad. So at the end of this period we were pretty fed up. We left our agent of the time and decided it was better not to be represented at all than to be . . . you know . . .

How did you get on without representation?

RW: Well, the third producer on *Limelight Blues*, with Tim Bevan and Eric Fellner, was a music guy called Rob Warr, who managed bands like ABC and Gang of Four, and he was the one who suggested the story of Derek Bentley and Christopher Craig. We only knew the story vaguely, so he got a researcher – called Will Self – to knock up a few pages about it.

NP: The interesting thing is that there weren't any long words in there.

RW: Anyway, Rob Warr didn't have any money, so we weren't sure whether to write the script, then one day we thought, 'If we can't get this made – a depressing period melodrama about a miscarriage of justice – we might as well pack it in', so we decided it was worth doing. It was a very dead case . . .

NP: There were no books on it: everything was out of print.

RW: . . . but what set it alight for us was a book we found in the library which had been written at the time – ghostwritten, really – by Bentley's father. This was a patriotic guy who fought in the First World War, worked hard all his life and tried to keep Bentley away from Craig, then had to stand by as his son was executed. His honest bewilderment at what had happened made us think, 'This is a great story.'

NP: They used to bump people off really quickly in those days. They got caught in November 1952, and he was hanged in January 1953 – within three months of doing it.

Or not doing it, depending on the interpretation of the words 'Let him have it'.

NP: Well, yeah.

RW: So we went back to Rob Warr, who'd become part of Luc Roeg's company, Vivid – which in turn was backed by Jeremy Thomas, who'd just won all those Oscars for *The Last Emperor* – and by writing our least commercial script, not trying in any way to be American, we ended up . . .

NP: . . . working in Hollywood with Tony Richardson. He had two swimming pools at his house, one on one side and one on the other, for when the sun moved around. He was a lovely bloke and one of the best people we've worked with, because he knew what he was doing.

RW: It would have been the first film he'd directed over here for ten years, but then he said, 'I need to make some money. Can I go off for six months and do *The Phantom of the Opera*?' Then Alex Cox came on board and we worked well with him – the script went down to a nice, tight 89 pages – but he walked out just as pre-production started.

NP: We were sitting at a café in Carnaby Street, which was one of our haunts . . .

RW: . . . and we saw him walking past with a big rubbish bag over his shoulder. He was just coming back from the launderette and he said, 'I'm off. I'm leaving the country.'

NP: The film would have lost its funding if there hadn't been a curious chain of events.

RW: We'd been talking to Malcolm McLaren about doing a film on Brian Epstein – because Malcolm McLaren is very interested in making films about rock managers – and he gave the *Let Him Have It* script to Peter Medak, who had just done *The Krays*. Peter read it with a view to working with us on this Brian Epstein thing, then rang up in the middle of the night and said, 'I hear that Alex Cox has walked off.' I said, 'Yeah.' And he said, 'I'd love to do it.'

Presumably he was in demand after *The Krays*?

NP: We were actually resistant to him . . .

RW: . . . because we thought *The Krays* was a good film, but we wanted *Let Him Have It* to be . . .

NP: . . . done differently. And he did do it differently, but it wasn't the film that we'd had in our heads – so it came as a bit of a shock.

RW: Peter is a very passionate director and saw the film as the slow and inevitable journey of a martyr, whereas our original script was all about two marginal figures who find each other and dress up as gangsters.

NP: The script went back up to something like 112 pages . . .

RW: . . . because he wanted it to be more explanatory and less elliptical, which meant that the flippancy we and Alex Cox and Tony Richardson had brought to it got lost. It's all about pleasing the director: if you clash with him you may get booted off.

NP: Then the film wasn't reviewed as a film; it was reviewed as a case.

RW: The case had been dead for a long time, but when the film got made the books started coming out.

NP: It was shown in parliament, and they clipped a bit on the news.

RW: And for Bentley's sister, Iris, it was great, because she had been campaigning her whole life to clear his name.

What was her reaction to the film?

NP: Well, we gave her the script . . .

RW: . . . but only after we'd got the project going, because we didn't want to intrude.

NP: We didn't know that she'd been campaigning all these years.

RW: She didn't like her brother being portrayed in a criminal way, but we weren't interested in whitewashing him. Similarly, we weren't saying that anyone lied at the trial, just that he shouldn't have stood trial because he had a mental age of eleven. That, in itself, was grounds for a pardon. But we didn't think that would ever happen.

Christopher Eccleston was also less than charitable about it.

RW: He slagged it off even as it was coming out.

NP: Which was completely unprofessional.

RW: He took it upon himself to be the sole custodian of Derek's true spirit, and his performance took no account of the fact that Bentley was a happy boy who was just mucking about. In the film, Christopher Eccleston . . .

NP: . . . never smiles . . .

RW: . . . but in every picture of Bentley, he's smiling. The whole point was that he didn't realise what was going to happen to him until near the end, but from the moment you see Christopher Eccleston he's carrying the weight of his future martyrdom.

NP: Someone told me that they thought it was like going to a funeral. I definitely think it was more depressing than it needed to be.

RW: Just because a film is serious, doesn't mean it can't be funny. The other problem was that after all the press interest in the case the distributors got overexcited about the film, and it ended up opening at the Odeon Leicester Square instead of opening in a few small cinemas.

NP: Or even opening wide straightaway. It just played for two weeks at one cinema.

RW: Two thousand, two hundred seats. When a cinema like that is half-full, it feels half-empty. And, on the same day, *The Commitments* opened at the Odeon Marble Arch – a very good film which obviously stuffed us.

You must have been glad of the credit, though.

NP: We managed to get a film made before we were thirty.

RW: We started when we were twenty-two, we wrote *Good News for Dreamers* when the Olympics was on in 1984 and *Let Him Have It* started shooting in 1990.

NP: Six years.

RW: It got some good reviews here and some great reviews in America.

NP: Where it was judged as a film, not by the evidence that we seemed to be putting forward. But after that there wasn't any work around.

RW: Excluding FilmFour, there were just four British cinema features made that year. So it took us a long time to decide what to do next. We went to LA for the opening of *Let Him Have It*, got an agent out there, Tom Strickler, a spec-script specialist . . .

NP: . . . and then spent months working on a spec script for America called *Return to Sender*. When we were researching *Let Him Have It*, we found that there was a conman who used to write to people on death row, gain their friendship and then auction the letters to the newspapers after they were hanged – so we wrote a character-based thriller about someone doing that con in America, which still has the death penalty in a number of states.

RW: We went to the Midwest and visited the death chamber at MacAlister.

NP: Which is an extremely nasty prison. And we went to death row in the women's prison in Oklahoma.

RW: It's a holding tank. They're transported to the male prison for execution.

NP: The fact that it was based on a real person made it very interesting. What makes you do something like that? How can you fall so low?

RW: The idea was Jeff Bridges.

NP: Or Michael Douglas. Someone who seems likeable despite their character being a complete bastard.

RW: But obviously the guy is going to redeem himself. That's what it's all about.

Did you have any problems adjusting your style for America?

RW: That seemed to come all right. It was very gratifying when we'd go into meetings with people who'd liked the script and they hadn't realised we were English. I don't know how we did that, because since then we've had some difficulty on that score.

NP: We did get the structure wrong on the first attempt. Until then, the writing had seemed quite easy, but when you get it wrong you start analysing things, and it becomes more difficult. For the first time we went and looked at those 'How to Write a Script' books.

RW: I'd read the William Goldman book when it came out.

NP: *Adventures in the Screen Trade*.

RW: And Edward Dmytryk, *On Screenwriting*. But when we got stuck, I think the book we looked at was *How to Make a Good Script Great*.

NP: And *How to Write a Script in 21 Days*.

RW: That was a good one. We've actually done that. We wrote *Let Him Have It* in three weeks.

NP: *Return to Sender* took nine months, but it was written in the days when we didn't have deadlines so we had the time to work on it.

RW: It was a real challenge but we're very proud of it.

NP: We gave it to our agent, and he gave every indication that it was going to sell, but we were just unlucky.

RW: It was marginally ahead of its time.

NP: There was a cycle of death-row movies later on, but at the time nobody would go with it except MGM. Warner were interested but they already had a death-row project, an adaptation of a book called *Just Cause*, which Sean Connery ended up doing. So the script went through all the right people at MGM, and Alan Ladd Jr, at the very top, just needed to OK the cheque. The next thing we hear is that Laddie – as he's known – had read it and found it 'morally repugnant'. And that was the end of that. But on the back of it we went out there and 'did the rounds'.

Did you consider moving to America?

RW: That was the time when we could have made a decision to move out there. We had a credit, and the British film industry . . .

NP: . . . didn't exist . . .

RW: . . . but the thing is that, if you're not part of that pool of writers, when you do go out there for a few weeks you get to see everyone you want to see.

NP: We spent four weeks out there pitching an idea . . .

RW: . . . for an anglophile producer called Mary Anne Page. She really liked *Let Him Have It*, and was producing a film written by Ian McEwan, *The Good Son*, so although her deal with Fox wasn't that great, we let her have a free option on *Return to Sender*.

NP: Meanwhile, she flew us out there . . .

RW: On a cheapo flight, paying half while we paid the other half.

NP: . . . and put us up in a granny flat . . .

RW: A 'grandmother unit'.

NP: . . . at the bottom of a friend's garden.

RW: It wasn't far from Venice Beach, but it was a long way from . . .

NP: . . . civilisation. There was gunfire during the night, and everyone drove around in cars with blacked-out windows.

RW: But she was doing the best that she could for us.

NP: So we were pitching this idea of hers, and from seeing people's eyes glaze over after about fifteen seconds it was quite clear to us that they didn't like it.

What was the idea about?

RW: It was about a man whose wife is in a coma, and he discovers that he can . . .

NP: . . . communicate with her while he's asleep. A bit like *Dreamscape*.

RW: So he finds out how she ended up in a coma and solves the crime in his sleep. But even talking about someone being in a coma lulls executives to sleep.

NP: We were doing one pitch and the woman who was sitting next to the main man put on some dark glasses and went to sleep. He was aware that she was asleep, and we were aware that she was asleep, but we had to carry on with the pitch.

RW: It was really embarrassing. And very funny.

NP: Pitching something is part of doing the rounds. It's not the done thing to turn up and say, 'How are you? How are you doing?' You're expected to do a rehearsed pitch. They just want to hear one.

RW: We were due to go home after a month and . . .

NP: . . . Mary Anne Page asked us to video the pitch so that it could continue doing the rounds without us being there. She actually got hold of a video camera . . .

RW: . . . but we refused to do it.

Did she manage to get anywhere with *Return to Sender*?

RW: Not really. By the end of this trip we had a choice of two producers: Stephen Woolley, who had just won a Producer of the Year award for *The Crying Game*, and Steve Tisch, who was producing a film with Tom Hanks which nobody knew would be very successful. Steve Tisch was saying, 'Go with me. I'm going to give it to my pal Michael Douglas' – which would have been perfect – but our agent told us, 'Go with Woolley. He's the guy.' So we went with him, which we don't regret doing, but Steve Tisch was the guy up for gazillions of Oscars the following year with *Forrest Gump*.

NP: Our future might have gone in a very different direction. Not that we're complaining.

Were any directors attached while the project was with Stephen Woolley?

NP: Vincent Ward was attached for a while.

RW: Vincent was a very unlikely choice because he's more interested in images than story, but we were pleased that he was intrigued by the script, and on our way to the first meeting we thought, 'We'd better have a new angle to offer him.'

NP: And, having seen a couple of his films, it was obvious that this angle had better be something a bit off-the-wall.

RW: So we came up with the idea that the kidnapping which forms the backstory was done by two blind people, and the hero finds this out after the heroine has spent five years on death row for the crime. It was really just something for Vincent to think about as we had breakfast, but he really liked it, so we spent the next six months trying to make it work. Some directors will tell you exactly what they think, but Vincent's way of getting more out of you is to make you guess.

NP: You had to dig deep to make something better, because you didn't know why he didn't like it in the first place.

RW: In fact, this flippant idea gave our trailer-trash characters more depth and texture. We sometimes have difficulty writing female parts, but that's a great part and hopefully we'll get a great actress to play it. Unfortunately, Vincent's casting ideas weren't really finance-able . . .

NP: . . . so we all went our separate ways. But the script was better for having worked with him.

RW: And now we've got Richard Loncraine.

NP: We're also co-producers on it.

RW: Which means we have formal say over choice of cast and director. We normally get consulted, which is good, but to actually have formal say is great.

NP: It's not about getting the thing made, it's about getting it

STORY AND CHARACTER

made right – hopefully not another of these pages in *Screen International*, Cannes edition, for a film that will just go straight to video.

RW: There was talk of sending the script to George Clooney. Now, George Clooney would be absolutely great, and it would give the film a chance of being really big, but if you go down that road everything gets ramped up.

NP: The expectations of the financiers increase, and if George Clooney says no – after the couple of months it took to even find that out – you've got to go for someone of the same stature, or else everyone thinks it's a B-movie.

RW: So we all decided, Richard and the producer and us, that we don't want to do that. The movie won't be as big, but it will be made in the right way.

After doing the rounds in Hollywood, did you go back to Britain?

NP: We were about to catch the plane out, when a British director called Stuart Orme, who we met through Mary Anne Page, rang up and said, 'I'm doing a sci-fi movie, *The Puppet Masters*, for Disney. Will you stick around and be my writers on it?'

RW: So we went in and pitched to the studio, Hollywood Pictures.

NP: Who had a terrible reputation. All their films were bad. The saying in Hollywood was, 'If it's Sphinx' – which was their logo – 'it stinks.'

RW: And it was true. The other outfit at Disney . . .

NP: Touchstone.

RW: . . . was making interesting movies. But this was Hollywood Pictures. The producer was the studio chief's personal heart doctor, and he was indulging his passion for Robert A. Heinlein. It was awful, really. They worked us like dogs.

NP: The studio would be all closed up except for one office with a light on. That was us and the director and one of the executives.

48

RW: The air-conditioning had been turned down . . .
NP: . . . so the exec had his shirt off . . .
RW: . . . and was walking around the corridors.
NP: We'd talk about a scene, then the exec would say, 'Could you run up a few versions of that for tomorrow?' and we would do three versions of the same scene by ten o'clock the next morning, having been given it at ten o'clock the night before.
RW: We ended up being there for quite a while, having told our respective partners that we were on our way home.
NP: Stuart was living in this nice villa in the hills, and we were staying in a room down by the pool.
RW: With two beds.
NP: One on the floor.
RW: Then my girl turned up.
NP: Rob moved to another fancy villa, and I moved to a motel in Hollywood – which is not a nice part of town. I changed rooms every week or so for a diffcrent perspective on the pool. It seemed like we were earning a lot of money, but we were probably on a fairly low scale.
RW: We did have twin convertibles.
NP: As part of our per diem we each had a white convertible, and because we were in different places we would meet up for breakfast on Sunset then drive along next to each other with the top down and the same music station on the radio. Only tourists have the top down, because LA is usually so hot and smoggy.

Were you working from Robert Heinlein's novel or an existing script?

RW: We were rewriting a script by a guy called David S. Goyer.
NP: An *SFX* magazine hero. And Goyer had rewritten . . .
RW: . . . the guys who wrote *Aladdin*, Ted Elliott and Terry Rossio.

NP: Who have since become really successful.

RW: We thought it was a load of crap – slugs from space without any irony – so we went in saying, 'This is about a guy who's spent his whole life looking for aliens and they've never turned up, and suddenly he's vindicated by the arrival of the slugs.'

NP: But in the end it was done as a completely straight B-movie.

RW: The pilot episode of *The X-Files* was made at the same time, but that was self-aware and this was anachronistic. Stuart brought us in to put his spin on it, and then we had these awful meetings where there was him and us and twelve people in suits.

NP: I think the same thing happened as on *An American Werewolf in Paris*. They like the first draft, which is the thing that gets everyone interested, then they have a draft done by somebody else, which is snazzier but lacks the something that they liked in the first place, so what they want you to do is to put that in again . . .

RW: . . . and make sense of it all. You can get to a point where the script is pretty good but not perfect – no script is ever going to be perfect – and if you go that little bit further you throw the baby out with the bath water.

NP: Then the studio realises that they've gone too far and try to go back.

RW: But they never go back to a previous draft. That's the stupid thing. There's never a problem about spending more money on another writer. They don't say, 'Let's forget this draft was ever written and go back to the first draft.'

I notice that you didn't receive a credit.

RW: We didn't want a credit.

NP: We were probably sent the arbitration thing . . .

RW: . . . but we didn't contest it.

NP: We saw what they shot. It's amazing how much you can

change in a short space of time. The interesting thing is what they kept. They only kept a few lines of ours, but nearly all of them were in the trailer – which shows you the sort of stuff we write.

RW: OTT. Lines like, 'Gentlemen, you thought you'd lost a town, but now you've lost a country.' The extraordinary thing was that after we'd worked our guts out we were fired.

NP: We did about six weeks and had fulfilled our contract, then we were given these pagers for the weekend – which we'd never been issued with before, even though we generally worked weekends – and on the Sunday we were paged . . .

RW: . . . by the head of the studio . . .

NP: . . . who told us that our contract was up.

RW: The only reason we were issued with these pagers was so they could get hold of us to fire us. It was weird. And it was awful, because it meant that the director had his authority undermined. We were his guys. But we could go home and carry on with our lives, while he had to stay out there for a year and make this movie.

NP: You have a choice. Either you walk off it or you try and make a good film out of it.

RW: For us it was the sort of thing where you felt, 'No one will ever know about that.'

Was that what prompted you to write another script of your own, *The Mabus*?

NP: We worked on that before and after *The Puppet Masters*, but mostly after. It was inspired by *The Golem*, a book by . . .

RW: . . . Gustav Meyrinck, which was a huge seller in Europe at the turn of the century.

NP: It was made into a German film in 1911, then remade seven years later. The look of that one was very influential on the original Hollywood *Frankenstein*.

RW: The book is all about the protecting spirit of the ghetto, which would walk . . .

NP: . . . through the town once every seven years.

RW: It's an old Jewish legend from Czechoslovakia, so after the Velvet Revolution we thought, 'Let's do a modern version where an American goes to Prague.' We did a lot of research, and one of the things we found out was that the Soviet psychic-weaponry programme had been based just outside Prague . . .

NP: 'ESPionage', they called it.

RW: . . . so our script starts in the fifties, where these experiments on gypsies unleash the monster, then jumps to the nineties, where the creature is back at this abandoned installation in the woods. The first sign that something has gone wrong is when a guy dies and they do an autopsy on him and find another head inside his.

NP: We had a great deal of trouble trying to explain that.

RW: But the idea of a skull inside another skull was really interesting. A producer who had been Richard Donner's agent at CAA . . .

NP: . . . said that it was the best thing he'd read horror-wise since *The Omen*. He really wanted to make it.

RW: We got to ride around the Columbia lot in his buggy, because he had an Arnold Schwarzenegger movie about to open. Then the movie opened, and it turned out to be *The Last Action Hero* – and he was off the lot a week later.

It sounds like a much more commercial spec script than *Return to Sender*.

NP: Well, a real case of trying to go for the money was *The Combination* . . .

RW: . . . a high-concept buddy-movie . . .

NP: . . . about two boxers . . .

RW: . . . the young white hotshot and the disgraced black guy who hate each other . . .

NP: . . . and are fighting the middleweight championship in Las Vegas.

RW: The wife of one of the boxers is kidnapped, and he's told, 'If you don't throw the fight, she's dead.' But just as he's about to throw the fight there's an earthquake and it's postponed for twenty-four hours, so he teams up with his opponent to find his wife.

NP: Then, having become a bit friendlier, they have to fight each other again at the end. We were trying to be like American writers, so there must be a lot of scripts like that. It was rather Shane Black-ey.

RW: Our American agent sold Shane Black's screenplay *The Long Kiss Goodnight*, which was the most expensive spec script to that date.

NP: Three or four months' work, and you know within a week whether it's going to sell. Then that's it. It didn't sell and it's dead.

RW: We spent much more time on it than that. A year, I think. We wanted to write a boxing movie, but what we wrote was too late and too premeditated.

NP: We tried to second-guess what people would want.

RW: Not a good idea.

NP: And *The Long Kiss Goodnight* was a complete flop.

RW: But we really learned from that.

What was your involvement in *An American Werewolf in Paris*?

RW: I'd always loved *An American Werewolf in London*, which is a brilliant mix of horror and comedy, and one of the things that Working Title had in development was *An American Werewolf in Paris*. I remember looking through *Screen International* and thinking, 'I'd love to be working on that', and suddenly Working Title called us in and said, 'We've got this great project.'

NP: At one point we were asked to take a wolf's head to America on the plane and got stopped at the other end.

RW: The producer was just using us as couriers.

NP: It was funny because they put the case on the X-ray machine and saw this thing with a mouth and a jaw.

RW: They were designing the monster at the Henson Creature Shop . . .

NP: . . . in Camden . . .

RW: . . . and we were shown around by these nutty bearded guys with spectacles. They demonstrated this talking pig for us . . .

NP: . . . and they explained that a pig wouldn't really be able to talk . . .

RW: . . . due to the articulation of the jaw. But they had managed to solve that. And this pig turned out to be Babe.

NP: They did all this explaining, then they realised that we were only the writers and completely lost interest in us. Everyone suddenly turned their backs.

Were you rewriting the original draft by John Landis?

RW: We never saw his script. What we saw was a draft by Alex Winter . . .

NP: . . . who was the non-Keanu Reeves character in *Bill and Ted* . . .

RW: . . . and had made a film called *Freaked* with the other guy who wrote this script. The director was Marco Brambilla, who had just done . . .

NP: . . . *Demolition Man*, which introduced the world to Sandra Bullock.

RW: Having worked on the script ourselves in London, we then spent a couple of weeks in Hollywood working on it with Marco.

NP: We stayed at the Château Marmont this time.

RW: I had Keanu Reeves next door to me.

NP: And I had the Marlboro Man outside my window, only viewable from the toilet. It was a fantastic view, so I spent quite a lot of time in there.

RW: Anyway, I thought we were really getting somewhere with the script. It wasn't as good as the original movie, because this was a kinetic thing whereas that was more character-based, but we were pretty excited about it. Unfortunately, during our rewrite the budget doubled – from $20 million to $40 million.

NP: We were concerned with the story and the gags, but the director was interested in special effects and car chases.

RW: It's the old Nazi excuse-me: 'We were just following orders.'

NP: So he got kicked off it. Then we did some work with the producers to try and bring it down a bit. And then it was sold on.

RW: Sony bought it from PolyGram, and a guy called Anthony Waller took it on . . .

NP: . . . who had only made one other film, *Mute Witness*, which did very well on the festival circuit.

RW: He's a writer-director, so he rewrote everything . . .

NP: . . . and they gave him *carte blanche* to destroy the franchise – with his company doing the special effects.

How much of your work did he use in the film?

RW: I've never actually seen it.

NP: The trailer was very bad.

RW: We came to it with the idea that this bunch of guys are doing a danger tour of Europe, so there was a sequence set in Pamplona and then there was a bungee jump off the Eiffel Tower.

NP: He certainly kept that bit.

RW: But how many times can you say that you've never seen a film which you worked on for six months? It's such a shame, because the idea of *An American Werewolf in Paris* was really nice and we were honoured to have been brought in on it.

NP: To go through all those years of drafts, with John Landis himself doing the first one, and then just toss the whole lot out of the window and say, 'You go off and do whatever you want as long as you keep it under a certain budget', was a bizarre thing to happen to something which could have been such a lucrative franchise.

Having written a sequel to one cult film, you later scripted a remake of another: _The Italian Job_. What challenges did that present?

RW: We were actually resistant to doing that. Working Title approached us about it first, and we thought, 'What's the point of remaking a classic, quirky movie which has its own special life?' But then an American producer called Donald DeLine became involved, and reminded us that the original film had not been a success in America. The Americans didn't have Mini Coopers, they didn't have a jingoistic attitude towards the Common Market and they hadn't just won the World Cup, which were three of the key elements in its success in Britain.

NP: The Americans didn't even like the ending of the original film, which the British all love. Looking at the American reviews, they obviously found it completely baffling.

RW: DeLine's desire was not to repeat the original film but to repeat the effect of the original film for an American audience, which was a way of doing it that we were able to get enthusiastic about. We thought that if the film was about new world versus old world, about America versus Europe, then when the cars arrive in Rome to do the job it would give the Americans the same feeling as the Minis turning up gives the British. We actually used old Minis, new Minis and American muscle cars, and devised a way they could all take part in the heist.

NP: Having written all those car chases, we were actioned-out. After a while, it's not a very satisfying way of spending your time. We were quite pleased with it, though.

Was the opening of your script, which is reminiscent of _Kelly's Heroes_ – Charlie Croker's father is murdered while stealing the gold during World War Two – a nod to the writer of both films, Troy Kennedy Martin?

RW: It was an unconscious nod. We were looking for an opening which would give Charlie Croker a personal stake in the job. In the original film he didn't really have any motivation besides being a crook, but these days you just can't have an amoral hero. There has to be a profound reason for him to do something like that. Also, because we weren't allowed to use the cliffhanger ending, we thought we'd use the cliffhanger at the beginning instead – with the gold in a truck on one side of the pivot. And then we said, 'Wait a minute. We're doing _Kelly's Heroes_. That's another Troy Kennedy Martin script.' We didn't talk to him at the time, but afterwards we mentioned what a good film he'd written . . .
NP: . . . and how it shouldn't be remade.

Which, so far, it hasn't been.

NP: From what I understand, Paramount have dragged it so far away from the original film that it now takes place in America and the robbery is in Hollywood. But that's the development process for you. You spend a year rewriting a script to the satisfaction of the producer and the studio, then you find out a few months later that they've ditched everything which you introduced bar a few elements – like the revenge aspect. 'Well, we really wanted an American film set in America, so it's a real shame that it's called _The Italian Job_ and takes place in Italy.'
RW: It was another case of throwing the baby out with the bath water. In the first few drafts we managed to keep the baby, and then it was gone and we lost interest in it. We were trying to write an American movie with affectionate nods to its British roots, but they wanted something so detached from the original

film that there was no point in doing a remake. They were
paying lip-service to the original film without any grasp of
what was good about it. That's why I felt we did a good job:
because we managed to keep those elements in there.

Another high-profile project which has spent a long time in
development is *The Grid*, from Philip Kerr's novel *Gridiron*.

RW: A lot of work went into that.
NP: We saw in the newspaper that Working Title had bought
the book for $1 million, so we rang Jenne Casarotto and told
her, 'We'd really like to work on that'. Then she rang Working Title and they said, 'We've paid a million for it so we're
going to get a really expensive writer.' In fact, they got Terry
Hayes, who wrote *Mad Max*.
RW: He did a fairly faithful adaptation of the book, which he
was honour-bound to do when they had publicly spent so
much money on it, but which wasn't the right thing to do
because the book wasn't actually very good.

Why did you want to work on it if you didn't think the book
was very good?

RW: [*To Purvis*] You quite liked Philip Kerr's previous book,
A Philosophical Investigation, didn't you?
NP: I liked the idea behind *A Philosophical Investigation*, and
we both liked the idea behind *Gridiron*, so it didn't seem
necessary to read the book before expressing our interest in
getting involved. Anyway . . .
RW: . . . Working Title have got an LA office as well, so they
brought in a couple called Donna and Wayne Powers, who
did a draft which was like a TV-movie version of the thing.
RW: It wasn't very imaginative, but it was very . . .
NP: . . . efficient.
RW: Then eventually it came to us. We reset it from LA to
Miami and came up with some new ideas: that the man you go

into the movie with is a tree surgeon, and there's a tree going up through the building; that the efficiency of the building drives its murderous impulse, because it's more efficient without humans in; and that the building has a 3-D wire-frame consciousness of itself. I think that made a big difference to the story, even though nothing happened with the film.

Is the script still in development?

RW: Roland Emmerich and Dean Devlin were considering it. Then they passed on it and we had heard that someone was rewriting it . . .
NP: . . . from scratch. You always think a script might come back to life like a zombie, but when it's being rewritten from scratch it's completely dead. There's no way back from that.
RW: I can't see it getting made now, after September 11th. But, by a nice irony, *The Italian Job* has apparently been rewritten by Donna and Wayne Powers.

You must be seen as action and thriller specialists – although in answer to that you can point to an earlier adaptation, of Iain Banks's novel *The Wasp Factory*.

RW: That was supposed to be Stephen Daldry's début feature film as director, and we were brought together by Stephen Evans and Caroline Wood at Renaissance. It was perfect material for him and a major project for them – their first contemporary script after splitting from Kenneth Branagh – but the problem was that Iain Banks didn't own the rights to the book. They were sold to a company which had gone into receivership some years before, then they were bought from the receiver by a Canadian company, and they were due to revert to Iain Banks on January 1st, 1996. So we wrote the script on the assumption that the rights would be in his gift . . .
NP: . . . killed ourselves to get it ready . . .
RW: . . . delivered it two days before Christmas, and on

December 31st this company turned over some footage and claimed they had begun principal photography . . .

NP: . . . which meant that they owned the rights in perpetuity.

RW: It then became a matter for the courts, with Iain Banks being the one who would have to sort it out, and I don't think he ever pursued it. None of his books had been adapted at that time and he had hoped this was going to get made, but then there was that successful TV adaptation of *The Crow Road* and suddenly it wasn't an issue any more. This company was probably angling for a quick fifty grand to shut up and drop the case, but it was a low-budget movie which wasn't going to take a lot of money.

NP: That's the quickest we've known that something's not going to happen.

RW: Immediately. That was very annoying because I was really proud of what we did. We normally say to people, 'It's an unadaptable book and we proved it with our script', but I think we actually did get the flavour of it and it was very enjoyable to write. Daldry is another director who makes you work hard by using silence as a tactic.

Were you fans of the book?

RW: I thought it was very interesting, but clearly the work of a young writer. You could understand why loads of students liked it, but it wasn't as good as it could have been because it was rather . . .

NP: . . . repetitive . . .

RW: . . . and excessive. We thought we could make it less repellent, so that you might actually engage with the characters, but we still thought it would make a big splash in the newspapers.

NP: Most of our scripts tend towards the dark side, and often have a thriller element, but this one really concentrated on the darkness.

RW: It's more a drama than a thriller. The ticking clock of the book is this boy's older brother coming back home, but it never really pays off, so we tried to tone that down and not have this spurious thrill. In a film you obviously can't deal with all the things in a book, so you make more of fewer. We were very much in tune with Daldry about having lovely William Walton music throughout, because the way this boy looks at the world is through war movies.

NP: There was one bit which was a pastiche of *Apocalypse Now*. He's standing among dead rabbits like Robert Duvall.

RW: 'It smelled like . . . Victory.'

NP: That's a good shot which will never see the light of day. It would have had to have said at the end, 'A large number of rabbits were killed in the making of this picture.'

Between *The Wasp Factory* and *The Grid*, you worked on one of your favourite scripts and least favourite films, *Plunkett & Macleane*. What happened there?

RW: A line producer called Selwyn Roberts came across the true story of Plunkett and Macleane and thought, 'That would make a great movie.' He knew Gary Oldman, and Gary Oldman took it to Eric Fellner and said, 'Could you develop this project? I'd like to be Plunkett.' So Selwyn Roberts did a draft, which began with a bit of highway robbery and then became about trying to marry Macleane off to make money from the dowry; then Peter Barnes did a draft, which was quite fun but basically *Carry On Dick*; then a British guy called Jonathan Darby, who had been an executive in LA, became attached as director, and for some reason he gave the job to an American . . .

NP: . . . who did a very long, not very readable draft . . .

RW: . . . and then it was basically dead. Working Title weren't pushing it. It was just one of those projects on the shelf. But we always liked the idea, and by going back to the Selwyn Roberts script we came up with a different take on the same characters. And that take was: 'Plunkett is cleverer than Macleane. Macleane is just a fop, so forget about marrying him off and instead find an interesting way for them to meet.' So we came up with the idea of Macleane swallowing the jewel which had been stolen by Plunkett, and Eric said, 'That sounds good. Go away and write it.' We've got several jobs just by concentrating on the start. A new opening gives you a new level of energy . . .

NP: . . . and sets the tone for the film. With that one, it gave you the darkness and the grime and the humour.

Were you still writing it for Gary Oldman as Plunkett?

RW: And Richard E. Grant as Macleane. Then somebody said, 'They're too old.' Then Jake Scott came on board, and the studio, PolyGram, wanted it funnier, and wanted to emphasise the romance between Macleane and the girl. I disagreed. I thought it was perfectly funny, and the whole idea was that we had written the girl as a bit of fluff, a reflection of the shallowness of the time and the emptiness of Macleane's worldview. The real romance is between Plunkett and Macleane.

NP: The most important thing was their relationship as friends. At the end of our draft, Plunkett gives his life for Macleane, having sold Macleane out beforehand.

RW: When we finally met Robert Carlyle on the set of *The World is Not Enough*, he said he committed to *Plunkett & Macleane* on the back of our script, and turned up in Prague a year later to find that his part had been made much more peripheral. He was very professional and carried on with the film, but there was really no way to make the romance work between Macleane and the girl while still keeping the importance of the relationship with Plunkett.

Did you go back to the true story as well as to the Selwyn Roberts script?

RW: Yeah, but there wasn't much to it. The fact that Plunkett had been an apothecary wasn't in any of the other versions, but most of that got lost in the movie. We did lots of research into seventeenth-century London, and had the Thames freezing over . . .

NP: . . . and a big chase across the ice . . .

RW: . . . a fantastic sequence, also not in the film. Jake wasn't confident about shooting it, so it went out of the window. Instead, they're shot at in a carriage and somehow disappear through the bottom.

NP: We looked very closely at the language, too.

RW: I was really proud of our dialogue. Movies don't often give you the opportunity to indulge in that sort of period language. But Jake wasn't confident about handling the dialogue, either, so if in doubt they had someone swear and be anachronistic.

NP: Our draft had one F-word, which we were told to remove.

RW: 'Stand and fucking deliver!'

NP: Then Jake came on, who viewed it as some sort of punk movie, and suddenly the film was jam-packed with swearing.

How did you feel about Charles McKeown's rewrite?

RW: I don't think we can blame him for what happened to it. If you come on to a movie which is heading towards production, you have to do what the director and producers ask you to do.

NP: It was still extremely depressing. The project wasn't our idea . . .

RW: . . . but we had brought it back to life . . .

NP: . . . so it felt like ours because we had put so much work into it.

RW: The thing did terribly compared to our hopes for it. In a mad moment, we'd even thought that if it did really well we could conceivably get Oscar nominations.

NP: Or at least something from the *Evening Standard*. It could have been a big British movie rather than a tiny film that happens to be a hit.

RW: But as it was we got . . .

NP: . . . some of the worst reviews I've ever seen.

RW: There was one review which said, 'Jake Scott struggles manfully . . .

NP: . . . with a woefully inadequate script.' You do remember the bad ones.

RW: These critics really know what they're talking about.

But your original draft was seen by . . .

RW: Barbara Broccoli and Michael Wilson. So the frustration and disappointment of *Plunkett & Macleane* led to the wonderful opportunity of being considered for Bond.

NP: Our draft had scale, humour, imaginative action, was character-based . . .

RW: . . . and British . . .

NP: . . . and that fulfils the Bond brief. And after *Tomorrow Never Dies* . . .

RW: . . . which strayed a little into other action movies and didn't really explore Bond . . .

NP: . . . they wanted to redress the balance and add more drama.

RW: The fact that we had also done *Let Him Have It* was quite a good thing, from their point of view.

Had you always dreamed of writing a Bond film?

RW: Oh, yeah. One of our early scripts, *Solid Gold Easy Action*, was a comedy about two working-class blokes . . .

NP: . . . both obsessed with James Bond . . .

RW: . . . who come across an old Aston Martin in a field up north, restore it and head down south . . .

NP: . . . one of them calling himself Roger and the other calling himself Sean.

164 RW: I even said to Neal a couple of times, 'We should write a

Bond film on spec' – and thank God we didn't, because the producers won't read such things for legal reasons.

NP: When we were invited in we hoped it was about Bond, but it was still a real shock.

RW: We went expecting to meet a development person, someone who checks you out before you meet the boss, but instead it was just Barbara Broccoli and Michael Wilson in this incredibly intimidating office on Piccadilly – like a villain's lair. We sat down and they said, 'What do you think James Bond should do next?' and because we hadn't prepared for that we were a bit flippant.

NP: 'You should see him around the house, doing his place up.'

RW: I suppose humour came through there, and we got on very well with them.

NP: So we came back a couple of weeks later, this time with ideas, including blowing up MI6 and the chase down the Thames. We even had a load of titles. Then we saw them again, with the executive from the studio, and we felt that nearly all of our ideas were criticised. We came out of the meeting, rang our agent and said, 'We don't think we did ourselves proud that time.'

RW: So that was it. We'd been going for thirteen years, and we always thought we'd be able to do the business if we got our foot in the door . . .

NP: Or our feet, because there's two of us.

RW: . . . and suddenly we did have our foot in the door, and when it came to it we blew it. But the next day – this was late November – our agent rang us and said, 'They want you to fly to America in January.' One question which came up in the meetings was, 'Would you be happy writing this in America for the next six months?' and I said, 'No problem', and Neal said, 'No problem', and I was surprised at him saying that because he had two young kids, and he was surprised at me saying that because I was getting married bang in the middle of those six months. So we turned up in January, with the release already announced for November the following year, with no story . . .

NP: . . . and a few ideas which would hopefully be included. The pressure was intense.

RW: We had our foot in the door but they could still cut it off, in the sense that if we didn't come up with a satisfactory story they could fire us.

NP: *Tomorrow Never Dies* had quite a few writers.

RW: It only felt like we had something when we spent a whole day doing a character description of Elektra. That galvanised everything.

NP: The draft we had by June 15th was pretty much the film which got made. Barbara rang us at the hotel and said that the studio liked it, which meant we hadn't screwed it up. M being held by the villains was the only real change from then on in.

RW: We'd all thought about that but hadn't gone down that road. It's wonderful when Bond shoots Elektra and M sees it.

You wanted to 'Flemingise' the films, I gather.

RW: [*Indicating Purvis*] He was quoted as saying that. I think you just read the books because you might find something that everyone else has missed.

NP: Of the books – and the films – the one we were heading towards would be *On Her Majesty's Secret Service*. It's a very faithful adaptation and a very good film, although people might not have liked George Lazenby.

RW: But you don't simply go away and write a Bond film. The producers are actively involved in shaping the story. They know all the movies inside out.

NP: Michael's co-written five of them, so we're there . . .

RW: . . . to stimulate something which wouldn't have been there if we weren't in the room.

NP: They spend two years on each film, from the very beginning to the very end, so they want something worth doing. They're open to all sorts of ideas. People talk about it being a formula, but in a sense it's almost a genre – and they want to push that genre.

RW: Also, Pierce Brosnan not only has to make this physically gruelling movie but he then has to promote it around the world, so you want to give him something he can get his teeth into and talk about in all those interviews. At a certain point, though, we had to decide, 'Does this film hinge on a nuclear weapon?' The nuclear option is, of course, the last resort, because you want to come up with something new, but we were running out of time because the film had to start shooting. I think the way it was used in the film was quite original, but nevertheless the villains were still stealing a nuclear weapon. We did give the villains psychological motivation, however, which was reasonably novel.

NP: Barbara said, 'Bond thinks Elektra is Tracy from *On Her Majesty's Secret Service*, but she turns out to be Blofeld.' Perhaps in focussing on character, you generate a certain sympathy for the villains. This woman was a damaged person.

RW: But you also needed the dementedness which makes it different from reality. In the final analysis, she was crazy and he had a bullet moving through his brain. But one thing we've found with both Bond films is that you seize on something which has interesting story potential, and suddenly it seems to be in the news all the time. Just as we started work on Bond 19, there was a series of articles in the *Los Angeles Times* – not the most highbrow of newspapers – focussing on the Caspian oil in Azerbaijan, and the deal to let the pipeline go through Georgia. Eduard Shevardnadze, the president of Georgia, actually survived a Bond-style assassination attempt when a dozen guys on motorcycles attacked his armoured Mercedes with sub-machine guns. Oddly enough, his numberplate was '007'.

Did you find it difficult to top the twelve-minute pre-title sequence?

RW: We've found that scripts tend to lose their pace two-thirds of the way in. You're rushing towards the end, but nothing much is actually happening. I thought one of the most interesting things about this script was . . .

NP: . . . M being caught. It gave it a new impetus. But perhaps the film went on too long, and you could argue that Renard should have been despatched before Elektra.

RW: We went back and forth on that . . .

NP: . . . and did different versions. We originally had a more low-key beginning, harking back to the sixties when the films didn't have a massive stunt before the titles. Bond just climbed on to the counterweight of a lift . . .

RW: . . . and descended into the shadows.

NP: Then we went into the titles. The Thames chase came later.

RW: It was supposed to set up an unease in the audience: 'What's going on? Why didn't we get a big explosion?' Then MI6 blows up.

NP: But in this day and age you'd be letting people down if you didn't wow them with something massive, so the Thames chase became part of the pre-title sequence. A low-key beginning is a nice idea, but what people want, what the Bond brand means, is really big entertainment, the rollercoaster ride.

RW: We felt that the ultimate opening was the bungee jump in *GoldenEye*, which is fantastic. *The Spy Who Loved Me* and *Moonraker* have equally good beginnings, but they were ancient history.

NP: I've been in three cinemas where, at the end of the Thames chase, the audience has broken out into applause. And the interesting thing is, Bond fails – so what are they applauding? They're applauding the excess.

RW: Anthony Lane, in his *New Yorker* review, described

those twelve minutes and the naked girls during the song as like going to the best party of the year . . . And after that you might as well go home.

You had more time to write the next one. Are you happier with it at this stage?

RW: We have had more time to write this one, but as it turns out it's a more difficult story to tell. Michael Apted didn't really bring an agenda to the last one, so the script didn't change that much, but Lee Tamahori came on board this one with lots of ideas about increasing the level of action, and it was a challenge to contain them within the structure. The more ambitious the action, the less room there is for the characters.

NP: And the harder it is to make everything credible. The interesting thing is that there are fantastical elements in it, but so far it's being shot in a fairly realistic way.

RW: Bond is betrayed, captured and tortured in North Korea, and when he comes out he has a beard and long hair. Now, that's an interesting idea, it's easy to write, but can you actually film it, can you really show him looking like that? In fact, they've handled it really well. The same is true of the villain, who's played by two different actors.

NP: Another case of doing the fantastic in a realistic way.

RW: We had to settle for a different version of our original opening, though. We were aiming for something to top the boat chase in the last one, and our idea involved these new hovercraft which travel five feet off the ground at eighty miles per hour, but it turned out to be impossible because it was too dangerous. Even for a Bond movie.

What impact did the events of September 11th have on the script development?

NP: The plot changed later anyway, although at that time we took out a scene of some American generals being . . .

RW: . . . melted . . .

NP: . . . by the superweapon. But the basis of Bond's character is that he will hunt down 'the hand that holds the whip' – which is exactly what the Americans tried to do straight afterwards.

RW: Oddly enough, the elements of our plot all tied in. Al-Qaida get their weapons from an ex-Soviet airforce officer, who controls all these transport planes, in return for African conflict diamonds. That's just like one of the key elements in our plot, except that the villain is from North Korea.

What difference has it made being involved with this film right into production?

RW: The scale of this film is bigger than the last one, so I think everyone can use a little help. For instance, we wrote a fight involving robot-laser diamond-cutters, but the machinery only arrived last week, and the realities of the robots don't gel with the fight we originally envisaged, so it's good to be on hand to contribute to the final action.

NP: And sometimes the way a set has been built is not the way we imagined it. In the Q scene, the entrance to the set was on the opposite side from where the business was going to take place, so they needed some dialogue to fill that dead time.

RW: There are also occasions when Pierce says, 'I'm not crazy about this', or, 'I'm not sure about that', and it makes you look at the scene again from his point of view and make some improvements because of it.

NP: It's like the old Hollywood studio system: typing up line changes, running to the set with them, shooting them an hour later. There was a scene when Michael Madsen was addressing the camera, talking to M, but we wrote it before he was cast. Having seen him do his thing over the previous couple of days, the scene suddenly seemed very un-Michael Madsen, so we quickly ran up a few line changes and took them over there. It's fortunate that everyone is prepared to look at things again, especially when the budget is more than a million dollars per page.

RW: Talk is cheap, but dialogue is very expensive.

Is it true that *Johnny English*, a comedy for Rowan Atkinson, is a Bond spoof?

RW: When we were introduced to Rowan Atkinson, we said, 'There are two things we don't do. Bond spoofs and advert spin-offs.' Then someone in the room put on a tape of the Barclaycard ads, which are Bond spoofs. So we said, 'We'll think about it.' We were still adamant that it shouldn't be a Bond spoof.

NP: We had him driving a Bristol . . .

RW: . . . but beyond that it was closer to Graham Greene: hapless foreign agent caught up in end-of-empire problems.

NP: Rather like a new Inspector Clouseau.

RW: We worked on it for a year in close consultation with Rowan, but by that time we were contractually obliged to start writing Bond 20, so Working Title hired Ben Elton, who wrote a very funny script which was more a collection of rants than a structured movie. Then Peter Howitt, who wrote and directed *Sliding Doors*, got involved, and in the two- or three-month hiatus . . .

NP: . . . while they were looking for a Bond director . . .

RW: . . . we did a draft which combined our old stuff with Ben Elton's new idea that the story should start with Lenin's body being stolen from his tomb . . .

NP: . . . in an attempt to rehang the Iron Curtain.

RW: Then we went back to Bond, *Johnny English* was in pre-production on the other side of Pinewood, and both films were due to start principal photography on the very same day in January . . .

NP: . . . taking up every single stage on the lot . . .

RW: . . . which would have been some kind of record. But in the weeks after September 11th, the idea of incompetent spies conspiring to rehang the Iron Curtain, together with the terrorist weapon which Pete had introduced into the plot, seemed irrelevant on the one hand and not very funny on the other. Then we were asked to re-jig the material, but we were still working on Bond, so we went to the producers and said, 'Is there any likelihood of us being given the boot? Because if there is . . .

NP: . . . we'll walk over the other side of the lot.'

RW: And Barbara said, 'Unfortunately not.' So Working Title brought in a chap called Will Davies, and the latest draft keeps a lot of our comic ideas but puts them in a new, non-controversial framework. It's less ambitious, in that it has a safe premise about stealing the crown jewels, but it's still very funny, and we've been told that our shared credit is guaranteed.

NP: It didn't start shooting on the same day as Bond – or at the same studio – but it'll hopefully be shooting at the same time.

Do you see what you do as an art or a craft?

RW: That's an interesting question. I think some of it is art and some of it is craft. The chances of being Oscar-nominated for a Bond script are absolutely nil, but you have fewer constraints writing something which comes from the heart than coming up with new things for a character everyone knows who has limits. That's craft, but it's hard. I'm not saying that *Let Him Have It* was a great piece of work, but people say to us, 'What a great film that was', because it was serious. That's art, but it's easier.

NP: I think in other scripts the characters are allowed to reveal themselves more. The difficulty with Bond is that you're not allowed to reveal too much of him but you've got to take him on an emotional journey, and if you go too far . . .

RW: . . . it's not Bond.

NP: Believe it or not, we try and approach Bond as dramatic
stories. If we approached it as banging out an action movie,

and all we did after that was other action movies, we would both be completely braindead.

RW: Someone came to us a couple of weeks ago and asked us to write a big-budget action-adventure film and we said no, partly because people will muck around with it more if it's not inherently serious and partly because we don't want to go straight into another action film. It's great to return to something like the Brian Jones project, which is unlike anything else we've done.

Because it's a rock biopic?

NP: It's not really a rock biopic, because nowadays Brian Jones, as the founder of the Rolling Stones, doesn't mean anything to most young people.

RW: There's a debate between the producer, Stephen Woolley, and us as to what extent it's a rock biopic. Steve, with his producer's hat on, is concerned that we dot the i's and cross the t's of the musical Brian Jones, and we're more interested in . . .

NP: . . . the power struggle between a rock star and his builder – backed by some good music and sprinkled with a bit of sex.

RW: It has two close antecedents: *Performance* and *The Servant*. It's both bizarre and banal. You've got the bizarre character of Brian Jones and the banal character of this builder . . .

NP: Frank Thoroughgood.

RW: . . . who basically took over Brian's life while some building work, which shouldn't have taken long, went on and on and on. Courtesy of Steve's contacts, we managed to talk to people who were actually there – people whom the authors of all the books about Brian Jones's mysterious death never managed to find. One of the challenges is that Brian was not a particularly sympathetic character, and neither was the man who killed him . . .

NP: . . . but at the end you want people to feel sorry for them and understand how two people can get into that situation. It's taken us a long time – eight years now, which is longer than Brian was in the Stones – to strike the right balance and make both characters sympathetic.

When you start a new project, do you usually write a treatment first?

RW: We don't like treatments. They're an art form in themselves.

NP: We used to have a no-treatment policy, but now we have to write them . . .

RW: . . . because we're being paid by the studios . . .

NP: . . . and they like to know everything, because there's so much at stake.

RW: Our treatments start out as beat sheets, with a line for each scene, then we flesh them out and they end up as treatments. Then, once we get to the point where we've got to give it a go to see if it works, we say, 'I'll take that bit and you take that bit.'

NP: About five pages each.

RW: Then we e-mail what we've done to each other, and I rewrite what Neal does and Neal rewrites what I do. When we started writing together our scripts were very wordy, but stylistically they've become more and more pared down until there's no style at all.

NP: Rob was recently cutting out the word 'the', and I was having to put it back again.

RW: You're affected by what you read, so don't read *Catcher in the Rye* before you write a Bond film. But economy is what it's all about. Shorter scripts are easier to read – and they're greener, because they use less paper. Also, you can . . .

NP: . . . hold them in your head. If they get too long you can't contain them in your mind.

Do you tend to start with plot or character?

RW: You have to start with character, otherwise you have no way in. There's a place in North America known in the insurance trade as 'Nub City' because it has a lot of people with missing limbs, and we were fascinated by the idea of people mutilating themselves for the insurance but we never found a character to build the story out of.

NP: Something we seem unable to do without in our last few scripts is backstory. You get to know a character better if they have a backstory, and it also lays the plot on the table from the outset, but it's hard to include backstories because the script instantly becomes more complicated.

It must be hard to establish a writing routine when there are two of you.

RW: The hardest thing about writing is getting yourself to do the work, isn't it?

NP: Yeah. [*To Wade*] You used to do your best work . . .

RW: . . . from about nine or ten at night to about two or three in the morning.

NP: But now you go to bed . . .

RW: . . . and that's it. No best work. [*To Purvis*] What about you?

NP: I used to start work at eight, do a few pages before ten and then take the rest of the morning off. Now, because of the school run, I can't really get started before ten and I'm struggling to do the pages by six. We don't need to speak to each other in the mornings because we have our work to do, but we were about to hand in a draft of something recently and we were on the phone at . . .

RW: . . . midnight . . .

NP: . . . trying to come up with the appropriate word.

RW: There's no peace. Nothing is ever truly dead unless it's been shot. You deliver a draft of a project, then, just as you've started the next one, the producer or the director of the previous one comes back with notes which you have to attend to. There's never a point where there isn't someone ringing you up about something . . .

NP: . . . even though the reality is that . . .

RW: . . . nothing happens when it's supposed to anyway.

Do you get fed up with rewriting scripts you already like to suit other people?

RW: Yeah.

NP: If you think that the film is going to get made, you're driven, because you can see the light at the end of the tunnel. Even with the worst jobs, you still believe that what you're writing is the best thing yet, because you're throwing yourself into it.

RW: It's like women and childbirth. Somehow they forget the excruciating pain and go on to have another child. So you will yourself into forgetting everything you know and thinking that this film is not only going to get made but get made within your lifetime.

NP: Putting out of your mind the fact that the child may be a horrible monster.

RW: We have been guilty of allowing ourselves to be pushed around too much. Some writers are quite obstinate and opinionated, but our approach is to see what someone is driving at and then see if it works. If you do all the work on your own and then some guy comes along and wants to change it, that can be pretty threatening, but because there are two of us we tend to be more distant from the material and not so threatened by the director. I was really pissed off about *Plunkett & Macleane*, though.

What's your attitude to the so-called 'vanity credit' taken by many directors?

RW: It's incredibly annoying.

NP: *Plunkett & Macleane* was 'A Film by Jake Scott'.

RW: There are certain instances, to do with the way the film is sold, where I think it's fair enough. If it's a Ridley Scott film, I think it should be 'A Ridley Scott Film' because he's a saleable asset. But if it doesn't contribute to the selling of the movie, I think it's really not fair.

NP: Directors have it written into their contract as standard now, and it's just rubberstamped, but if you know about movies you can tell when a film really is 'by' someone. Ninety-nine times out of a hundred it isn't.

RW: Peter Medak came on board *Let Him Have It* a few weeks before it was shot and it was still 'A Peter Medak Film', but to be fair he did make it into a Peter Medak film. It wasn't our film.

You originally wanted to direct. Would you still like to make a film of your own?

NP: It's finding the time to spend a year on something.

RW: And finding the thing you're prepared to spend a year *on*. With writing, you can do something and then go and do something completely different. But to get bogged down for more than a year, really, doing just one thing, it has to be really worthwhile. We still need to try it, but Working Title would like us to do a silly comedy . . .

NP: . . . and unfortunately we're going through a Bergman phase.

Shawn Slovo was born in 1950, in South Africa, and later moved to England with her exiled parents, ANC executive-committee member Joe Slovo and journalist Ruth First. She now lives in London.

FILM

A World Apart (Chris Menges, 1987, UK)

Captain Corelli's Mandolin (John Madden, 2001, US/Fr/UK)

UNCREDITED

Elizabeth (Shekhar Kapur, 1998, UK)
The Hi-Lo Country (Stephen Frears, 1998, UK/US)

Bridget Jones's Diary (Sharon Maguire, 2001, US/Fr/UK)

SCREENPLAYS

Jamie (Working Title)
Orphan Train (TriStar)
Hand Over Fist (Orion)
Dancin' Across the River (Paramount)
Virgin of the Rodeo (Warner Bros)
Rake's Progress (Majestic)
Mitigating Circumstances (TriStar)

Bang Bang Club (Intermedia)
Sin City (Working Title)
Count Zero (Warner Bros)
Busby's Babes (Working Title)
The Poetess (Working Title)
Hippy Hippy Shake (Working Title)

You started writing comparatively late in life. What were you doing before that?

I always wanted to be a screenwriter, but it took me years to sit down and start writing. In the meantime, I worked in the industry. The first job I had was with a producer called Elliott Kastner, who was based at Pinewood, and that gave me a fantastic crash course in feature-film production. Elliott was prolific in the seventies, making four films a year both here and in America, and I was his development person. I worked with writers, I worked with directors, I read an enormous amount and I learned how films are made. I was with him for about four years, and then I was offered a job by his former partner, Arnon Milchan, who was going to base himself in America. I thought if you were serious about working in the industry you had to be in America, because in those days there wasn't much of an industry here other than the American films shooting at Pinewood, Elstree and Shepperton. Arnon had optioned *The King of Comedy* and was wooing Robert De Niro, so he and De Niro and Michael Cimino – who was attached to direct the film at that point – came over here to do a feasibility study. Arnon was based in Paris, I was working from home and De Niro needed an assistant, so I got myself the job. Arnon paid my salary but I worked for Bob, and I was with him during post-production of *The Deerhunter*, then on *Raging Bull*, *The King of Comedy* and *True Confessions*. Then, in 1982, there was a personal tragedy in my life which brought things into focus. I was thirty-two, I'd always wanted to write and I thought, 'It's time.'

It was another five years until *A World Apart*, though.

I did other work in between. I was story editor on *Supergirl* and *Revolution*.

Oh, God!

I know. But it was invaluable experience, focussing on story and reading scripts over and over again. It surprises me how many people write scripts without having read one, because it is a technical endeavour: learning how to tell a story in an audio-visual way. Anyway, when I decided it was time to write, I applied to study screenwriting at the National Film School in Beaconsfield. This was at the time when Colin Young was still the head of it, and it was very dynamic, very well funded and taken very seriously. I started to write the script which became *A World Apart*, and it was an amazing milieu in which to write because you got wonderful support and criticism: from your peers, from the staff and from outsiders like Stephen Frears. It was a three-year course, but at the end of the first year I'd finished the script and got an agent, Jenne Casarotto, and together we went looking for a producer. Because it was a low-budget story about South Africa, before films like *Cry Freedom* and *A Dry White Season* had been made, there was quite a lot of interest. So we chose Sarah Radclyffe at Working Title, then Sarah and I went looking for a director, and Chris Menges wanted to make his directorial début with my script. The whole thing came together really fast. Then the film was made, which negated my status as a screenwriting student – and I've been writing ever since.

Why did you want to write films? Why not write novels, like your sister Gillian?

Because film was my passion. My mother was a great cinema-goer, and I grew up going to the movies. That was what excited me most, for real and unreal reasons. Now, I couldn't begin to write in any other form, and I don't think crossing over is all that easy. Novelists rarely make good screenwriters, and vice versa, because the disciplines are so different.

I assume that your mother's assassination not only made you start writing but also told you *what* to write – in the sense that you wrote *A World Apart* and nothing else.

Yes. I didn't have much desire to do anything else – or much choice, it seemed to me.

It's heavily autobiographical; it's also partly fictionalised. Why did you do that?

I think any autobiographical film has to be partly fictionalised. Events move slower in life, and there is more mundanity in life, so in order to create a drama you impose a different structure of some kind, and you make decisions about which characters you include. The mother was obviously my mother, and then there was me and my two sisters and my grandmother, but everyone else was fictional. Fictionalising it gave me a sense of objectivity which enabled me to pull it together, otherwise it would have been too raw and too personal. It was also a way of protecting people. My sisters have their own version of those events, their own experience of what happened, but this was my story so I made them quite peripheral. It felt right to do that.

The film was occasionally criticised, like *Cry Freedom* and *A Dry White Season*, for being a white take on a black issue. What do you make of that attitude?

Political correctness taken to the point of inverse racism. I'm white; is that less of a reason to tell my story? Spike Lee really attacked me at the time, and I thought it showed an ignorance on his part of the role which white South Africans played in the liberation struggle. Interestingly, black South Africans who saw the movie reacted differently. Their take on the piece was how isolated the white girl at the centre of the story was. Had she been black, there would have been a strong support system put in place when her father was exiled and her mother arrested.

The majority of the film is seen from the point of view of the teenage girl, Molly, except for the scenes where her mother is arrested for opposition to apartheid. Why did you decide to break that point of view for those interrogation scenes?

That was partly the input of Barbara Hershey, the actor who played the mother. She felt it was important to dramatise the time in solitary confinement in order to give more depth to and understanding of her attempted suicide and her relationship with her daughter. Also, while her mother is in prison for those 117 days, the child's life is on hold in a sense – and that could be monotonous to dramatise.

How much of that detail did you take from your mother's own account of her time in prison, *117 Days*?

Everything was taken from *117 Days*: the characters, the form of the interrogation. There didn't seem to be any point in inventing it when it was all there, like her gift to me. I just shaped it to fit the story I was telling.

Did you set out to write a personal story more than a political one?

I don't think you can separate the personal from the political in this kind of story.

The political detail is mainly in the background, though, and you avoid captions which explain it any further. Were you worried that audiences might not get it?

There was a lot of anti-apartheid work going on outside South Africa, and awareness was high around the world of the nature of the struggle. I wasn't writing about some obscure corner of the planet and historical events which no one had ever heard of. *Captain Corelli's Mandolin* needed more explanation than *A World Apart*, because American audiences in particular couldn't understand what the Italians were doing fighting with the Germans.

I notice that you describe all that background detail: posters and leaflets and so on.

That was very much part of my world, and I think it was helpful to the art department. Because it's seen through a child's eyes, it's fragmented but quite specific.

You place as much emphasis on what is seen as what is said. Do you prefer writing in pictures or in words?

The former. I don't have difficulty writing dialogue, but I don't think it comes as easily to me as it does to some writers. I think the most successful scene in *Captain Corelli* is the only scene with no dialogue in it. Pelagia is dancing in the square, and there's all this stuff between her and Corelli and her father who's watching them. But getting the words right, when there *are* words, is still of paramount importance.

In your introduction to the published script, you talk about putting together a writing support group – including your sister Gillian. Do you rely on that sort of outside input now?

It was partly lack of confidence – this was my first script – but I think it's invaluable to have someone good reading your stuff while the work is in progress. Having someone around you who has the whole story in their head, someone with whom you've had intense initial discussions, can keep you on track and speed up the process – and make it less lonely. The Americans are particularly good at story. They can really 'work' a script. The danger is that they can work it out of existence.

What role does the producer play in this process?

I think the main role of the producer is to facilitate the writing of the screenplay, hands-on or not. Tim Bevan is pretty hands-on, but he doesn't have time to sit in on story meetings day after day because he's too busy doing the business which keeps his company going. Working Title were much smaller then, only doing one film at a time, whereas these days they're in pre-production, production and post-production on God knows how many at any given time. But they have a story department in place which is there for this purpose: to provide a context in which the story work can happen.

Is that the role which Sarah Radclyffe played in developing A World Apart?

Sarah was completely hands-on with *A World Apart*, but as the producer she also respects the working relationship which develops between the writer and the director. I think that's the primary relationship in film-making: by taking the script to the next level, the director can bring out the best in the writer.

Why did you choose a British producer rather than an American?

The Americans we submitted the script to didn't 'get it', although the completed film was very well received over there. Anyway, because the film only cost $5 million, we managed to raise most of the money here.

How much did the script change once Chris Menges had committed to direct?

I had really worked the script, with drafts into double digits, by the time it got to Chris. Then there was a lot of polishing and tightening, but very little major structural work. The ending – the final mother-and-daughter confrontation – was not properly written, because it was the most difficult scene to write, but the script had undergone an incredible metamorphosis from the first draft I wrote to the first draft Chris read.

In what way?

I knew I wanted to write something based on the relationship between myself and my mother, and the events which took place during that particular year in my childhood, but I wasn't entirely certain what the story would be – and that's what the rewriting was about. Initially, the girl was either too passive or too much of a victim, and, because it was a personal story, I had all these un-worked-out personal feelings – about the role of my grandmother in our family, for example. I remember someone saying to me, 'You can't make the grandmother more of a villain than the policeman.' I had to make it less raw, basically, so I did a lot of learning on the job.

Did you ever make use of screenwriting manuals, with their emphasis on things like character arcs and three-act structure?

Syd Field's book *Screenplay* was my bible when I first started writing. In those days, a manual on the mechanics of the form was very helpful and comforting. I still enjoy dipping into screenwriting manuals, and reading about other screenwriters' views and experiences, but I think in the end every rule is made to be broken. It's all down to story.

What about watching other films to give you ideas?

Someone sent me a book the other day and said in all seriousness, 'This is a cross between *An Angel at My Table* and *GoodFellas*.' I just thought, 'Why on earth would I want to write a film that was a cross between *An Angel at My Table* and *GoodFellas*?' They've been done, so why would you want to do them again? I think you watch films to reinforce your love of film-making rather than in an attempt to emulate them.

The thing which struck me most about the script is that many of the scenes are quite short but each one does a huge amount of work. Did that balance of story and character emerge through this process of rewriting and polishing?

I've always been quite an economical writer – I call it being economical; some people would call it underwriting – but obviously through that process you find ways of compressing the events and harnessing the emotions, and the scene becomes stronger.

The writer is often long gone by the time a film is shot, but you were on location all the time. What was your role in relation to the director?

The method we used is that every evening I would hand Chris a page of prose about the scene he was going to shoot the following day – because obviously we weren't shooting in continuity – and then the main relationship was between him and the actors and he would call on me if necessary. I did spend a lot of time with the actors but we didn't really talk about the film. We played tennis and smoked pot and went looking for the elusive white rhino.

How did you handle it when some of the actors wanted to be in more scenes, or wanted the scenes they were already in to be rewritten?

It's up to the director to handle that. Some directors will shoot the extra material in the interests of peace and harmony, knowing full well that they'll leave it on the cutting-room

187

floor, some will be confrontational and others will wear the actors down through talk. No names named here.

Were you around during the editing as well?

I used to be called in when there was something to view, but I don't really understand the process of editing. It's down to the director and the editor. Once you have a cut, then you can bring in the writer and the producer and everybody else.

You said that the ending needed work. In your introduction to the script, you talk about two more difficult sections: a pair of polemical speeches in a church and at a graveside. Had you actually written any of these scenes?

There were words down on the page, but none of the scenes were right. I come from an ANC family, so I've been to many funerals and heard many speeches, but I didn't feel confident about writing in that kind of rhetorical way. It was really just a technical thing, getting something down on the page which was succinct and moving. The mother-and-daughter scene was a different challenge, because it was hard to find the words to sum up the film.

In fact, hard to sum up the confrontation which you and your mother never had, the reason why you wanted to write the film in the first place.

Exactly.

Did you receive any help from your father?

He was based in Mozambique and Zambia, running special operations in Umkhonto Wesizwe, the military branch of the ANC. I would send him the screenplay, and ask for his help with certain scenes, and he would say, 'I'm too busy! I'm trying to run a revolution down here!' When Sarah and I first went to

Zimbabwe, which is where we shot the film, the Zimbabwians informed us that they would only give us permission to shoot there if we had script approval from the ANC. I called my father and said, 'We can't proceed unless we get a letter from the ANC.' He said, 'I'm too busy. I'm trying to run a revolution down here.' I said, 'Well, I'm getting on a plane.' He said, 'Fine, but I'm too busy to meet you at the airport.' Anyway, he meets me at the airport, takes me to ANC headquarters and in ten minutes I have the letter. That was Joe's manner: he was always reluctant, and he always came through.

What did he make of the script — and the film?

He got a tape of the film before it was released, and the writer of one of his obituaries — I think it was Anthony Sampson — describes being part of a delegation which met with him, and how he made everybody sit down and watch it. Joe was a tough man, but the film moved him to tears. While we were shooting it he spent three days on location in Bulawayo, because he was so fascinated by our reconstruction of these events.

And what do *you* make of it now?

If I have a criticism of *A World Apart* — and this is *not* a criticism of Chris Menges, who did an absolutely superb job — it's that the film is possibly missing the next level. Chris deferred to me the whole time out of respect for the fact that it was my story. On the other hand, there's a certain innocence about the way it's directed which is part of why the film works, and if someone else had come in with all sorts of radical ideas perhaps the story would have been corrupted somehow. Watching it recently, I thought in parts it *felt* like a first screenplay. The black friend of the mother is a bit of a cypher, really, and some of his dialogue comes across as rather leaden. I don't entirely dismiss that dramatisation, because my favourite scene is the one where Molly eats with his family and sees the cultural differences between them, but I do think his character wasn't properly written.

The film won several awards at Cannes, didn't it?

The actors got the Best Actress award, and the film got the Jury Prize and the ecumenical award – and my script got a BAFTA for Best Original Screenplay – but nobody got to see it, because we fucked up the distribution. There's no other way to describe it, and I think Tim Bevan and Sarah Radclyffe would be the first to admit that. This was before Miramax or Fox Searchlight or any of the classics divisions, and there were something like sixteen prints and that was it. But it got a great critical response – according to my experience of these things – and it didn't *lose* any money, so you think, 'I'm made!' It's probably the worst thing that can happen to your first script, because it gives you a false perspective on the industry.

In fact, there was a gap of thirteen years before you had another film made.

That's the most common thing people say to me about *Captain Corelli*: 'It must be so great to have a film made after so long!' It shows an ignorance about how this industry works; about the fact that it takes a miracle to get a film made; about the importance of luck and being in the right place at the right time. I haven't been out of work since *A World Apart*, and I think that's a major achievement. I've been writing productively, earning a good living and having a good time – so I'm fed up with having to justify this gap. [*Smiling*] That's my little rant.

Were you typecast as a writer after *A World Apart*?

The first thing I did after *A World Apart* was an adaptation of a novel called *Jamie*, for Working Title, about a boy on a farm in Kenya who loses his father. Then I rewrote a script for Barry Levinson and his partner Mark Johnson, *Orphan Train*, a true story set in the thirties about orphans who were relocated from New York to the Midwest and used as child labour. So I *was* typecast: I became the children-and-Africa expert.

Do you have any favourites among your unproduced scripts?

Well, I did an adaptation of a book called *Virgin of the Rodeo* for Paula Weinstein at Warner, a love story between a rodeo rider and a girl who's transformed from a duckling into a swan. I loved that script, but again the studio decided not to proceed. And I did a rewrite of a script called *Mitigating Circumstances* for Jonathan Demme's company and Agnieszka Holland, which was a thriller about a woman who kills a man and gets away with it. I thought that was an excellent story and I enjoyed working with Agnieszka, but she went off and directed something else instead. I've also adapted a science-fiction book, *Count Zero*, for Michael Mann, and done a rewrite of a football story, *Busby's Babes*, for Working Title.

You can hardly be less typecast than writing science-fiction for Michael Mann.

I had the best time working with him; I thought I was in heaven. He's one of the great living directors and I would adapt *anything* for him, but in the end this William Gibson story turned out to be unadaptable. I only did one draft, and then Michael went off to do *The Insider*. But my favourite of the scripts I've rewritten is *Busby's Babes*, which I worked on with John Roberts, the director of *War of the Buttons*. It's the story of Matt Busby's desire to build a postwar team which could take on Europe, but it isn't about the football, it's about the passions and conflicts involved in putting this team together. There's a young player who has no belief in himself. There's the tragedy of the plane crash at Munich. And it culminates with the realisation of Matt Busby's vision when England wins the European Cup in 1968. I don't know if

Working Title lost confidence in it, or if their taskmasters at Universal thought it was too English, but I spent quite a long time on it: four passes over the period of a year.

I believe you also made a pass at *Bridget Jones's Diary*.

I only had a month to do that because I was still working on *Busby's Babes*. I made Working Title send me and the director, Sharon Maguire, to a luxury retreat, and we spent a week going over the script, then I had three weeks in which to write it. It went from Helen Fielding to Andrew Davies, then I rewrote the Andrew Davies script, and then they got another writer in while they were waiting for Richard Curtis to become free after doing Comic Relief. It's basically his script, but a synthesis of everybody else's work.

Did you recognise any of your work in the finished film?

The fight. There was always a fight in it, but I said to Sharon, 'It can't just be a biff here and there. It's got to be a completely over-the-top, bodies-through-plate-glass-windows kind of a fight.' I think I can write comedy, you see. Nobody else does, but I do. I actually did a lot of work on the subsidiary characters but I don't think there was space for subsidiary characters, in the end. I love polishes, though. I usually spend at least three weeks procrastinating before I even write my outline, but with a polish you have this incredible focus and just fly through it. I could definitely spend the rest of my life doing polishes.

When you were approached to adapt *Captain Corelli's Mandolin*, had the novel already become a bestseller?

No. Kevin Loader and Roger Michell optioned the novel in 1995, and it didn't become a bestseller until the late nineties. It wasn't reviewed particularly well, but it was a word-of-mouth phenomenon. Kevin and Roger were passionate about the material.

By the time the film was made, you must have felt a huge weight of expectation.

It was only in this country that we felt a weight of expectation, because it was only in this country that the book was such a publishing phenomenon. *Captain Corelli*, as the book was called in America, didn't do crossover business like *Bridget Jones's Diary*.

What were your first impressions of the novel? It's not an easy book to adapt, after all.

I don't think you make your decisions about the work you're going to do based on how easy the material is; I think you make your decisions based on all kinds of other criteria – including who's attached to direct it and what the possibilities of it being made are. I thought it was a rich, epic, character-filled saga which would be not uninteresting to adapt, but I also thought it was so long since I'd had a film made that having a director attached from the start and Working Title passionately committed to making it would immediately increase my chances.

And avoid the necessity of changing the script to suit a director attached later.

That's right. You're writing the film which the director wants to make. I must stress how important both Roger Michell and John Madden were to the development process. From the very first meeting, where Roger and I literally went through the book with a red pencil deciding what we liked and what we didn't, they led the discussions, and when it says above the title, 'A John Madden Film', it *is* a John Madden film. I was simply there to help them realise their vision.

193

What else attracted you to the project, besides its epic scale and the possibility that it might actually get made?

I thought that the occupation of Greece by the Italians and the Germans was an interestingly obscure story of World War Two, but I suppose the main hook was the love story: two people who aren't meant to fall in love. Love stories are a mother to write, though, because people in love speak such gobbledegook.

So what kind of film *did* Roger Michell and John Madden want to make?

Roger stayed much closer to the Louis de Bernières story – in terms of the beginning, the middle and particularly the end, in which the lovers are reunited after forty years – whereas John hadn't read the novel before he came on board. I suppose the book is quirky and comic, and John wanted to make something mainstream and dramatic. It seems odd to say this about the novel, but there isn't much drama in it. There's drama in the events going on around the characters, but not in the interaction between them. For example, in Roger's version, Corelli moves into the house with Pelagia and basically stays there, and John felt we needed to separate them in order to raise the stakes.

Do you think that by making the film less quirky and more mainstream, you may have lost the element which made every-one want to adapt the novel in the first place?

Well, *you* obviously do.

No, I thought the film worked just fine on its own terms.

And so did audiences. What the critics thought about it is another story, but we got a very positive audience response in all the previews; not from the core group of 18 to 25-year-old males, but from an older kind of audience. *I* think the movie is very successful, a brave attempt to make a film which is actually *about* something. It may not have stormed the box office, but I'm proud of the work I did and I'm most proud of the fact that I survived the transition between two directors – which is almost unheard of.

Presumably, though, you were quite happy with the last draft which you wrote for Roger Michell?

Tweaking and fine-tuning apart, that was the film Roger wanted to make. Because the whole process was director-led, and because the story was Louis de Bernières's, I felt that my role was to serve the director's vision. Then Roger had a heart attack and was forced to withdraw, so John Madden came on board and had a different take on the material. Which is exactly the way it should be: any director of any merit will want to make the story their own. But he came on board in December, and we were locked into a May start date for principal photography to accommodate Nicolas Cage, which left us no time at all to effect what turned out to be pretty radical changes to the script.

Is that why John Madden brought in Irena Brignull as story editor?

Yes. The three of us would meet, then I would go away and write while John and Irena looked further ahead. I'd produce pages, we'd de-brief those, I'd retire to write, John and Irena continued meeting. It was an intense process and Irena was very important to it; she was like an extra pair of hands.

For Roger Michell, you wrote five drafts over four years. For John Madden, you wrote four drafts in five months. That must have been rather daunting.

I loved it. We met at John's house in West London, and sometimes on the drive home I'd be in tears from exhaustion, overwhelmed by the amount of changes he wanted. But it was incredibly exciting, and I learned an enormous amount. I enjoy having the pressure of that kind of deadline, of having to step up to the mark. During the four years of development with Roger, he made two other films and I wrote or rewrote three other scripts, so I didn't feel that I'd necessarily cracked it – although that's unfair to the work he and I did do.

Were there any changes which you regretted having to make?

I regret that the Carlo story was lost. I think it's the most interesting part of the book, the silent unrequited love which this big lonely man has for Corelli, and it was more to the forefront in Roger's version of the script, but John didn't feel that there was enough room to incorporate it. I didn't think it needed much. I originally wrote a few scenes where he observes the developing affair with Pelagia, and the enormous pain that this causes him obviously showed his utter devotion to Corelli. I felt that the power of the final shootout, when he puts his arms around Corelli to protect him from the bullets, was not as strong as it could have been had we developed that relationship.

There's also a scene where Pelagia is raped by her rejected fiancé, Mandras, which is in the book and in the published script but not in the finished film.

The rape survived right through to the previews, but then there was a lot of pressure from America to remove it because the scene was quite brutal. I really felt the loss of that scene, because I thought it made Mandras unbelievably sympathetic. That's not to excuse what he does, but the rape is his way of responding once he realises that his love has been betrayed. It seemed to make him more real, rather than nodding and accepting it and walking away into the night as he does, and it gave the film some kind of grit.

You'd already removed other atrocities which he commits in the book, though.

On a personal level, I felt that the more dignified Mandras was then the more real the love triangle would be. If he's a two-dimensional, corrupt character, of course Pelagia will choose Corelli, whereas if he's a three-dimensional, conflicted character, who goes from being a simple peasant to a committed fighter, it makes her choice more poignant. On a political level, I felt that if you were telling a story about the Second World War you could not present the Greek Partisans in a worse light than the Nazis. This issue received a lot of coverage in Greece, and I met some of the people who were involved in the conflict, so I was very sensitive to their reaction: that there are bad apples in every barrel, but basically the Left was fighting the forces of Fascism.

Yet you also invented a new character, Eleni, who is executed for flirting with a Nazi. Why did you add that when you had to cut so much existing material?

That *was* a way of showing that atrocities were perpetrated on both sides, and I think it was a successful invention because she was minimally done but not marginal.

How important is your own research in tackling an adaptation?

It depends on the project: there are some stories which you *have* to research. The object is to immerse yourself in the world of your subject, and to reach a point where you feel confident enough to start writing. I felt during location recess to Greece, 'I really shouldn't be here. I should be at home attacking the story.'

The novel is told from various points of view. Did you try to stick to just one? The film opens with a passage of voiceover by Dr Iannis, for example.

There was never any doubt in my mind that the main character was Pelagia. The voiceover was a post-production addition.

A way of explaining why it takes Corelli ten years to return to the island?

Exactly.

Which, as you mentioned earlier, was scaled down from forty years in the novel and in the original script. What was the thinking behind that decision?

John felt very strongly that ageing up the actors would take the audience right out of the film, and he also felt that after everything the characters had gone through they deserved some sort of redemption and happiness.

What was your experience of being on set this time around?

Boredom, mainly. A film shoot goes on for a long time, and the only person on set with absolutely nothing to do is the writer. Everyone else is working from five o'clock in the morning until ten o'clock at night, and unless you're pounding away at the typewriter doing major rewrites that the actors are waiting for you're just standing around like a spare part. It's great to visit a set, though. I know of one writer who's just had a film made, and he wasn't allowed on set and he wasn't allowed to see the rushes. That's absurd. That's discrimination. The writer should be treated with respect, should be called on to solve any problems – which is what I was doing on *Captain Corelli* – and should be invited to have a look at the various cuts. But really your job is done when

you hand in the script; the rest belongs to the director and the team.

In your introduction to the published script, you conclude by saying that as the writer you take full responsibility for the script. That's a bold statement to make, given the number of things in a film which may be beyond your control.

I would now amend that to, 'I take full responsibility for my role', which was to serve the visions of the directors. But it was a fantastic experience and I developed some very strong working relationships, which is what screenwriting – and life – is all about.

Louis de Bernières wrote an introduction for the 'Making of' book which was published to coincide with the film, and his comments on screenwriting might be described as condescending at best . . .

Ignorant at worst. Ignorant *and* opinionated, not a good combination. In fact, when people ask why he didn't adapt the book himself, he says that screenwriting is an even lower profession than teaching – so he not only insults screenwriters but teachers as well. It's extraordinary. I don't think he realises what he's actually saying, because if he did I don't think he'd be able to say it. I was deeply upset by the contempt he showed for me in that introduction. He mentions everybody *but* the screenwriter: Nicolas Cage, Penélope Cruz, John Madden, Roger Michell, Kevin Loader, Tim Bevan. That doesn't take away from the fact that those are my words up there, via his novel. Thinking about the critics' problems with the film, though, my feeling is that perhaps we didn't change it enough.

When I first read the novel I found it absolutely captivating, but when I re-read it I found it extremely self-conscious. The accusations of stereotyping levelled at the film, for example, seem to me to be equally true of the book.

I was very conscious of that in adapting it. I think there's a process here: what's on the page is then cast and directed, so if we *are* open to accusations of stereotyping I can't take full responsibility for it. It's an extraordinarily successful novel, but I don't think it bears terribly close scrutiny. Its politics are shameful.

What have you been working on since the release of *Captain Corelli*?

Another couple of rewrites, again for Working Title: *The Poetess* and *Hippy Hippy Shake*.

Do you agree with this tendency to bring in writer after writer?

If there's a problem with a script, the knee-jerk reaction, particularly from the studios, is to get another writer in to solve it. I think I have the objectivity and the skill to take someone else's work and see where it's not working, but I'm fully prepared for the fact that after I've finished my rewrite they'll bring in another writer because it's not working in other areas. The wrongdoing occurs when the original writer isn't given a chance to realise their vision, and I'd probably feel quite differently about rewrites if I'd had an experience of not being allowed to finish the work I'd started. As soon as Universal and Miramax gave *Captain Corelli* the green light, there was tremendous pressure on Working Title and John Madden to bring in somebody else. In fact, another writer *was* brought in – for two weeks. He was paid handsomely, and nothing he wrote was used.

Have you ever talked to the original writer of a script before starting a rewrite?

No. I did ask Working Title if I should call the original writer of *The Poetess*, but they said, 'For God's sake! He's quite happy about it! He's sick of this project!'

You're about to write your first original script since A World Apart. Why now?

I've had the story in mind for twelve years, but the timing has never felt right before. It's partly to do with wanting to express my own voice after the experience of *Captain Corelli*. It's partly to do with having more confidence in my writing because of that film; I'm very certain about what I achieved, even though it was not critically embraced. But it's mainly to do with the story: I'm very fired up about it and I feel I'm the right writer to do it, and if I didn't have my Working Title deal I think I'd go ahead and do it anyway.

Can you tell me what the story is?

I can, but I won't – because things change. You see your words in print and think, 'Why did I speak too soon?'

Do you think originals can be more satisfying than adaptations – or rewrites?

I don't think doing an adaptation or a rewrite is any less of a skill or a craft than writing an original. I'm not one of those writers who has a million stories they want to tell, but I can recognise a good story when I see it.

In your introduction to the published script of A World Apart, you point out that Chris Menges had no problem working with women. Is that unusual?

The same would apply to John Madden, or to Michael Mann. It's something to do with the quality of their relationships with the women in their lives, their wives and their daughters. But women are discriminated against in all areas of life, whether it be business or politics or education or the police. The film industry is dominated by men, and men are often more comfortable working with other men. A lot of male directors have probably never worked with a woman screenwriter, but then there are very few women screenwriters. The same is true of women directors: they're not adequately represented. Where women have made a huge impact is as heads of studio, like Sherry Lansing at Paramount and Stacey Snider at Universal.

Why do you think there *are* so few women screenwriters?

I think it's to do with confidence. It's an enormously competitive industry, and you're either seen as a produced or an unproduced writer, so it takes a certain amount of confidence to survive without the constant approval of getting films made. I think that every project I start writing will get made; you have to in order to keep going.

Are there any jobs which you don't get offered as a woman screenwriter?

They don't offer big-concept jobs to women: *Die Hard* and *Face/Off* and *Con Air* and *Men in Black*.

Would you want them?

I fantasise that I would. It's ballsy writing, well crafted and technically very strong. If those films work, it's because the writing works. American male screenwriters have really mastered the form.

Do you have any ambitions to direct?

I've always answered in the negative, for reasons like, 'I don't have that kind of stamina', or, 'Who needs the pressure?' or, 'Too many questions!' But, in the end, I think it's because I enjoy the life of a writer.

All the time?

Of course not. Every writer experiences moments of despair. But that's part of the process. You *will* find a way to break through. If you don't believe that, you're fucked.

William Boyd was born in 1952, in Ghana, to Scottish parents, and educated at Gordonstoun School and the universities of Nice, Glasgow and Oxford. He is married and lives in London.

FILM

Stars and Bars (Pat O'Connor, 1988, US)
Mister Johnson (Bruce Beresford, 1990, US)
Aunt Julia and the Scriptwriter (Jon Amiel, 1990, US)

Chaplin (Richard Attenborough, 1992, UK)
A Good Man in Africa (Bruce Beresford, 1994, US)
The Trench (William Boyd, 1999, UK/Fr)

TELEVISION

Good and Bad at Games (Jack Gold, 1983, Channel Four)
Dutch Girls (Giles Foster, 1985, ITV)
Scoop (Gavin Millar, 1987, ITV)

Sword of Honour (Bill Anderson, 2001, Channel Four)
Armadillo (Howard Davies, 2001, BBC)

SCREENPLAYS

An Ice-Cream War (spec)
The Galapagos Affair (spec)
Cork (spec)

The Blue Afternoon (spec)
The Gunpowder Plot (Universal)
Hitler (BBC, F/X)

FICTION

A Good Man in Africa (1981)
On the Yankee Station (1981)
An Ice-Cream War (1982)
Stars and Bars (1984)
The New Confessions (1987)

Brazzaville Beach (1990)
The Blue Afternoon (1993)
The Destiny of Nathalie 'X' (1995)
Armadillo (1998)
Any Human Heart (2002)

Do you consider yourself as much a screenwriter as a novelist?

No, I consider myself a novelist, but after spending a year alone writing a novel I find it tremendously refreshing to hang out on a film set for a while. I've always loved movies, and after I'd published my first novel and a collection of short stories – and my second novel was in the works – I hoped that this would open the doors to film or television, but of course they say, 'Have you written a script?' and you say, 'No, that's what I *want* to do.' I did write a couple of trial scripts which my agent could show people, but then came a lucky break: Channel Four started up and approached non-screenwriters to write scripts, and their remit was that it had to be British and it had to be contemporary and that was it.

Why did you choose the subject of public school?

The original plan was to write a series of short stories – I wrote one called 'Hardly Ever', about putting on a Gilbert and Sullivan operetta, which was in my first collection – but I decided that I would use some of my ideas for a film, *Good and Bad at Games*, a very dark piece about revenge and torture and madness. After that I was approached by an independent producer, Sue Birtwistle, to do a comedy about public school, so I wrote a lighthearted look at sexual conditioning, *Dutch Girls*, and that used up the rest of my material. I published the two scripts, wrote a long memoir about my own schooldays and discovered that I'd done what I'd set out to achieve: a completely honest account of what it's like to be in a single-sex boarding school. Having spent nine and a half years in one of these institutions, an experience common to a huge number of writers, it was astonishing to me that if you looked for anything remotely true or realistic about them in literature, let alone in film or television, you could count them on the fingers of one hand. With the exception of *If . . .*, and a TV film which Frederic Raphael wrote, called *School Play*, everything was a bit Victorian or romanticised. It's very odd, this absence, a sort of collective act of unre-membering by British artists who will not look closely at these incredibly powerful institutions. My schooldays are a long time ago now, but they still have a resonance – nothing has changed that much. The public life of these schools has changed, in that the kids are more sophisticated and they go home at weekends, but the private life of every closed society is by definition not available for scrutiny and can be a particularly nasty and unpleasant place. It doesn't have to be 1965, it could be 2001.

Your early fiction was compared to the work of Evelyn Waugh, some of which you later adapted into the television dramas *Scoop* and *Sword of Honour*, and he also wrote about public school in *Decline and Fall*. Did you want to bring something of his satirical style to these scripts?

Decline and Fall is about prep school, which is a sub-category of the genre. Waugh's own diaries, which he kept as a schoolboy, are a harrowing and realistic portrait, and the same savage indignation is at work in *Good and Bad at Games*. It was based on a boy I remember who was hideously persecuted for five years. I always wondered what had become of him, so I invented a fate for this character: he goes mad and exacts revenge. I know quite a few very successful, apparently well-balanced, adults who are still tormented by their schooldays. It does have a profound effect on you, and it was quite a controversial film when it came out. I was actually attacked for it – like a class traitor. *Dutch Girls*, though, is a comedy, and is meant to make you laugh and say how ridiculous it is to bring up boys with this attitude. There are satirical elements in it, but I want all my work to be grounded in the real. However dark or absurd it is, I don't want it to take off into fantasy or magic realism. I'm very pleased with the films. They're still requested by schools, and I go and talk about them.

What did you learn from working with directors Jack Gold and Giles Foster?

I learned how the industrial process of film-making can influence the way it turns out onscreen. Because they were television films – and because I've always worked with people I've got on well with – my role was far more respected than if I'd started out writing for the movies. I was a welcome presence, as involved as I wanted to be, and in fact on both films I was on set almost every day. They were original scripts, so I was the source of all wisdom, and they're very close to what was written. But once you know how a film is physically made that shapes a lot of your thinking, especially if you're working on a low-budget independent movie.

Scoop **was your first experience of adapting a classic. How did you find it?**

When I saw the finished film, I said to Sue Birtwistle and the director, Gavin Millar, 'You can relax. Not even the most dyed-in-the-wool Waugh pedant is going to object to this.' And boy was I wrong. It got a real hammering. It's never been repeated, unfortunately, but I still think it's a good adaptation: lavish, brilliantly acted, faithful to the narrative shape of the book and true to the spirit of Waugh. One of the only things I left out was a literary joke. William Boot writes his country column about the badger, and his sister changes the word 'badger' to 'great-crested grebe'. It's hilariously funny, but the only way it can work onscreen is if you show the words – which is manifestly not filmic. But there seems to be something about Evelyn Waugh which gets the most jaded hack asking to write a piece for their editor. Having been a TV critic for two years with the *New Statesman*, I know the thought processes that go on, and when we were really pleased with *Sword of Honour*, I said, 'Beware!'

In fact, you were one of the few critics who disliked the TV adaptation of *Brideshead Revisited*.

I was teaching at Oxford at the time and knew the novel inside out, so I was probably a bit self-righteous. It was a memorable event in television history and was compelling in its own way. It was nine hours long, which seems extraordinary today. Again, the problem is one of adaptation. It's a first-person novel, so everything is in the voice of Charles Ryder, which is why there was masses of voiceover.

What do you think of voiceover, by and large?

Voiceover is one of the tools in your toolkit and should be employed whenever it works well. I remember having an argument with someone who put money into *The Mission*. He said, 'I didn't have the faintest idea where this country was.' I said, 'Why didn't they use a map?' Shock! Horror! I'm a great believer in maps or captions if they do the job, otherwise you have to explain it all with dialogue. 'Of course, you used to be the ambassador to Indo-China and then you were fired. What was it for, now? Yes, it was because of . . .' That's classic bad screenwriting, and you can cut through that nonsense by putting, say, 'The Libyan Desert – 1942'. Captions are very succinct and very effective. With voiceover, however, I think there are certain ground-rules. It should be present from the start: often it's a rescue attempt, bolted on here and there, and usually that doesn't work. I've been guilty of this myself, so I know what's involved. And it should have nothing to do with what's happening in the scene: there's nothing worse than seeing a man going into a house and hearing him say, 'When I went into my house . . .' But you should use everything that's available to make your film work, and you can always cite classic films where these devices are used to tremendous effect. There's a map at the beginning of *Casablanca*, for example. *The Third Man* starts with quite a sustained bit of voiceover by a character who doesn't even appear in the film, because nobody knew what was going on in Vienna. French movies use voiceover all the time without a qualm. These devices are attempts to undermine what I call the 'tyranny of the lens'. Film is absolutely objective – there is basically one point of view, the camera lens, which is relentless and unsparing – and voiceover is a way of being subjective. When a character onscreen is telling the individual members of the audience what he's thinking, then you're hearing a voice in your ear which is close to the voice in your ear when you read a book. You have penetrated the character's unconscious, but you're not seeing him speak the words.

With a 250-page book, it's presumably easier to be true not just to the spirit but also to the letter. Waugh's own dialogue and description, for example.

Particularly his dialogue. Often it's unimprovable. The only thing is, dialogue in a novel can sound unconversational when spoken, so in the interests of realism what you do is roughen it up a bit, add a few 'um's and 'ah's. But mostly you hardly need to alter it at all, so it's usually a case, as it always is with adaptation, of structure and what you leave out. These are the decisions which the screenwriter has to make, and that's where the most brutal changes occur, because you have to fit the total liberty of a novel into the confined parameters of a film. If you decide to adapt a classic or much-loved book, your working maxim should be, 'How will it work best as a film?' However faithful it is to the original, if it's not interesting onscreen then you've failed. Film-novel adaptations suffer in a way that no other adaptations between art forms do. No one goes to see Verdi's *Falstaff* then comes home and compares it to *The Merry Wives of Windsor*. No one goes to see the ballet of *Eugene Onegin* then comes home and compares it to Pushkin's epic poem. The two art forms are allowed to coexist. But the first thing people say about a film adaptation of a novel is, 'Why did you leave out the bit about . . . ?' It's a mistake, a complete category error. 'Did it work as a film?' is the question you should be asking, and if you say, 'Yes, I enjoyed myself and I was engaged', end of story. Having been a victim on numerous occasions of that sort of critical misunderstanding, I feel this can't be said often enough. You have to make it work as a film, not as a simulacrum of the novel. The two forms are quite distinct, and there are different aesthetic pleasures to be derived from each.

Scoop was adapted from a single novel into a single drama. *Sword of Honour* was adapted from three novels into two parts totalling four hours, with adverts, yet a trilogy would seem to lend itself to three parts. Whose decision was that?

It was Channel Four's decision. Initially they asked for six times one hour – it was going to be weekly – but then there was a change of thinking: 'Channel Four audiences do not tune in every Sunday night to watch the classic serial, so could we do it as two film-length episodes back to back on consecutive nights?' For me, having written my six-hour version, moving the goalposts in this way was something of a kick in the teeth, but in fact I think it was the right decision. I said to the director, Bill Anderson, 'This is the David Lean version. Think of it as *Lawrence of Arabia*.' And, of course, when you think of it like that you can strip away all the stuff which you'd normally do in a leisurely TV way and concentrate on the essence of the story. The novels are wonderful but incredibly uneven, full of longueurs. Guy Crouchback's war is essentially Evelyn Waugh's, and when Waugh was bored rigid from 1942 to 1944 there's an enormous sag in the books. He left a seven-year gap after writing Volume Two, and was jaded and embittered and close to the end of his life when he wrote Volume Three, but because we had our new format we were able to make the narrative lines more graceful and more telling. But there's a lot left out.

Whether it's six hours or four hours it's still a difficult story to tell because it's about lives intersecting randomly, one of your favourite themes.

To a certain extent that's my interpretation of it. Evelyn Waugh might disagree with me. What makes the books endure, I think, is that they're like an English *Catch-22*. War is horrifying. Armies can't function. You think something is going to happen and the opposite will happen. You try to be brave but you're forced to be a coward. These are very cynical, disenchanted, Joseph Heller-esque points of view. Waugh would argue, as he did in the preface to the novels, that he was actually writing about the collapse of Roman Catholic values in contemporary Britain, but what you take away from the trilogy now is its modernity, its sense of the cruel and absurd, its dark and ruthless observation of human beings in a war zone. I stressed that angle because as a devout atheist I wasn't remotely interested in Evelyn Waugh's tormented workings-out of a Catholic gentleman attempting to cling on to his faith when the hideous modern world was trying to trample it underfoot.

Did you tailor the script to suit the budget?

I don't think you really do tailor your first draft because these decisions often come later on, but you know you're not making *Gladiator*, and you don't have $185 million to spend, so you save your bravura shots for things you can actually deliver. The Battle for Crete was going to be our big set-piece and would need a cast of thousands, so there was no point in writing earlier, 'A convoy steams over the horizon and we see it from the coast of Africa.' That's just common sense. But because of special effects you can now do stuff which looks fantastic. We had two Dakotas, one with American markings and one with RAF markings, but we couldn't get a Stuka in Majorca because Spanish air-traffic control wouldn't allow us to fly one into their airspace. So we did the Stuka attack with CGI and it actually looks better, because we had *three* Stukas coming out of the sky. These decisions are often taken on the hoof. You don't really think about them when you're writing. But there is a scene on board a destroyer off the coast of Africa, and I knew that could be done on a blue screen, so the whole scene was written shooting out, as it were, from two men leaning on a railing. It works well, it looks great, it didn't cost a lot and it's underpinned in the writing by a sense of, 'What's the best way of shooting this that will give us the biggest bang for our buck?'

Do you prefer writing for the big screen or the small screen?

I would never say, 'I'll only write movies', like certain actors say, 'I don't do television.' It's really a question of what works best – and what's available – although for me that choice is a luxury because I'm primarily a novelist: that satisfies so many urges and needs.

Mister Johnson and Aunt Julia and the Scriptwriter were based on novels by Joyce Cary and Mario Vargas Llosa which both feature highly exotic settings, something they share with your own fiction. Is that why you were approached?

Commissioned work is often very attractive because the book appeals to your tastes or chimes with your interests. *Mister Johnson* is set in Nigeria, and I'd lived in Nigeria and written an introduction to the Penguin World Classics edition of the book, so it was an easy decision. *Aunt Julia* came about as a result of my relationship with David Puttnam, because the adaptation of my novel *Stars and Bars* was with his company, Enigma, before he went off to run Columbia Pictures. It was suggested that I might be the person to adapt it, so I read it and loved it but knew it was going to be a bold adaptation. By then it was no longer at Columbia but with an independent company, and they said it could be set anywhere in America but not in Peru, so it seemed to me that New Orleans delivered the same polyglot mix as Lima. That was one of those nice jobs which comes your way, and the relationships I built up at that time endure to this day. Mark Tarlov, who produced *Aunt Julia*, also produced *A Good Man in Africa*, and we have any number of irons in the fire.

I believe you actually discussed the changes to *Aunt Julia* with Vargas Llosa.

Yes, I did. There's a character in the novel who writes soap operas for the radio, about fifteen different stories which get progressively more surreal and outlandish, and there was no way the film could cope with that. Vargas Llosa, who had approved the Americanisation of the novel, just said, 'Go for it. Do the best you can.' He knew the book would be respected and he was very pleased with the film. What got him furious was that the American distributor changed the title to *Tune In Tomorrow*. It was a real no-brainer, but they thought that they had a comic hit on their hands and they felt that the original title was a bit too arthouse. I protested vehemently; Vargas Llosa refused to have anything to do with it; the film did no business at all; and every review started with, 'What idiot changed the title?' But it's good work and I'm proud of it. I've got a full-page ad for the film from *The New York Times* which is chock-a-block with raves. We got across-the-board raves for *Mister Johnson*, as well – Bruce Beresford said he's never had such good reviews – but it didn't even do a million dollars' business in the US. It did nothing here. It played for just four weeks in one cinema. If you looked up *Mister Johnson* on some database of US critics you'd say, 'Why didn't this film do better?' Well, because of the financial precariousness of the distributor, and the fact that the guy at Fox who commissioned the movie had been fired. The main achievement was to get the films made, so I'm quite philosophical about these things.

Three of your novels have been filmed: Stars and Bars, A Good Man in Africa and Armadillo. Are you able to take more or less licence with your own work?

More licence. Because the book is always there, the adaptation is a wonderful bonus and I can authorise myself to strike a pencil through this or that character and this or that episode. I also find that as soon as a character becomes flesh and blood, once you see the contribution of a talented actor in the role, all sorts of beneficial and productive things can suggest themselves. A minor character can bloom with the right casting, and you might exploit that by bringing them into a scene and giving them lines to say. In *A Good Man in Africa*, Sean Connery brought something to the role of Dr Murray which simply wasn't there on the page. So we worked on his part together, and wrote a few more gags for Dr Murray, because it would have been a terrible shame not to exploit that acerbic and laconic sense of humour.

How did you stay philosophical when Stars and Bars and A Good Man in Africa failed both critically and commercially?

They were not great critical or commercial successes, but I don't think of them as films which have failed. Bits of them don't work, but they both have tremendous casts and they're both really entertaining, which is not bad given the vagaries of the business. Again, getting the films made was probably the great achievement. We had hellish problems setting up *Stars and Bars*, then it was flushed down the toilet by Columbia, post-Puttnam, so it never had a chance. It might have been ahead of its time. If a quirky comedy about an Englishman abroad had been released in 1999 instead of 1988, it might have been seen in the context of all these British films which play to their strengths in the same way. Lots of works of art are perceived not to have delivered at the time of their presentation to the marketplace but can be savoured later on, when all the fuss has died down. The effect of criticism is transient and ephemeral, but these films pop up on television in their post-release life and are watched and appreciated. You want everything you do to be as big a success as possible, but you should also be trying to make the best film that you can. If you try to second-guess the market and write a sub-Hannibal Lecter film and it bombs, then you must feel like a complete whore, but if you've done your best and you're pleased with the film, then it has to take its chances. *The Trench* didn't get a US distributor, but there's nothing I can do about that. It's the film I wanted to make and if it's too dark and sad to play commercially then so be it. You're striving all the time – I think this is true of every artist – to be popular *and* preserve your integrity: 'Can I have both, please?'

That aspiration was certainly true of Charlie Chaplin, whose life you tackled for Richard Attenborough. What attracted you to that project?

It came at a very good time for me because I'd just finished writing *Brazzaville Beach*, my brain was empty and I literally had nothing to do. Everybody knows a bit about Chaplin – about 'The Tramp' and United Artists – but the true story is unbelievably dark and intense. 'The Tramp' was not Charlie Chaplin. He was very left wing but ran his studio like a fascist dictator. He was vastly wealthy and became obsessed with young girls. Having written *The New Confessions* by then, I found that whole period of American film-making fascinating. Also I really, really liked Dickie. You think, 'I get to work with Richard Attenborough. How fantastic is that?' He has this habit of saying, 'Steve used to say to me . . .' and you think, 'Who's Steve?' and after a while you realise it's Steve McQueen. He has a phenomenal history, he's known everybody and is an amazing man.

Did you read Bryan Forbes's first draft?

No, I was told to go back to source – which was the biography by David Robinson. I also used lots of other sources in the public domain.

In *The New Confessions*, you had several hundred pages to explore the life of its fictitious director. In *Chaplin*, you only had three hours or so.

The biopic is the hardest genre to pull off without it ending up as some sort of documentary. Again, it's an adapting problem, but instead of having a book to adapt you have a life, so it becomes a question of choosing key moments or filmically interesting moments and somehow alluding to the rest. The studio executive on the project, Barry Isaacson, came over here and we thought, 'Let's choose a template, given what we know about the man.' We decided to choose *Raging Bull* – which sounds silly, but that film also covers a long period and is very dark and intense. To a degree, it distorts Chaplin's life just to look at his neuroses, but that's what's really interesting about the man.

Presumably the character played by Anthony Hopkins, a book editor going over Chaplin's autobiography with its elderly author, was invented as the means of 'alluding to the rest'?

The scenes of Chaplin as an old man were exclusively the work of William Goldman. I didn't write a single word of them. My first draft started with Chaplin as a boy of seven, and ended in his late sixties when he was banished from America. My thinking was that his banishment was the end of the story: 'We made you, so we can throw you out.' After that he lived in Switzerland and had lots of kids. We thought that Robert Downey Jr could pick it up at seventeen and age up to about seventy, but taking it to eighty and having him wear twenty pounds of prosthetic make-up was stretching credulity a bit far, in my opinion. The history of the film was fraught, because it collapsed and Attenborough had to set the whole thing up again. It was ready to go, but Universal were unhappy with the budget. Tom Stoppard did a pass at it before they put it in turnaround, then a year later it went to Carolco and his revisions were lifted out and William Goldman was brought in to write the extra scenes.

Including the scenes where Chaplin accepts a Lifetime Achievement Oscar?

We always envisaged that as a bookend device: Hollywood admitted that they were wrong and welcomed him back. We showed him preparing for the ceremony, then had a huge flashback, and right at the end he picks up the award.

Were you present while the film was being shot?

I flew out to LA with Dickie to look at the locations, I got to know Robert during the making of it and I went to see it being filmed here. In spite of its terrible ups and downs, a very happy group worked on the film, and what emerged is a really intriguing portrait. It's possibly Attenborough's darkest film, and Downey is absolutely brilliant, but powerful men just wanted to get their fingerprints on it. Look at the first version of *Blade Runner*: 'Let's stick in a voiceover.' Look at the director's cut: you don't need a voiceover. These things happen.

The screenplay credit actually reads . . .

Me, Bryan Forbes and William Goldman. It was decided in arbitration. In theory the first writer should get the first credit, but in fact I was the second writer.

Can you explain how a Writers Guild credit arbitration works?

There can't be more than three writers credited, unless two of the writers scrabbling for those three credits are a writing team, so if you're claiming a credit you have to write a declaration of why you think you earned it. You never write to claim a shared credit, you always write to demand sole credit, however unjust that may be. And you have to do it, because if you opt out, your credit is gone. You then submit all the drafts of the script you've written, and it goes before a kind of secret Star Chamber court.

Comprising other screenwriters?

The Writers Guild publish a list. Any member of the Guild could be called upon, but there seem to be about two or three hundred writers who make up these committees. You don't know who they are, and there's no right of appeal, but certain things usually apply. The first writer nearly always gets a credit, even if there's not a comma of theirs in the script, then the subsequent writers need to have changed something like thirty per cent of the script to even qualify for consideration. But, by definition, the last writer on the script is going to have more of his work in the film, so if there have been seven or eight writers before him the whole process can be very unfair. There are instances where a well-known writer has written an entire film and not got a credit, and the credited writer has picked up an Oscar or a Golden Globe. It's a source of great bitterness, this tendency to rewrite, and is one of the besetting sins of Hollywood. It pits writer against writer and involves an unseemly scrabble for prominence. I was subsequently asked to rewrite a script – a comedy called *Hot Water*, which has never been made – and I decided to meet the original writer to clear the air and make it non-adversarial. His advice was, 'Tear it apart.' The time when I was rewritten, in the case of *Diabolique*, I withdrew from the arbitration, and they gave sole credit to a very interesting writer, Don Roos. I'd probably have got a credit because I was the first writer on the film, but I didn't want my name associated with it in any way and just thought, 'To hell with this!'

Why is there this tendency to rewrite in Hollywood?

Hollywood is governed by a fear of failure, and what happens is that as a film is being greenlit the studio hires another writer at vast expense – a quarter of a million dollars, half a million dollars, paid by the week – to put in some more gags or to look at the beginnings and endings of scenes, to 'put it through their machine', as the saying goes. Most celebratedly, Robert Towne was called in to polish *The Godfather*, and wrote the scene before Brando keels over in the garden. I won't name any names, but when *Kindergarten Cop* was being greenlit the studio hired a very well-known screenwriter to put in a few more one-liners. The work came in and it was utterly useless, but if you've paid a celebrated screenwriter hundreds of thousands of dollars, what could be wrong with that? I call it the 'only a fool' syndrome. If you've got a really crap script, but Brad Pitt and Julia Roberts will accept huge sums of money to be in it, then, well, only a fool wouldn't make that film. It takes the curse off the decision. And sometimes it pays dividends. If you're a hugely intelligent person, like Tom Stoppard, you can tinker with anything and improve it: come out of this scene a bit earlier, start the next scene a bit later. A script is endlessly malleable. But the process is driven by a fear of failure, it seems to me, rather than a genuine search for excellence.

In the case of *Diabolique*, there was already a classic adaptation of the novel by Boileau and Narcejac, so why did you agree to give it another shot?

I knew the film well; I didn't go back to the novel. The brief was very clear: update it from fifties France to contemporary America. Again, it was a good moment; I can't remember what I'd just finished. And it was for Warner, who I hadn't worked for. When you take on these studio jobs you look for something challenging. *Chaplin*, *Diabolique* and *The Gunpowder Plot* are all very interesting assignments. In updating an old film all sorts of things had to be considerably altered, while at the same time delivering the mood and the menace of the original. The headmaster's wife dying of fright has to be made ultra-plausible today, so you have to lay in her medical history. And, in contemporary mores, would you tolerate your husband openly sleeping with another teacher at the school? The updating was really quite complex. I did a lot of hard work and wrote a script which everybody seemed pleased with, then the studio put it in turnaround and it was picked up by a large independent company – who brought in Don Roos. I was sent the shooting script when the credit arbitration approached, as I was obliged to be, and it was apparent that they had basically remade the old film. All my stuff, the modernity, the plausibility, had gone, so I said, 'It's all yours.'

How long did it take you to write?

I worked on it for several months, made two trips to LA and did a lot of free work because I liked the producer. You're contracted to do a first draft, a set of revisions and a polish – three passes – but I must have done at least another three polishes to try and get it right. This is another thing the Writers Guild is up in arms about. Writers want a film to work, and it's very easy for producers to say, 'Maybe if we just fiddle with those scenes in the middle', so you do the extra, unpaid work in good faith and it turns out to be a waste of time. I now resist polishing and polishing because there will always be more work to do when a director comes on board. It would seem sensible to wait before you say, 'This is the finished script.'

What did you find challenging about *The Gunpowder Plot*?

I read Antonia Fraser's book, and it was a bit like *Chaplin*: everyone *thinks* they know about the Gunpowder Plot, but again you're saying, 'Actually, no, it was like this.' That kind of demythologising is something I do a lot in my novels, and that's what sets the creative juices flowing. You run the movie in your head and see a fantastic film about Jacobean England, which has all the pageantry, derring-do and men in tights you could want, but is really a hugely relevant story about how a decent man becomes a ruthless terrorist.

A historical political thriller.

Yes, it is. It's like Z set in 1605. Just look around the world: that story is relevant today. It was unbelievable that the film got commissioned and that we got as far as we did. Hollywood is changing hugely, and now you wouldn't get past the door with that type of film unless you had major talent attached. Again, we did a lot of work on it, and again, we were a victim of a studio Night of the Long Knives. Everybody at Universal was fired, and with them went their projects.

We've talked about the film adaptations of your novels, but you've also written a couple of unproduced adaptations of your short stories. *Cork*, first of all.

In a lot of my short stories, I take real characters and write something fictional about them. *Cork* was inspired by a Portuguese poet called Fernando Pessoa, who led an extraordinarily schizoid life. He wrote under different pseudonyms – he called them 'heteronyms' – and took on different identities. He'd take on the personality of a rustic pagan poet, for example, and then a tortured intellectual poet, and he'd write in that particular style. It's unapologetically complex, intensely erotic, has an unhappy ending and requires two brave actors. Various directors have been attached to it, and in the course of its life one of the actors we saw was Catherine McCormack. When the project languished, Catherine rang up and said, 'Could I option the script?' I think she was sick to death of the kind of movie roles she was being offered and thought, 'I must find interesting work which I can have some sort of influence over.' I'm often asked to option my short stories and always say no, because you never get them back, but I said, 'Let's see if my producing team, with you added, can put it together.' The more we talked about it, the more we realised she had very strong opinions about it, so Mark Tarlov said to her, '*You* should direct this film.' Of course, I think she was hoping for someone to offer her that, and without a second thought she went for it. The current state of play is that she's going to direct and star in it, which is unusual because not many women do that. It's not unprecedented, but it's a tall order for your first movie as a director. So we now have a script, a producer, a director and a leading actor; we just need to cast the other role and get some money. I've also adapted another of my short stories as a short film, a ten-page script, which in a funny way was more challenging than taking a short story and expanding it.

What was that?

Two young film-makers approached me and asked if they could option a story of mine, *The Care and Attention of Swimming Pools*, about a mad pool-cleaner in LA. I thought the producer wanted to do it as a feature film, but she said she wanted to do it as a short, so I said, 'Why don't I write it for nothing and let's see how we go?' I wrote it, we got it financed, they spent six weeks out in LA setting it up and then it all fell apart. There was a Screen Actors Guild strike at the time, so the cast and crew were all sitting around, prepared to work for scale, then overnight the strike ended and everybody was working again. Rather than blow the money – there was a lot of private equity involved – the producer thought, 'Let's come back and fight another day.' They were young and very enthusiastic, and I thought, 'I can move this process forward a huge amount by not insisting they pay me to option the story or write the script.' It was just an interesting experiment.

Do you find it more or less satisfying, adapting a story rather than a novel?

More satisfying, in a way, because you tend to add on rather than cut out. If you're looking to literature for inspiration for a film, a short story is better than a novel because you have the germ but there's often not enough material to fill 90 or 100 minutes, so you're forced to open it out and think about other elements which can work filmically. It's more creative expanding something than boiling it down, which is what happens with novel to film adaptations.

Presumably *Cork* is a full-length script, 90 pages or so?

Cork is actually very tight, about 80 pages, but because of the nature of the material it will run to a full-length feature. I used to think 120 pages was about right, but now I think all scripts should be between 90 and 100 pages, because any film which crosses the two-hour barrier brings all sorts of industrial problems in its train. A film will always expand from the script. *The Trench*, which was a 90-page screenplay, is a 97-minute film. *The Gunpowder Plot* would be a long film – two hours fifteen, two hours thirty – but the script was only 105 pages, because I knew the film would balloon if it got to 115 or 120. All our scripts for *Armadillo*, which is three one-hour chunks, were 54 or 55 pages, and as a result we have no length problem. It's better to make these tough decisions on the page than in the cutting room. Of course, there's usually a chunk you can lift out during editing if you have that problem, but it's always soul destroying to lose a sequence which cost hundreds of thousands and took nine days to shoot – and you can usually spot the joins and have to do a bit of reshooting to smooth things out. In some ways, length depends on the genre. *Chaplin* was always going to be two hours-plus, but a comedy or a thriller which is much over an hour and forty minutes is asking a lot of itself.

In fact, your next project as writer-director is a thriller.

It's called *Stone Free* – which is quite a good title, I think, quite an intriguing title – and is a sort of contemporary *film noir*: an ensemble piece about a bungled kidnap attempt which is set in London and has nothing to do with gangsters from the East End. It'll be an independent film which shouldn't cost more than two or three million pounds – which is cheap – and then you're left alone and nobody forces you to make compromises. In theory!

Why do you think the scripts you write for yourself to direct are less exotic and more confined than the scripts you write for other people?

It's knowing my own strengths and, by definition, weaknesses. *The Trench* minimised the hassles for me as a first-time director. We shot a lot of it in the studio and it was fantastic working on a set. You started work at eight and knocked off at seven. You didn't have to worry about rain or aeroplanes flying overhead. Offices were there. Cutting rooms were there. It was a great experience and, so, planning my second film, I thought, 'Softly, softly.' This one will be maybe seventy-five per cent studio-based and twenty-five per cent location-based. I won't be going to live in a hotel for six weeks, so I'll be able to do the work without all that endless hanging around involved in film-making. And having cut my teeth on the war movie, I thought that the kind of film I'd like to do next would be a complicated and sophisticated thriller. *Chinatown*, *Body Heat*, *The Parallax View* and *Three Days of the Condor* are films which made a big impression on me. Film does genre really well: that's where it seems to excel and is particularly true to its own art form. I've also got this hankering to make a film about Billy the Kid, which again is genre, but nobody wants to make Westerns these days. I wrote about the Kid in *The New Confessions*, where the hero makes a film about him, and I've read a lot about the real Billy, revolting little scumbag of a human being that he was.

Many screenwriters try their hand at directing in an effort to exercise greater control over their work, but your screenwriting experiences have mostly been very positive – so what drew you to become a director?

I originally wanted to be a painter, so this desire to direct may be satisfying the painterly side of my nature, reflected in the compositional and choreographical elements of film-making. I remember seeing *The Conformist* when I was nineteen, and being struck as much by the look of the film as by the story it was telling. One of my favourite films is *Electra Glide in Blue*, which is beautifully shot and blew me away when I saw it in my early twenties. I think that aspect was drawing me towards being a director rather than thinking, 'I must have more control' – although, of course, directing a film as well as writing it is very alluring. I would never abandon writing novels to become a film director, but, as time has gone by and yet another director drops out of a project, friends have said, 'You should direct this', and I realised that one day I would direct, but I wanted to do something tailor-made for me. And, in the end, I enjoyed it so much that I want to do it again. But because I'm a novelist, and have the ultimate creative control there, I don't mind sharing the burden sometimes. I enjoyed the making of *Armadillo*. Howard Davies is a brilliant director, and I've learned a lot from him and other directors. I enjoy being a benign presence behind the scenes and I'll always write scripts for other people to direct, but I would never direct an adaptation of one of my novels and I would never direct a script by anybody else. I would only direct an original script of mine.

Why would you never direct an adaptation of one of your novels? An adaptation of your second novel, *An Ice-Cream War*, has spent many years in development hell for example. Why not take the director's chair for that film?

Because I know what's involved in adapting. For me, creatively, it's truer and fairer to the art form to write something which is purely a film. *The Trench* can sit on the shelf with any of my novels because, although it's a huge collaboration, it's exactly as I hoped it would be. I couldn't say that a film version of *An Ice-Cream War* would be part of my body of work in the same way.

Why did the project languish?

It was with Working Title, but when Working Title was bought by PolyGram the new men at the top deemed that they were going to make American movies, and a lot of what you would regard as classic Working Title projects were rejected – including *An Ice-Cream War* and *The Galapagos Affair*. I'd feel more upset if the book and the script were owned today by someone else, but I never optioned the book and was writing the script on spec so nobody has a piece of it except me. It's now on a very crowded back-burner. Gavin Millar was going to direct it and had actually cast three of the six principal parts but then the money fell away. The usual stuff. One of these days the right elements will cohere and we may be able to do it.

You could direct The Galapagos Affair, too. What prompted you to option such dark and difficult material yourself?

I have a desert-island obsession. These myths are buried deep within us: *Robinson Crusoe*, *Swiss Family Robinson* and so on. I read a review of John Treherne's book and thought, 'What an extraordinary story.' A nymphomaniac baroness, an American millionaire in his white yacht, the mad German philosopher who swaps partners; the ingredients intrigued me. And at this stage in my screenwriting, I was thinking about optioning books to give myself more independence. The book had in fact been optioned by Nic Roeg and the option had lapsed, so I took it over and wrote a script, then set about seeing if I could find a producer and director. It eventually wound up at Working Title, and Tim Bevan and Mel Smith were hugely taken with it. We worked on it for a long time and they spent a lot of money – Mel had even done location recces in Australia – and then it all fell apart because of the nature of the material. It revived with Sarah Radclyffe as producer, but by then the PolyGram writing was on the wall, and because I'd signed no contract and received no money, I was able to take the book and script away and live to fight another day. I occasionally think about directing it, because it's been on the go since 1985, but again it's an adaptation, and something makes me think that any films I direct will be original.

Have you learned anything from writing these original screen-plays for yourself to direct which you can bring to bear on writing adaptations for other people?

I really don't know. I'm reluctant to create rules like, 'If you're writing a scene and it's seven pages long and it isn't over yet then you're in trouble', because in fact you may not be. Or to insist, 'Don't put in any camera moves', because camera moves might actually be useful. But I'm now much more aware of the issue, 'Is this going to be a problem to shoot?' When I was writing for other people, that was their problem not mine. Take a dinner-party scene, for example, with ten people chattering away around a table. There's really only a bog-standard way of filming that kind of scene, and because I know how long it takes and how much coverage you have to shoot and how it still looks like a bunch of people talking at a table, I now think, 'Maybe this scene shouldn't take place at a dinner party after all. Maybe it would be more interesting if they were walking through a park.' It's not going to justify the sheer effort of shooting it, because you can do it in a more elegant or intriguing way. If you look at the opening of *Reservoir Dogs*, Tarantino set himself exactly that problem and obviously thought, 'To hell with this', and got someone to walk round and round with a steadicam. If you weren't in shot when you were talking and he didn't have coverage for it, so what? It's actually quite a good way of shooting a lot of people talking at a table, although you may find when you come to cut it that a really crucial line is masked by some-body's head, whereas if you'd storyboarded it and shot it from five or six different static positions you'd have got your coverage. The directorial influence makes itself felt more in the details than the big picture. Some establishing shots are key, for example, but do you really need to see people arriving in their cars and unlocking their front doors? You know you'll cut that during editing, so why write it in the first place? Unless you happen to be Michael Mann and have seven cameras running simultaneously, there's no interesting way of shooting someone arriving home. So maybe a better way of writing a scene like that is to have someone inside the house hearing the car pull up, followed by the driver bursting through the front door. Everyone will be able to envisage what happened outside. That sort of writing decision is all as a result of having stood behind a camera.

The vast majority of your scripts are adaptations. Do you think that Hollywood somehow perceives British screenwriters as more literary?

I think that's a fair point. Maybe the classic serial generates that feeling. *Masterpiece Theatre* is hugely popular in America. But I also think it's an industry-wide taste – or problem. For every original script commissioned there are four or five adaptations. Again, it's driven by this fear of failure: 'It's a really successful book. Let's make it into a movie.' The art of film is not best served by constantly doing adaptations, because of the problems inherent in shifting from one form to the other. It's like putting pop songs on soundtracks. Isn't it better to have a proper score? Isn't that what film music is all about? It's not about taking ten hit records and sticking them on so you get a great CD. Similarly, I feel, in a vaguely purist way, that film is best served if the script was always destined to be a film.

Which, looking at your filmography, is rather ironic.

That's my point. That's the nature of the beast. I bet most screenwriters would rather write something based on their own ideas than on this bestselling novel or that work of non-fiction. It's not just books; they're adapting TV shows, comic strips, other films. *Traffic* is an adaptation of a British television series. That's why, in any scriptography, there will always be three to one in favour of adaptations. I was quite lucky that the first two scripts I did were original scripts. I think you have to separate adaptations and original scripts, because there are totally different sets of mental gears engaged in producing them.

How quickly did you adapt to writing scripts?

You can learn the grammar of a screenplay incredibly quickly. That's why there are so many screenwriters out there. Any resting actor can produce a screenplay which looks exactly like a Robert Towne screenplay in terms of format but ultimately you have to fall back on whatever storytelling ability you have. You also have to understand what you can do with film and what you can't. You'd have to be a very talented director, for example, to make a forty-five-page dialogue scene work. My advice to aspiring screenwriters is that if you see a film you really like, get hold of the screenplay and read it watching the movie simultaneously, with the remote control close at hand. You begin to understand the rhythms and cadences of film. Why is this scene so arresting? Stop. Rewind. Look again. Because you're hearing this person talking, but you're actually seeing the other person listening. And you realise it's much more powerful that way. You learn.

Though that might not be written down.

It's surprising how much is written down. I know, having directed myself, that you do a master shot and close-ups and reverses so that you can cut it any way you want. But if, for example, one character is announcing the news of the other character's wife's infidelity, then you will often write in the script, 'Hold on a big close-up of John.' That's simple story-telling. It's more important to see John's reaction than it is to see Fred speaking the words. And if you, the writer, think the moment should be played that way, then you haven't even got a chance of getting it done like that if you don't write it down.

The rule of thumb is: if you want it in the film, make sure it's in the script. Of course, stuff that's in the script often doesn't get shot, which is particularly galling for the writer. You come to the editing stage and say, 'Where's that close shot of Sally turning round as he walks off?' 'Oh, we never did it.' 'But it's on page forty-three.' 'Well, we were pressed for time.' But a good film writer will put these shots in, all the same.

Or not, depending on the advice you listen to. Aspiring screen-writers are often told precisely the opposite: the fewer camera directions the better.

In fact, the first screenplays I read were by Harold Pinter, who's extremely sparing with directions, so my first screen-plays were similarly spare. I don't think William Goldman even puts scene headings in, it's just 'Cut to . . .' But there are moments where a scene has no dialogue so you have to write directions, and you would be better off writing them in a way that you think they would be well shot.

Of course, a script – particularly a spec script – isn't simply a blueprint for a film, it's also a sales tool for a project, so it has to be as readable as it is shootable. For example, direc-tions in parentheses to indicate how the dialogue should be spoken.

It's called 'grandstanding' in Hollywood. When I was writing for Universal and Warner it was understood that this kind of thing would go in. It makes an easier read for overtaxed executives, because you're telling them what the emotion is and they don't have to deduce whether a character is happy or sad. Now, because I've worked more with actors and I understand an actor's take on a script, I tend to strip that stuff away. Actors hate things like, 'Ted (with a thin smile)', because you're saying, 'This is how I want you to act it.' But if you're writing a film for a Hollywood studio you write it in a different way. A script has to be so many things in its life, and is going to be read by so many people who have a vested interest in saying no, that you want to give it your best shot – and there are all sorts of ways you can garnish it so it seems user-friendly. Hollywood is very conventional, in its own way. They want the script to be presented in the right typeface – courier – to be printed on the right paper – American letter-size is not the same as our A4 – and to be bound with two clips – brass not silver – else they'll say, 'Foreign', and throw it away. British screenwriters who take their scripts down to KallKwik and get a plastic binding are handicapping them-selves. When I was writing a lot in Hollywood, I used to buy great stacks of American paper and brass clips precisely so that it 'looked right'.

You also get the impression from screenwriting manuals that if the spec writer doesn't place the heroine in jeopardy on page twenty then the executives aren't going to read any more of the script. Or even that much.

And not just spec writers. As a gun-for-hire screenwriter you can find yourself having to do things which you regard as mind-bogglingly stupid to satisfy some berk at the studio. In my opinion, these screenwriting courses are designed so executives can come back from them and say knowing things to writers about 'character arcs' and 'three-act structure'. It's just jargon, really. Why not have a five-act structure, like Shakespeare? I don't know any screenwriter who doesn't regard these courses as laughable, but they have to take the jargon on board because they know they'll go into meetings with people who'll be spouting it. Fundamentally, all these decisions are to do with telling a story. Does the story demand that the heroine should be in jeopardy after twenty minutes? That's the only true criterion.

Do you have a rigid writing routine?

I do for writing novels. I have the same approach for screen-writing, to a degree, in that I spend a long time figuring everything out before I start. That's true whether it's an adaptation or an original. As a rule, I make notes and draw diagrams and do scene lists, so that when I sit down to write the script I have the whole thing planned. From page one, I know exactly how it's going to end. Then I write the first draft as quickly as possible, which may only take two or three weeks, because compared to a novel a screenplay is so short. There are maybe 10,000 words in a screenplay: a couple of chapters, if that. And then I can look at the 110 pages and reorder them and fiddle around with them. That's where the similarity ends, in a way, because the script is now at a stage to show people and talk about. It's unfinished in the sense of, 'Who's going to direct it?' or, 'Who's going to put money into it?' You know that there's going to be more changes required, so you consciously don't make it word perfect.

Though you have said that the first draft should be fairly close to the final draft.

I think so. You shouldn't submit a first draft which wouldn't make a perfectly good film. There are always changes – often nothing to do with the story but to do with the input you get from the producer and the director and the actors – but if in a parallel universe the film company said, 'We'll make this', the draft which you present should be the film which you want, not just something 'along the right lines'. Then, if you're going to make changes, they're usually not substantial. One of my working maxims is, 'All intelligent suggestions gratefully received', but if you present something which is polished then it has to be really quite a bright idea for you to say, 'Actually, you're right.' If somebody says, 'I don't like the ending', you say, 'Why? Come up with a better one.' That sort of script note drives you mad: 'I just feel the character of Julie isn't sufficiently developed.' 'Really? In what particular areas? Because I think she's pretty damn developed.' There's an endless process of tinkering required as the various investors are given notes by their script readers, and one of the main attractions of being a writer–director is that you can say, 'The director is very happy with this script as it stands.' But if you're working with people you're sympathetic with, that process is mostly beneficial. We did a lot of work on *Armadillo* before we submitted it to the BBC, so the notes which came back were pretty valid – or else we had cogent counter-arguments if we thought that some suggestion was a mistake.

When you choose to adapt something or are offered something to adapt, do you respond to the material in an emotional or an intellectual way?

I suspect the two are related. If a story appeals to me, it's bound to have things in common with the stories I write myself, to a greater or lesser degree. As a novelist you always write the books that you would like to read yourself, so that feeling probably governs your choice of commissioned work too: 'I wouldn't mind seeing this movie.' I don't think I would write a horror film, for example, because I don't particularly enjoy that genre, but there are all sorts of other genres I *would* tackle. You might not think I'd like to write a Western, but I've got this very dark Western in mind. Your choice is shaped by your own tastes and inclinations, and if you're not in-trigued or stimulated then sure as hell the work you do is going to be similarly lacklustre.

Hossein Amini was born in 1966, in Iran, and educated at Bryanston School and Wadham College, Oxford. He is married with two children and lives in London.

FILM

Jude (Michael Winterbottom, 1996, UK)
The Wings of the Dove (Iain Softley, 1997, US/UK)

The Four Feathers (Shekhar Kapur, 2002, US)
The Great Raid (John Dahl, 2003, US)

TELEVISION

The Dying of the Light (Peter Kosminsky, 1994, ITV)

UNCREDITED

Gangs of New York (Martin Scorsese, 2002, US)

SCREENPLAYS

Khanjar (BBC)
In a Lonely Place (Sony)

Shanghai (Miramax/Phoenix)
Mila 18 (Miramax)

When did you first get into movies?

When I was twelve, maybe a bit older. My mum and dad are both Iranian, educated in England and France, so after the revolution they went to their natural second homes, which were London and Paris. My brother and I used to spend our school holidays with my dad. He didn't really know what to do with us so we'd literally walk down the Champs Élysées and go to a two o'clock showing, a four o'clock showing, a six o'clock showing. There was a whole period where all I did was sit and watch movies. That was between about 1980 and 1990, so my knowledge of eighties films is pretty good.

That's a very cosmopolitan upbringing. How did it influence the development of your writing and the type of material you wanted to tackle?

I guess growing up on Hollywood movies and French movies, as opposed to those great British television series, I imagined a big screen as soon as I started writing. I tend to write in pictures, trying to transcribe what I'm seeing in my head. Dialogue I find extremely hard. I'm not brilliant at the technical side of film-making, but I've always been interested in it. I did History and Italian Literature at Oxford, and you're supposed to go to Italy for a year off – but the job I had with this Italian professor of cinema fell through, so I went and worked with a cameraman friend of my dad as an assistant on a seedy French soft-porn programme called *Charme*. I spent most of the time trying to get out of the way of the actresses.

When you were at Oxford, you also won a BP Short Film Award.

It was a pretty poor short film. We got some money from the Oxford Film Foundation and set up a drama society, but no one really knew how to use a camera. So we put up a notice at the

National Film School and got this Polish cameraman, who said he would do it if we listened to everything he said and he got to use whatever film stock he wanted. He was about forty and I don't think he'd ever worked professionally, but he pretty much helped me direct the thing. I saw him years later and he'd just shot his first movie in America, a low-budget film called *Reservoir Dogs*. I remember thinking, 'What a stupid title!' But that cameraman was Andrzej Sekula, and he subsequently became really famous. Even after we finished the short, I used to spend afternoons talking to him because neither of us was working. He probably taught me more than anyone else has.

Do you think you learn more about writing from talking to people in the industry than from reading screenwriting manuals and taking screenwriting courses?

They're both useful in different ways. Talking to editors you realise how much stuff is cut out, flab which you don't need to write, people walking into rooms and sitting down and so on. The notion that you can start in the middle of a scene should be common sense, but it takes quite a lot of courage and was one of my biggest breakthroughs as a young writer. Books on screenwriting are a good way of reminding yourself about things like that, but when I'm stuck I've never thought, 'Oh my God, I haven't hit my act-one turning point on page twenty-eight!' I always take them with a pinch of salt.

Presumably you wrote the short film as well as directing it?

Yes. It was about a hit man who's hired by this woman to kill her husband – we think – but it turns out that she's actually committing suicide and trying to frame her husband. It was a fairly convoluted plot with just one actor, one room and a telephone, but it won the short-film competition and gave me the confidence to carry on. I've been quite lucky like that. Every time I'm about to give up there's a little bit of luck which keeps me going for another year or two. So much of getting by in this industry is persistence, and so many people give up for financial reasons or just through lack of confidence. I've had an enormous number of rejection letters, because I started writing when I was nineteen or twenty.

A screenplay?

A play. Like a lot of students, I was obsessed with Baudelaire, so I wrote a play which was put on at the King's Head and got some quite nice reviews, and I thought I'd adapt that into a film. The second script – another terrible one – was an adaptation of *Macbeth* set in South America, and the one that got me my first job was a two-hander between a psychiatrist – all the clichés again – and an old lady who's murdered her husband. All these scripts went out and none of them was accepted, but a producer at the BBC called Ruth Baumgarten liked one and set me up with this fantastic Chinese director, Zhang Zeming, who had made a film called *Swan Song* and was being courted by lots of British producers at the time. I went off to China and Hong Kong for four months to help him with English dialogue in the film he was writing, but it never got made. After that, again through Ruth Baumgarten, I was commissioned by Michael Wearing to do a four-part mini-series called *Khanjar* about terrorism and the Persian community in exile, which was and is the most personal thing I've written. It was the first one I wrote more than a draft of, for a start.

I take it you had an agent by now?

I got an agent after the short film. He was someone who had been a couple of years above me at university, and within a year he found out he didn't really enjoy what he was doing – so I was agentless. But another university friend had been working with my present agent, Nick Marston, and recommended him, so I sent him a draft of one of these scripts. Rather than sending it out and seeing if anything stuck, he made me rewrite it. He was one of the first people who forced me to understand what it is to write second, third and fourth drafts. What happens later is that so many other people start telling you how to rewrite it that it becomes a relief to have someone read it and just encourage you. That's what he does now.

Why didn't the BBC make *Khanjar*? Was the ethnicity a problem?

It didn't help. *The Buddha of Suburbia* had just come out, which did well critically but not commercially, and there was a feeling that there were too many foreigners in this. People liked it, but it was too big and too expensive. A lot of it was set in Paris, and there were some flashbacks to the Iran–Iraq war. Having said that there wasn't much television I was inspired by, the one thing which absolutely blew my mind was *Edge of Darkness*, so I tried to write something along those lines about a subject I knew. It starts with a British cop investigating what he thinks is the drug murder of an Iranian, then gradually he finds out about this mythical assassin called Khanjar, who is feared among the community in exile as the retribution sent by the Mullahs. The cop feels he's been chosen to capture this guy, and you learn that they're both fanatics, in the sense that they'd both sacrifice everything to get what they want, but you don't know until the end whether the terrorist exists or is a figment of this obsession. I suppose another inspiration was *The Day of the Jackal*, which was the film that most stuck in my mind as a kid. I've got this fascination with thrillers and *film noir*, and I thought that was the only way you could make this story accessible for a British audience.

Were you aiming to articulate any political point of view, or do you never start a script with something like that in mind?

I did with that one, and around the time of the Salman Rushdie fatwa I suddenly got really worried: 'Have I written anything which could offend the government in Iran?' HBO once offered me the most dangerous assignment ever, about plutonium smuggling by Islamic terrorists and the Russian Mafia – two groups of people you don't want to offend. My grandad was Prime Minister of Iran in 1961, and even though he'd been a fairly liberal one who'd got in trouble with the Shah, he'd also done one or two things which didn't stand him in very good stead with the present government, so he was somewhere low down on their hit list. The revolution overturned my world completely, and if I have anything to say a lot of it is informed by that fear and confusion. I'm adapting *Mila 18* for Miramax, from the Leon Uris book about the Warsaw Ghetto Uprising, and obviously it's a very different world, but there's still this sense that a way of life people took for granted was inexplicably ripped out from under them with horrific consequences. I'm drawn to these big subjects. You hope that someone is going to say, 'I'll take a chance on this', but they didn't with *Khanjar*. It's the only thing I actually own, because when you write something for the BBC it eventually reverts back to you. I was so disappointed when it didn't get made that I gave it to my brother, who's just come out of film school in the States, and he's now adapting it as a movie. I have a lot of faith in him. He's probably my most reliable script editor.

I believe he also helped you out on the television drama *The Dying of the Light*, about the murder in Africa of aid worker Sean Devereux.

My brother had been in Liberia – he was a photojournalist and gave up because lots of people he knew were killed – and so had Sean Devereux. He used to tell me all these surreal things about completely stoned soldiers wearing cowboy hats, and it seemed like this mad *Apocalypse Now*-type world. Peter Kosminski, the director, read and liked *Khanjar* and hired me to do this docudrama, and I was literally thinking in terms of, 'How can we make *Apocalypse Now* or *The Killing Fields* out of this story?'

He's a really talented director, but his whole style as a film-maker is to get very involved with the people he's making the film about, so he took out anything which wasn't quite heavily documented. I was almost exactly the opposite. I didn't want to meet the family. I wanted to use the real character as a stepping stone to a dramatic character. But a lot of the fictional elements were cut and a lot of the documentary stuff stayed in, and it became much more a docu than a drama, which was disappointing. The essence of the thing was about what an extraordinarily giving person he was towards these young children, and one of the liberties I took was having him killed by a boy soldier at the end. I thought that made for a strong dramatic irony, but they did their research and the suspect had to be a much older man, so it was done like that.

Did you actually go to Liberia as part of your research?

It was still a no-go area at the time. Some of the people who did the research went there but I'm not the most courageous person. I watched a lot of videos. A rebel leader called Prince Johnson had killed a previous president, Samuel Doe, and there was an actual video of his interrogation doing the rounds in various countries for a while. It was the most appalling thing I've ever seen but I still tried to do a scene based on it, and that was one of the things which was either cut out or cut down. The most terrifying thing about this interrogation was the banality of it. They're having a bizarre conversation about nothing, dotted with occasional threats, then they suddenly cut off something. You don't see it but you know they're cutting off an ear, and you expect the reaction of the person having it done to them to be scream, scream, horror, horror, but there was a calm about him which was eerie. Moments like that, if handled well, can be mind-blowing on film.

What was your way into the story?

Heart of Darkness: going into an incredibly dark place and finding an answer, and that answer being completely different to what you expected. It's my favourite book, probably the book which has influenced me the most, so it creeps into everything I write. I suppose it's the quest story: a young university student with a big heart and big ideas goes in there and finds a world which is dark and corrupt and unforgiving. But that's a difficult story to tell on television. It's hard to be honest about the brutality and still get a positive message out of it, and obviously a nervousness about accusations of racism crept in too. The screenplay had a much bleaker ending and the film is more hopeful, about the achievements of Sean Devereux rather than his frustration. This was the first thing I had made, and it's such a shock when you see how different something is to how you imagined it. Kosminski is a big-screen director, but I think the medium reduced it to some-thing smaller. At the time, I thought that if it's on the big screen it's going to be bigger and better, and that isn't always the case either.

You didn't immediately warm to the idea of adapting *Jude*, though, did you?

I had no personal connection to the material at all. There isn't always one when you accept the commission, but you have to care about it to be able to write it. Then, coincidentally, my girlfriend got pregnant, and this whole notion of how children and commitment can suddenly turn your dreams upside down gave me that connection. I was at the beginning of my career, I'd got a BAFTA nomination for *The Dying of the Light* and I thought, 'I need to be single, I need to be focussed.' It was very similar to Jude wanting to go to Christminster, and that gave me an 'in' into writing a more personal adaptation. It really felt like I was telling a story which was uniquely mine, which helped me forget that this was Hardy's story and he'd done all the hard work.

The script is 124 pages; the novel is 500 pages. Where did you start?

First I went through the book and broke it up – which is what I still do with adaptations, especially ones like this or *Mila 18* where the scenes are clear – then I went through it again to boil it down. I like adaptations because somebody else has created the story and it's a question of interpretation and reinvention, but I very rarely stick rigidly to my outline because it's nice for there to be a process of discovery while you write. That script would be too long in Hollywood, because they always try to get a page count of about 115. The script that I used in terms of style and layout was Eisenstein's *The Battleship Potemkin*, where each image has its own line, but when I began working in America I had to condense the scripts, running lines into each other.

On the other hand, you added things like directions in parentheses to indicate how the dialogue should be spoken. *Jude* has none of those.

That's interesting. Again, it's the transition to writing in America. Studio executives are bright people, but they read very quickly because they read such a lot. Directors, too. I tend to strive for quite spare and elliptical dialogue – my favourite dialogue writer is Pinter – and when actors deliver it with the right intonation it becomes very clear. But reading it on the page, people would often ask, 'Why is he saying that?' and you go, 'Well, it's ironic.' So, parentheses, 'Ironic'. I don't like them, but I'm using them more and more because they're sometimes a helpful way of making yourself clearer. A lot of writers probably have the problem that what you think you're saying is very different to how people are reading it.

Were you aiming to distinguish *Jude* from the so-called heritage cycle?

Michael Winterbottom's intention right from the start was to turn costume drama on its head, and he chose *Jude* because it wasn't your traditional period film dealing with the middle classes. He wanted to make something tough and gritty, and there were things in it, like a very graphic birth scene, which everyone told him to cut and I really admire him for keeping. He started playing around with a strong set of genre conventions, largely created by Merchant Ivory, and to a certain extent I followed his lead. Both of us, quite independently, were inspired by Truffaut films like *Jules et Jim*, and he used a couple of things which weren't scripted, like freeze frames and the homage where Sue is smoking a cigarette. I contemporised the language, not going too far but keeping it neutral, because in most costume dramas I'd seen the language felt very flowery and crafted. I hate dialogue which feels written, where someone has spent hours trying to come up with the perfect phrase, and I love dialogue which sounds like something you overhear, however much dramatic significance it has.

Of course, a lot of people like those films because of that.

Yes, and I think we were a bit smug about sticking two fingers up to that audience. That's why it didn't do very well commercially. We lost the older audience and we didn't get the younger one. They put it in the multiplexes, not in the Curzon Chelsea or Mayfair where these films usually end up, and when it first opened I went to a cinema to see, in a paranoid way, who was going in to watch it. Groups of people would turn up, and one of them would say, 'I've heard that's really good', and another would say, 'I've heard that's really bad', and the common denominator was that they would all go and see *The Nutty Professor*, which was also on at the time. I love going to matinées on Monday afternoons, and when I read the book I thought, 'This is a perfect Monday-afternoon film', forgetting that most people go in groups on Friday and Saturday evenings, which is when most films make their money. So many people love the novel that there's no reason why a film version shouldn't get an audience, but I think it would have to be a different adaptation.

When I saw it at the cinema, a woman in the audience started having hysterics during the scene where Jude and Sue find that their son has hanged himself and his siblings. How can you reach a mainstream audience with a story like that?

If you can make them cry. Michael's one of our most talented directors, but he's not one of the most audience-friendly, and he very deliberately didn't allow them to cry – at least, not in a manipulative way. The head of Fox Searchlight was interested in doing the film before PolyGram came on – if that scene was changed or taken out. I remember thinking, as an arrogant film-snob, 'God, what an idiot', then sitting in an audience and seeing how that moment takes them out of the film. Some of the most moving scenes actually happen after that, but who cares? There were scenes in the script which pushed the film towards a more conventional tragedy, complete with a heart-breaking weepy scene at the end where Jude journeyed to find Sue even though he knew he was dying, and had this conversation with her but never told her. That would have got the heartstrings going. You're waiting for him to say, 'I'm dying. Come back to me', and he never does. There was something noble about that, but Michael felt it was just too manipulative.

Were you pleased with the film?

The first time I saw it I thought it was fabulous, then the reviews came in and I started questioning my own opinion. Even though I loved what Michael had done, I thought, 'Well, 247 it could have been great if . . .' It's very easy to lay blame and I have a tendency to do that, but *Jude* is still the thing I've written where I was most thrilled by the result – and most shattered when nobody else seemed to think the same way. I had almost the opposite experience on *The Wings of the Dove*. I was a little disappointed with it, then the reviews were good and I forgot all my criticisms. You become very dishonest, in a way. I was less happy with *The Wings of the Dove* than *Jude*, but I saw it at an earlier stage. When I saw *Jude*, it was pretty much what was released. When I saw *The Wings of the Dove*, it was a year from being released. No matter how many times you've seen rough cuts, you can't help comparing them to finished films. It's difficult watching a film without a proper score, without a proper mix, with tons of re-editing to be done. Everyone else was pretty happy with it, but I was depressed for days.

I assume the producers of *The Wings of the Dove* hired you because of *Jude*?

Because of the script. The film hadn't come out. Also, both on *Jude* and *The Wings of the Dove*, Nick Marston chased the projects very aggressively – more aggressively than I did. That's how things tend to come about when you start off. They're making the phone calls, saying, 'This guy is right.' *The Wings of the Dove* took quite a while because I'd only done one film which no one had seen yet. It was my agent saying, 'You're making a huge mistake', which convinced them.

Were you familiar with the novel?

No, I hadn't read it. I started to read it, and I was pretty bored until I got to one of the last lines. There's a scene where they break up and Kate says to Merton, 'We will never be again as we were.' I haven't read enough Henry James to be an authority, but apparently in a lot of his books everything suddenly comes together right at the very end. That's how it was for me. I went back and re-read the book, and because of that last scene I suddenly knew how to do it. Even though it was originally written as two people facing each other across a mantelpiece, the language was so dark and so sexual that it seemed appropriate to adapt it as a post-coital scene. They've probably had really good sex, but it felt hollow and weird and now they're talking and the relationship is breaking up. The idea of ending a costume drama with two people naked in bed baring their hearts to each other seemed exciting and contemporary. The way it was shot, with this very harsh light, shows the corruption of their love. The book starts off with two people who are desperately in love with each other and will do anything to get married, and what they do is so corrupting that they end up falling apart. It reverses the traditional love story: being separated and then being united.

A story that remains oblique until the final scene presents certain problems for a screenwriter, I would have thought.

Henry James doesn't really write scenes; he writes states of mind. The great thing about that is the characters are so complex and their motivations are so strong that it is actually very easy to invent scenes. Most of the scenes were invented; very few of them exist in the book. When you read *Jude*, I'm sure everyone can imagine it as a movie. Or most books, because they've got concrete scenes which your imagination can turn into a filmic equivalent. *The Wings of the Dove* really wasn't like that. There aren't scenes or set pieces you can latch on to, so you're not really sure where you are. But you're very clear about what they're thinking and what they're plotting.

The dialogue seems less modern in *The Wings of the Dove* than in *Jude*.

It's probably more effective but it's the same idea: I wanted to get away from period dialogue which sounds very literary, and try get back to something which sounds real to contemporary audiences without being anachronistic. Unfortunately, in *Jude*, one of them says to the other, 'Stop being so confrontational', and I had no idea that 'confrontational' was a very modern word. My ear didn't pick that up at all when I was writing it, then half the reviews must have used that as an example of jarring dialogue. I was a little bit more careful on *The Wings of the Dove*. I based it more on *film noir*, very clipped and quite spare. Henry James writes like that anyway, so it was easier to find the right tone for it. That's one of the advantages of adapting a great book. I remember thinking, 'I'm writing really cool dialogue. I can do this with anything', but when you start adapting a less well-written book with less well-written characters, you realise you can't.

What elements of *film noir* did you bring to *The Wings of the Dove*?

I've always loved *film noir*, and I thought, 'I need to reinvent this story for the screen, so why don't I try and change it according to my favourite genre?' You couldn't do that with *Jude*, because there was no connection between the two, whereas there was something of *film noir* in the plot of *The Wings of the Dove*. It particularly reminded me of *Double Indemnity* and *The Postman Always Rings Twice*. They both have scenes where the woman is trying to push the man into committing a crime, and the book *The Wings of the Dove* had that too. What's interesting is that Merton and Kate hint at it without actually saying it, so they are both complicit but neither of them wants to come out and say, 'murder', or, 'kill'. But that's what they were doing: they were murdering Milly, breaking her heart.

Visually, *The Wings of the Dove* is much more in the Merchant Ivory tradition of sumptuous costume drama than *Jude*. Otherwise, were you and Iain Softley as keen as Michael Winterbottom to escape that approach?

Not quite as aggressively as it probably was with Michael. I actually think Merchant Ivory films are pretty damn good. What they did was create a genre that the costume dramas which followed could try to subvert. Iain made it contemporary, but it wasn't as in your face as Michael. I'm not saying one is better than the other, just that Iain's style was, 'Let's subvert this through the story and characterisation', whereas with Michael it was, 'Let's shock and surprise people.' That's just the kind of film-maker Michael is.

Did you work more closely with Iain Softley than Michael Winterbottom?

On *Jude*, I was literally there for one rehearsal and then not at all. On *The Wings of the Dove*, Iain let me into rehearsals quite a lot and I went to a few days of shooting. He became, and still is, a really good friend. He's a very writer-friendly director. He's very bright, but he doesn't impose his ideas. He encourages you to find your own way, rather than saying, 'Let's do this', or, 'Let's try that', and trying to become the writer without actually having to write. One of the things I'm more and more wary of is those brilliant directorial ideas which haven't been thought through and can send the script in completely the wrong direction. It's much harder to write than it is to have ideas. The execution of the ideas is worth far more than that great flash of inspiration.

The film is set a few years later than the novel, isn't it?

That was partly based on the Tube scene, which is just a couple of lines in the middle of the book. I remember thinking when I read it, 'Wouldn't it be great to end a costume drama with two people naked in bed and begin it with two people flirting on the Underground?' People sometimes say, 'I saw this girl on the Underground and we were looking at each other, then she got off and I didn't', so that's where the scene came from. But when we did the research, we found that although there *was* an Underground when the book is set – 1904 – the trains looked clunky and ridiculous and wouldn't have had that contemporary resonance, so they updated it. Also, I think the costume designer, Sandy Powell, had some things she wanted to try out, and Iain wanted to bring in some paintings from 1910, 1912, so it was shifted mainly for design reasons. They did that after the script was finished.

In terms of gaining audience sympathy, Kate is an extremely difficult character: she asks her lover to seduce a dying woman so he will inherit her money.

She's probably softer in the film than she was in the book. It's this notion that we want something and we're ashamed of the way we get it and we lie to ourselves to justify it. Even when she tells Merton, 'She's going to die anyway. You're making her happy', she convinces herself that's true and pushes the more sordid aspects of what she's doing to the side. That's something we all do. I don't think you necessarily have to have a sympathetic character, but certainly one who's human and understandable. That was what was interesting about her: in a genre sense she was your *femme fatale*, but at the same time she was just a kid. In the script she was eighteen, nineteen.. Innocence and corruption coexist, and she isn't in control of what she does in the way that she is in the book. Another thing in the film which isn't in the book is that she's suddenly scared of losing Merton and sabotages her own plot. She's a bit of a bungling villainess, and again that made her seem more human and more understandable – if not more sympathetic – as a result.

In the book, Merton is more of a travel writer than a radical journalist. Why did you decide to give him that background, since he later dismisses those principles in a single line during a conversation with Milly?

That scene is almost like a confession. He can't tell her that he's actually part of this dreadful plot to make her fall in love with him and eventually get her money, so what he does tell her is, 'I'm not the person you think I am. I'm corrupt at heart.' I think he really believes that at that stage, too, in the sense that they're away from London society and values become much more primitive. He starts off believing very strongly in his left-wing ideals, but they're all abstract and he writes about them at a distance. The erosion in his belief in his own morality is why his redemption is so important, and why the ending imposed on the film was so confusing. He's too weak to stand up to the stronger personality, but in the end he's so guilty that he gives up the money and Kate. The happier ending, which was different from the script, muddled this idea of 'I don't want the money and I can't live with you'. In effect, 'I want to live with my guilt'. One way to read the imposed ending is that he's going back to Venice to remember Milly, but the way it was perceived by a lot of people was that he accepted the money. When I was writing it and when we were making it, it was clear that at the end there may not have been a moral redemption but there has been a moral realisation.

In other words, the film should end with Merton alone on the bed after refusing to tell Kate that he has no feelings for Milly.

That's what it was. I still don't like the ending, but in its favour I have to say that when I went and watched the film in New York, where a lot of the audience were older ladies, I noticed that they were chatting as they came out of the cinema. I think that was Harvey Weinstein's rationale behind it, and he's very good at judging that sort of thing. He told me that you need to give your audience an 'out'. I'm not saying that was the right 'out', but there was something really sudden about *Jude* – and possibly the original ending of *The Wings of the Dove* – and what you tended to see if you watched an audience coming out of a cinema were these slightly dazed faces. If they come out talking about the film, with something to discuss, you wonder if somehow that finds its way into the box office.

It could have been a lot worse. The film could have ended with both of them going to Venice and meeting each other and getting back together.

Oh, yeah. I've worked with Miramax a lot, and I think their instincts and their intentions are always fantastic. I was just disappointed at the time because you're fighting for the ending you want. I had this passionate speech prepared, and I went to see Harvey at the Savoy, where he was staying, and he sat there and nodded, and at the end of it he said, 'Hoss, how many people saw your last movie?' I was speechless, and everyone else in the room was trying not to giggle, and then he said, 'Do you want to be the king of no box office or do you want to get an Oscar nomination?' And oddly enough . . .

You got an Oscar nomination.

Yeah. Harvey really does look out for the people who work for him, and it's fantastic to have someone like that behind you. But I think it's right to have the battles because that's part of the creative process. You sometimes need someone to bully you into looking at the script again or looking at the film again. You start lying to yourself and saying, 'This is brilliant and perfect as it is', which is very rarely the case, and that honest person or that powerful person who comes up to you and says, 'It's not good enough', is often a very useful ally. I wrote him a letter when I was trying to keep the ending as it was. I thought, 'I have to be diplomatic about this', so the first paragraph said, 'I've enjoyed working with Miramax and your support has been great'; the second paragraph said, 'Please don't change the ending'; and the third paragraph said, 'I'd really like to work for Miramax again and have really enjoyed this experience.' And I got a reply from Harvey's office saying, 'Harvey thanks you for your first and third paragraphs.'

What was it like being nominated for an Oscar?

I used to stay up and watch them and have bets on them with my family, so it was fantastic. It was a four-hour ceremony, and I didn't go to the bathroom once because I didn't want to miss a moment of it. They're the last of the awards to be announced, and there were two or three things I'd been nominated for in the period leading up to them – which made it even more tense. I lost to *L.A. Confidential* every time, but when Walter Matthau was announcing the Oscar there was a brief moment where he stumbled over the name. No one else had a difficult name to pronounce, so when he said, 'And the winner is . . .' just for an instant I thought, 'Could this be an upset?' I'd forgotten about Brian Helgeland. I vividly remember sitting in the same row as Brian Helgeland and Curtis Hanson, who won for *L.A. Confidential*, and we all knew they were going to win it and deserved to win it, but I felt this urge to go and grab their Oscar. And I desperately want to go back.

Did it make a big difference to your career?

It made a huge difference in terms of pay and the quality of stuff being offered, but it's funny because I haven't had a film made since – apart from *The Four Feathers* and *Gangs of New York*, which were both rewrites. It's very important for an English writer going over to the States to get the lie of the land. The big advantage that a writer who lives in Hollywood has is an awareness of the various relationships going on: which company is about to go under or how many other projects are the same as yours. I was incredibly lucky to get the Oscar nomination, but there was a moment where I could have capitalised on that and got something made here. There was a three-year gap between *The Wings of the Dove* and anything else going into production, and a lot of that was trying to break into Hollywood and not really knowing the rules.

In fact, you already had two projects in hand by the time the film was released: *In a Lonely Place*, an adaptation of the book by Dorothy Hughes, and *Shanghai*, your second major original screenplay.

I wrote *In a Lonely Place* before *The Wings of the Dove* came out, and was writing *Shanghai* when it came out. Hollywood is amazingly fast at being interested in new talent. Over here, it can take for ever to get a meeting with some of these production companies or commissioning editors. Over there, a script is read overnight and you usually get an extensive set of notes. Everything moves much more quickly. Within a week of *Jude* getting its financing at Cannes, I had calls from all the major American agencies, and Nick Marston hooked me up with UTA and a fantastic agent called John Lesher. This happens to a lot of writers who go from here to America. Your agents set up several days of meetings out there, so you're literally going from one studio to another, and half of these executives don't know who you are, but they're always really enthusiastic. I ended up working for two big producers: Stanley Jaffe, who had a deal at Sony, and Mike Medavoy, who was head of a company called Phoenix. Stanley wanted me to do *The Four Feathers*, which was in development for a long time before I eventually came on board, and I was totally uninterested in that, but I saw that one of his other projects was a remake of *In a Lonely Place*. I'd always loved the Nicholas Ray film with Humphrey Bogart, and had read the book out of curiosity, so I pitched for it and Stanley took a chance on me. It was on an open assignment list, and the good thing about that is you know what the studio wants – or what you think they want.

It was also a *film noir*. Why do you like that genre?

It's the love stories I find most interesting, that journey from innocence to corruption, which is an aspect of *film noir* that's not often explored. I like the look of it as well, but that's less important to me than the relationships: the emotional torture which people can inflict on each other without meaning to, the fact that you can love someone and destroy them at the same time, and the idea of not knowing how to love and loving too much. *In a Lonely Place* has a hero who is bright and good-looking and the most romantic person but still a monster, so totally disfunctional that he doesn't know how to organise his emotions. There's a scene at the end of the script which is based on *Breathless*, and the psycho Belmondo-like character saying, 'I love you. Why don't you love me back?' It's set in a diner the last time the couple gets together, and she's saying, 'Who are you? I don't know who you are', and all he can talk about is how much he loves her. I found that very moving. It wasn't in the book but it was where I felt the book was going, and of all the scenes I've written that one is my favourite.

Was it hard shifting gears from a pair of costume dramas to a modern thriller?

The book is so different from the original film that I thought we should just change the title and do a straighter period adaptation, but the brief was a modern adaptation and when I accepted that it was like being a beginner again. I'd always wanted to write for an American studio, but this was my first attempt at contemporary American dialogue and it was quite hard. I like doing period stuff, because I know as much about the setting as anyone else does, but I've never lived in America, so they could turn around and say, 'We don't talk like that.' They express themselves more clearly and openly, which is why you get that big speech in a lot of American films where people say how they feel. I find those really hard to write. Towards the end of the script there was a roadside argument between the cop and the killer, who are best friends, but I wrote a very quiet scene which was all about the way these two people looked at each other without saying anything. I remember Stanley saying, 'You were afraid to write this' – and he was absolutely right. I've never had a worse reaction to a first draft. Over here, everyone loves the script when you hand it in but you start hearing things behind your back, whereas he was so straight-up and honest about the whole thing. He phoned on Boxing Day – he spared me on Christmas Day – and said, 'The only reason I'm not considering another writer is that there are two scenes in this I absolutely love. We've got a lot of work to do.' End of conversation. I've been a huge fan of his ever since.

What was the studio reaction?

Producers have these deals with studios but they don't necessarily see eye to eye, and it quickly became clear that the studio's notes were very different from Stanley's. He was saying, 'Let's make the audience fall in love with this character then let them know he's a serial killer', and they were saying, 'Can't we tell this story from the cop's point of view?' I assumed that as a powerful man with a big career Stanley could get anything he wanted greenlit, but I should have stopped to think, 'What studio in their right mind is going to make a movie where the hero is a serial killer?' Stanley's idea was that if the part were not only written sympathetically but played by a star whom the audience would naturally respond to, you'd have that audience on a roller-coaster ride of not wanting that star to get caught. I've always been quite snobbish about the value of stars because I tend to watch movies for the director, but over the past year or two I've noticed that although stars may not be the best actors they do so much of the work for you as an audience. Unfortunately, a star was unlikely to play that part, so you instantly become one of hundreds of scripts chasing ten actors, and the chances of it getting made are minus one per cent before you even put pen to paper. It's a cliché that when someone sends you a book you say, 'Is there a part for Tom Cruise?' but that actually becomes a reality you have to be aware of.

Was it sent to Tom Cruise?

There was a week or so – I don't know how much of this is true, but this is what I was told – where he'd read it, was intrigued by it and there was a good chance he'd do it. Once upon a time the arty film-snob in me would have said, 'I don't want to write for Tom Cruise', but now I was thinking that if Tom Cruise did my movie my fee would double. I literally started talking to my wife about looking at houses. Then it got slowly watered down: 'Tom Cruise is having second thoughts. His next three films are lined up.' There was also a period when Adrian Lyne was interested in directing it. Stanley wanted him right from the start because of their relationship on *Fatal Attraction*. I was out there for the Writers Guild awards and Adrian Lyne was in New York and Stanley wanted to set up a meeting, so my whole family was flown first class and put up in a suite overlooking Central Park. I was having the time of my life. I thought I'd arrived. The meeting went pretty well and, again, for a week or two he was definitely doing it – and if the studio had been more in love with the material they might have pushed it further. If I ever get a chance, it's the script I'm most interested in directing. There's still something about the subject matter which really appeals to me, and I think it was just a couple of drafts away from being right. The problem is that it's been impossible to get the project out of Sony, because it's what they call a 'library picture'. They've made it before, so they can't give up the rights and it doesn't get put in turnaround.

How did the *Shanghai* commission come about?

In that week of meetings during the first go-see period, Mike Medavoy said he wanted to do a *Doctor Zhivago*-type story set in Shanghai. I didn't want to do that because *Doctor Zhivago* is not in my top twenty, but I said I'd love to do a *Chinatown*-type story set in Shanghai. That idea had stuck with me, and the fact that I got excited about it must have stuck with him, so I committed to do it after *In a Lonely Place*. Before I finally accepted the commission I woke up a couple of times in the middle of the night thinking, 'Don't do this', but there are all these parties around the week of the Oscars which make you feel extremely good about yourself and able to do anything. I did tons of research on thirties Shanghai, and had the idea of showing the city as a landscape of the imagination like *Blade Runner*. I wanted an opium den. I wanted a big casino with stripping booths. I wanted bars where Russian prostitutes dance with American sailors and snub Japanese officers. I was so in love with this world that in the first draft the central character almost became a guide through it, which meant that in the second and third drafts I had to concentrate more on the characters and the story and less on the description and the atmosphere. The research is my favourite part of the process, though. I sit there with a stack of books and lots of those coloured cards and take notes – white for plot, green for images – then finally, when I feel really guilty about not writing, I start the screenplay.

Why did it take you two years to write?

I read a book about writing crime thrillers which said, 'Imagine you're the one being sucked into the mystery', so I thought, 'I'm just going to riff', and got very stuck. I've never been able to imagine the whole script in my head before I start writing, so the problem with not sticking to my card outline was that I spent a lot of sleepless nights agonising about what to do the next morning. *Chinatown* is a very tough model to follow. The script is so intricate and Robert Towne makes it look so easy. In a complex thriller each scene has to do several different things, which is why they take a long time to write. The real craft is the relationship with the audience. Hitchcock said, 'Don't confuse the audience. If they're asking too many questions then they're not emoting.' That's a very important rule. *Chinatown* works because of that – and so does *L.A. Confidential*. Although they're incredibly complex, you're never asking questions you shouldn't be. Curtis Hanson actually gave me some advice about the script. He told me that the problem he had was that he felt detached from the central character because he was a spy. He said, 'What if his two friends are spies, but he's not involved in their world? Then you have audience identification, because he's an innocent and you're discovering things with him.' An obsessive hero who will not stop no matter what people tell him always makes for a powerful thriller. I've also realised from working on *The Four Feathers* that when a film's under financial pressure you can lose up to a third of the script in cuts, and a complicated plot-led thriller like *Shanghai* probably couldn't take that, so in the next draft I think I'm going to go through and simplify it.

Were you more comfortable with the dialogue scenes than the action scenes?

No, I was actually more comfortable with the action scenes. It takes me quite a long time to write dialogue. If I know I've only got action to write the next day I can relax the night before, whereas if I know I've got a big dialogue scene I get very stressed. I think better in pictures than in words. I'm still slightly concerned that my Japanese villain talks too much like an Oxford professor. The characters can't all have lived in America for five years or trained at an American naval academy. A film that works fantastically well in terms of accents is *Schindler's List*. The dialogue was written with a slightly foreign tilt but was still spoken extremely articulately. Your characters become less interesting if they're trying to express themselves in some weird pidgin-English. I tend to avoid that and assume that the actors will slightly adjust the dialogue to what they can do or what they want to do.

It's an intimate epic until the final scenes, depicting the evacuation of Shanghai in the aftermath of Pearl Harbor.

For me, the thing was about a man investigating what he thinks is a crime of passion, which then spirals into this huge conspiracy but is actually as simple as two people in love. There's a line where the villain says to the hero, 'It all comes down to two people in the end.' Out of context it sounds quite cheesy, but it was all leading to this moment – probably my favourite thing in the script – where the hero's escaping with the girl he's in love with, chased by the villain who's just lost the girl he's in love with. They're about to get on the boat and think the guy's dead, then they spot him waiting by the gangplank and think that's it, but he sees them together and reflects on his loss and lets them pass. I'm usually a sucker for unhappy endings, but it was worth having a happy ending so that the bad guy could become a good guy just for a moment. It's like *The Wings of the Dove*: the baddies have intensely human characteristics which makes you question who they are and what they are – and makes them more compelling. It's also the sort of sequence which will tempt a director, I think.

Mike Newell, for instance.

Mike came on board *Shanghai* with big reservations, and the script moved away from *Chinatown* and towards *The Third Man* – which he knew better and liked more. It became much more internalised, about a spy lying to himself and betraying people, and the forward momentum of the thriller genre got lost. I was so desperate to have him fully commit to the movie that I was ready to make changes which I disagreed with. *Donnie Brasco* is a fantastic film so I felt that he had to be right somehow, forgetting that someone can be a brilliant director and still be wrong about a script. I was one draft away from getting the script I wanted, but when he came on board he wanted something else, so I went from the third draft to the first draft of a completely different film. Then, two or three weeks before we were supposed to hand the script in, he suddenly said, 'I think we're making this worse.' I panicked because *The Four Feathers* commitment was looming, ended up doing an incomplete fourth draft which I would never show to anyone and was lucky to get paid for, then Phoenix said, 'We're going to get another writer.' I fought a bit and said, 'I know this script better than anyone. Let's just wait three months and if we lose Mike we lose Mike', but they weren't prepared to do that. So I suggested Becky Johnston, a friend of mine who wrote *Seven Years in Tibet*, and although she did a fantastic job it was very different, and I felt pissed off that they would go with a director who wasn't even fully committed. It's like snakes and ladders, and it can go on for ever until the project loses its heat or they run out of development money. Directors have an extraordinary amount of power – unless you've got a producer who is brave enough to say, 'I can get another director. We like this script the way it is and we refuse to change it the way you want to.'

Who was the producer on the project before it was bought by Miramax?

We were working with a brilliant producer called Barry Mendel, and he stood up to Mike more when Mike had a bad idea. Unfortunately, he wasn't there for very long, so I've now realised how important producers are as a buffer between the writer and the director. Mike's a great director and a lovely guy, but at the end of the day I'm a writer and he isn't, so I should be as convinced of my abilities as he is. It's almost unheard of for a writer to have a screenplay bought back for them, but hopefully now that I've got a second crack at it I can get back to the *film noir* story which was beginning to find its shape before he came on board. After that experience, though, I wouldn't particularly want to write another original which I didn't at least have a chance of directing myself. It just pisses you off the way people love the script one moment, then the hot director says, 'Something is wrong with it', and they say, 'You're so right', as if the writer's not in the room. If a director comes on and says, 'This is my next film and I'm in it as deep as you are', then of course they have to make it theirs, but if they come on and say, 'I'll think about committing to it if you make the following changes', it's very difficult to get passionate about writing it. That was one of the problems with *The Four Feathers*. The only people who'd lived it, breathed it, really truly believed in it, were Stanley and Bobby Jaffe. They were the ones who found the book and thought it would be great to remake it. They were the ones who paid three writers and went after the director. And when they're gone, what's left? Me, who turned it down three times and only did it for the money, and a director who came in saying he didn't like the script.

What did you learn about Hollywood from those three years writing *Shanghai* and *In a Lonely Place*?

I learned that contrary to popular belief American executives are much more able than their British equivalents in terms of script development. American screenplays tend to be far more polished than British ones, because they have to be liked forty million dollars' worth as opposed to one million dollars' worth, and most of the notes you get are about character not plot. Part of the skill of screenwriting is learning to deal with producers' notes. The ease with which you can be replaced, especially in Hollywood, means you have to take some of them on board, but you have to be very disciplined about which you take on board and which you ignore – judging a bunch of executives and trying to work out which are giving you notes because they genuinely believe it and which are just trying to impress their boss. The second stage, I think, is learning to deal with directors' notes. You can be seduced by people whose films you love, so you spend a long time working on a script then some great director says, 'What if you do this?' and because you really admire them you accept it without questioning it hard enough, whereas if it was anyone else you'd say, 'Screw you!' I've promised myself I won't do that again. The best thing about notes is that they're a great stimulus for writing another draft. When you finish the second or third or fourth draft you've pretty much written it as well as you can and it's always hard summoning up the energy to write another one. If someone gives you fantastic notes they can be like a bucket of water waking you up to have another go.

Why do you think Stanley Jaffe wanted you for *The Four Feathers* – because you were known for adaptations, or because the script needed a touch of ethnicity?

I think Stanley wanted me because he wanted a British writer. There was a very telling moment when I was in a meeting in

LA and the executive said, 'We've just had one of your fellow countrymen in here', and I was thinking, 'Which Iranian film-maker could that be?' and then he said, 'Mel Smith'. I'm proud of my Iranian heritage but I don't feel that I'm an Iranian writer, and what's so great about the American approach is that it's colour-blind and you're just seen as British. Stanley loves British writers and British subject matter. Alan Plater wrote the first draft of *The Four Feathers*, but what they got was something beautifully written which they wanted to turn into an adventure movie. Then an American writer called Michael Schiffer did several drafts – he wrote *Crimson Tide* – and having got an adventure movie they wanted to go back and give it some Britishness. It was supposed to be a technical rewrite, but I just got sucked into the whole thing. I read one draft of Alan Plater's and one draft of Michael Schiffer's and I felt I had to put in a call to Michael Schiffer, which was pretty uncomfortable. He was incredibly sweet, but you're promising someone that you won't do much to their script – and you know you will. I'm surprised it's the third thing I've done which is coming out, because it doesn't feel like mine at all. It's not one of my favourite old films, and that's one of the reasons I didn't want to do it.

Was there a director attached at this point?

They'd sent it to various directors, all of whom had passed on it, so it wasn't going anywhere. Paramount and Miramax were both interested but neither had made a firm commitment. Stanley and Harvey were both pressuring me to do it and I owed the two of them quite a lot. So I said to my American agent, 'There's no way I want to do this. It's just not my kind of thing', and he said, 'We'll ask for a ludicrous amount of money. They'll move on to somebody else.' But they didn't. They came up with the money and I thought, 'This is never going to get made but I might as well do a good job.' Then I started writing it and I really got into the material. I was working with Stanley's son, Bobby, and he's terrific at getting you excited about something. I love Westerns and thought that the British army going off to war in the Sudan was the equivalent of a Western setting. It was a very African war which has always been presented as Arabic, so I started researching the various Sudanese tribes, and there was one scene where tribe after tribe of the Mahdi's army were riding out in different uniforms. Unfortunately, it was too expensive to film.

When did Shekhar Kapur commit?

Shekhar was the first director they approached with this draft and he was interested straight away, so there was this overwhelming desire to get him involved and get the thing going as quickly as possible, because it was one of those projects which had been around for a long time. I was working on *Gangs of New York* by this stage, and had a commitment to do one more pass for Mike Newell on *Shanghai*, so I said, 'I'm not going to be available until June', and they said, 'We'll wait.' Shekhar, who is very charming and seductive, said, 'I only want to do this script with you', and Stanley and Bobby were saying, 'Don't worry. It's ready to go. It'll be a tiny rewrite.' June came, and I hadn't finished the Mike Newell draft of *Shanghai*, and I couldn't do any more work on *Gangs*, and I was more desperate to be involved in either of those projects than to do a rewrite on *The Four Feathers*. Then there were all sorts of creative disagreements, and for three months – which should have been four weeks – Shekhar liked every scene I wrote which the Jaffes disliked, and vice versa. There was a real will on everyone's part to make it work, but the Jaffes saw it as a heroic story about courage and friendship, and Shekhar, who's Indian, saw it as a great opportunity to subvert material related to colonialism and turn it into something anticolonial.

Did you manage to subvert the material?

However much you try to subvert it, the story is structured in a heroic fashion: a man has everything, loses everything, goes off and finds himself and regains everything. That was one of the big problems I had doing Shekhar's version. For example, in one draft, the first time we cut to the Sudan he wanted British soldiers killing Sudanese prisoners of war. This actually happened, and there was documentation to prove it, but it left you nowhere to go with the story. So then you get into a juggling act: can you make the army look unsympathetic but keep your hero sympathetic? And then you get into something really anachronistic: turning against what your country's doing, like Vietnam, which wasn't the case at the time. Whatever intentions we started out with – Shekhar more than me; I don't have quite the same anti-colonial attitude he does – we found that the story would still be the same. I've just started to watch some of the assembled footage and what's really striking is that the story still comes through. You can subvert it in the details, but what hooks you is the heroic stuff.

So it turned from a technical rewrite into a production rewrite?

A very troubled production rewrite. The tension between the director and the producers reached an impasse, Stanley and Bobby left the picture and Paramount handed over creative control to Miramax – so there was a whole new set of chiefs. Luckily for me they were people I get on really well with, but they wanted it rewritten again because Shekhar felt that it was the Jaffes' script not his. In a way it was nobody's, because it had been used in this political battle. It's the first time I've been involved in a script where, even if no one says it directly, there's a sense that it's something which requires constant fixing. Every day everything was up for grabs, which meant an ego-battering few months of on-set rewrites. Shekhar has a very improvisational style, and when the British actors im-provised they sometimes came up with far better stuff than I would have done, but when you have American actors ignor-ant of the language and the culture improvising period lines, you get stuff in the rushes which makes you tear your hair out. It's not just the improvised stuff: a lot of the lines I don't like are my own. I love what's not said and for a line of dialogue to create an energy in the pause that comes after it, but some-times the actors just needed to know what their characters were about and the lines weren't doing it. I felt that you'd get it in the edit, and in the scenes I've seen you do, but try telling an actor that they can say everything they want to say in one line. On the page it feels flat and bland, but with the silence and the music and all those other elements it becomes huge.

What was Miramax's attitude?

Miramax were behind me in the sense that they were as worried as I was about the lines being changed. There were some brilliant executives on the film, thank God, but there were no producers who had invested in the project like the Jaffes. Miramax were protective of the script, but quite often there's nothing you can do if the director wants to try something on the day. The problem with doing that on something like *The Four Feathers* is that the narrative is what makes it work, so you might gain a moment of magic but you lose something key to the story and the continuity of the next scene suffers. Shekhar's ambition for the film was also twenty or thirty million dollars more than the money we had, so at some stage the completion-bond company got involved and we had to lose a lot of scenes. The bond company insures a film up to a certain amount and once it goes over that they start paying all the extra costs, so the studio was giving me my creative instructions but the pro-ducer who replaced the Jaffes was conveying messages from the bond company like, 'This scene has been bonded at two-

and-three-eighths of a page. If it runs two-and-four-eighths we're not responsible for the overages.'

It's a slightly unusual position for a screenwriter to be in.

It's very unusual and not very comfortable. I saw scenes which worked less well than they should have done because the side of me which wanted to cut this scene in order for that scene to be shot had taken out some crucial stuff. The one thing I will say about Shekhar is that he's a fighter, and he finally ended up championing the script much more than me. My attitude was, 'If we don't lose this scene then we're going to lose this scene further down the line', whereas he said, 'I want this and I want this and I want everything'. I was compromising because I was prioritising, and now I hope that something interesting comes out of all this hassle and heartache. Although it's the material I've cared least about, it's the production I've been most involved in – where my being there in a production capacity actually made a difference. I've got to champion Miramax, because they were fabulous at holding together a film which was on the point of collapse. The one thing I admire about them, Harvey particularly, is that they're so passionate about movies. I think his job's fairly safe, so he's fearless in a way that a lot of people in the industry aren't, and he will take a risk. He has on this and he has on *Gangs of New York*, which is a huge commitment.

Is that why you rewrote *Gangs of New York*, because it was with Miramax?

Harvey got me in there, but Miramax can't impose a writer on Scorsese. He's running the show.

What was it like working with him?

It was like a dream come true. I spent a month in New York staying in a brilliant hotel, walking to his house every day and working with him. He's always been a big hero of mine, and he's an incredibly generous person creatively. I would write in the morning and show him stuff in the afternoon, and he would start by being very excited and very positive about what he liked, so the first thing that hits you is, 'Wow! Martin Scorsese loves my scene!' Then, slowly, he starts fiddling with it and changing it and, 'How about this?' and, 'Maybe we can do a bit more there', and by the end he could have moved the scene around a complete 180, but the fact that he has instilled this confidence in you means that you feel like the greatest writer in the world working with the greatest film-maker. I had a few weeks in Rome doing the same thing. It was hard, because I like to have my books and my videos and my familiar environment, but there's also an adrenalin rush, because you've got to get a certain amount of pages for him to have a look at.

How long did you work on it in total?

I probably did about seven or eight weeks. Basically, Jay Cocks and Martin Scorsese spent years writing seven or eight drafts of it. Then I came on and did a draft, getting it to a stage where it could be greenlit. Then Steven Zaillian came on and did two drafts, completely transforming the structure and dialogue. Then I came on and did another quick draft, working on character stuff just before shooting. Then Kenneth Lonergan rewrote it as they were shooting and put in a lot of humour. It wasn't one of those messy rewrites with too many writers. Scorsese was always there, every writer was reporting back to him and he was one of the writers himself – so the script did get better. I suppose they'd hit a wall with it, or maybe the studio thought they'd hit a wall with it, and they just wanted a fresh pair of eyes. And then another fresh pair of eyes. And then a third fresh pair of eyes.

If the structure and dialogue were overhauled by Zaillian, and the humour and human touches were provided by Lonergan, what were you approached to do?

It was character, I think, more than anything. The first draft I did, I worked quite a lot on the love triangle involving a character called Amsterdam, the Leonardo DiCaprio character. The second draft I did, I was dealing with Amsterdam's character because he was a bit like The Man With No Name, very silent, and DiCaprio and Scorsese wanted more emotional vulnerability. It was also an availability thing. After I did my first draft, I was very flattered because he asked me to do some more work on it, but I had to go off and do *Shanghai*, the Mike Newell draft. When I look back on it I think, 'God, I could have worked flat out on *Gangs of New York* instead of doing a botched draft of *Shanghai*', but you can't really think like that. The second time around, I was brought in because Steve Zaillian wasn't available, then suddenly *The Four Feathers* was in trouble and I was taken off again. I doubt I'll get a credit but it was a fantastic experience, and I was as passionate about it as other stuff I've worked on.

You went to see Scorsese shooting the film. What did you learn from that?

He has a fantastic movie-brain – and brain generally. You can see how much thought goes into each shot. A lot of directors move the camera because they're bored or they think the audience is going to get bored. With him, each time the camera moves there are so many ideas behind it. There's a very good reason why he is who he is and has made such consistently great films. He is the master.

Have you contributed to any other scripts recently?

It's embarrassing to talk about uncredited work, not necessarily because of the films themselves but because you're supposed to be invisible. It's not like *Gangs of New York*, or even *The Four Feathers*, where you put your heart into it; it's literally, 'Fix a scene here', or, 'Fix a line of dialogue there', but you sometimes get paid as much for two or three days' work as for an entire script, and it's very hard to resist. What tends to happen is that you're not brought on by the director, and however gracious they are about it they don't want your stuff anyway. I actually wrote some scenes for *Enemy at the Gates*, but only one or two lines survived. Jean-Jacques Annaud is a terrific guy, so I was made to feel very welcome, but you don't know who's really hiring you and you don't know why they're hiring you. You don't know if it's the director trying to pacify the studio or the studio trying to push the director – if they're ever going to use what you've written.

Which scenes didn't survive?

There was originally a deeper friendship between the Jude Law and Joseph Fiennes characters, and I thought it would be great to have this moving, tragic scene at the end between these two enemies who had once been friends. So I wrote this incredibly long scene, and when I see the rough cut they get through the lines in the official version of the script, then Joseph Fiennes opens his mouth to say the first line of my speech, and suddenly a bullet crashes through the window and blows his head to pieces. Which I think is a very effective way of saying, 'We didn't like your dialogue'.

Tell me about your recent deal with Miramax.

I have to write one more script for them, and the next one I get to write and direct. *Mila 18* is also for Miramax, but I'd agreed to that before this deal came into play.

Were they simply impressed by *The Wings of the Dove* and *The Four Feathers*?

I think it was more to do with *Shanghai*, because there had been a situation where John Madden wanted to direct it after *Shakespeare in Love*. This wasn't like the thing with Tom Cruise. I'd met John, and he was ready to commit, and everyone was very excited. But he had a similar deal with Miramax to the one I've now got, so if Phoenix – via Sony – wanted to get John Madden they had to set up a Sony–Miramax co-production. Harvey really liked the script and wanted to get involved but at that stage Sony decided they didn't want Miramax involved, because the studios all spend ages developing projects and then Miramax just waltzes in through these talent-based deals. There was an agonising few weeks where Sony and Miramax were negotiating, and in the end Mike Newell was attached instead of John, who went off and did *Captain Corelli's Mandolin*. But the combination of the fact that Harvey had read and liked *Shanghai*, and a degree of frustration that he wouldn't have been shut out if I'd developed it for Miramax, helped the deal – as well as *The Wings of the Dove* and *The Four Feathers*.

Did you sign the deal because they were willing to give you a shot at directing?

Partly. They also seem by far the friendliest home, not only in terms of the executives who you deal with but also in terms of investing in films which are ambitious as well as mainstream. The kind of people who have deals there are John Madden and Anthony Minghella. *The Talented Mr Ripley* was incredibly ambitious, and no one else would have touched that material. It's also a place where you can get a decent amount of money and stand a fairly good chance of the films being made. I do want to move into directing, but I have no idea how one short film will translate in terms of feature films. I sometimes wonder if the arrogance you have when you're starting out in your early twenties is still there. A fear of failure creeps in, and although I want to direct as much as ever I feel far less secure about it than I did at twenty-four or twenty-five.

Do you think those kind of insecurities can wreak havoc on your writing?

I think they probably do. There are very few fun moments in the whole thing. The first draft is probably the most fun, because after that the criticism starts – and waiting for the film to get made has its own miseries. Then the film does get made, which is a high point. Then the film starts shooting, and you look at rushes and the fear sets in again. Then the film comes out, and you ignore the good reviews and memorise the bad ones. I'm plagued by those kind of insecurities, and I'm curious to know what the effect of one great film would be, one knockout success that gets the reviews and the audiences and the prizes, because a fear of failure is one of the things which keeps me going as a writer. I genuinely don't think I've achieved very much. When someone asks, 'What do you do?' and you say, 'I'm a screenwriter', and they say, 'What have you written?' it's almost embarrassing to say, 'Well, *Jude* and *The Wings of the Dove*', because then they say, 'Oh. I saw *Titanic* the other day and that was a great movie.'

Wouldn't you rather have written *Jude* than *Titanic*?

I'm not so sure. My ambition may be to write something like *Chinatown* or *The Killing Fields*, but the working writer in me also admires scripts like *Ordinary People* and *Dead Poets Society*. It's not so much that I want to write more commercial movies; it would just be nice to come up with a film which people have actually seen.

Have the tone and routine of your writing changed now that you have a family?

I'm far more aware of the need not necessarily for a happy ending but for something with a promise of catharsis. The more you see – sometimes through looking at kids – an audience's enjoyment of what they're watching, the more you start to respect that and the less it becomes about thinking, 'I'm going to write whatever I want and screw the world.' There's a famous saying that the worst thing that can happen to a writer is a pushchair in the hallway. I don't think that's true. I've probably taken on more jobs for the money than I would have done otherwise, but I'm too selfish to let my family affect my routine too much. For example, sleep is crucial. If I haven't had six or seven hours' sleep I write absolute crap the next day. Normally I write from about nine until two, but if I haven't slept well I'll have a very bad day from nine until two and then keep trying to write. There have been days when from two until six I've literally written the same line again and again and again, changing words around and printing it out until I lose all perspective and go completely nuts. I used to think that was because of difficulties with scenes, but actually quite a lot of it is to do with sleep.

Simon Beaufoy was born in 1966, in Keighley, and educated at Ermysted's School, Sedbergh School and St Peter's College, Oxford. He lives in London with his partner and their baby daughter.

FILM

The Full Monty (Peter Cattaneo, 1997, US/UK)

Among Giants (Sam Miller, 1998, UK)

The Darkest Light (Bille Eltringham/ Simon Beaufoy, 1999, UK/Fr)

Blow Dry, based on the screenplay *Never Better* by Simon Beaufoy (Paddy Breathnach, 2001, Ger/UK/US)

This is Not a Love Song (Bille Eltringham, 2002, UK)

When did you first become interested in screenwriting?

It was an accident, really. I actually trained as a documentary director. My first paid job was making a documentary for the BBC series *40 Minutes* – or, rather, completing a documentary which I'd started at Bournemouth Film School. I began writing drama because there was a lot of space between documentary projects, but my documentary background means I've always been interested in people first and story second.

In fact, *Among Giants* started out as a documentary idea.

Yeah. I was sorting out my paperwork the other day and I came across the original treatment for it, a ten-minute documentary about pylon-painters. I submitted it as a *10 × 10*, which was the BBC's short-film slot, and it was turned down, but a drama called *Physics for Fish*, which I'd written with Bille Eltringham, was accepted instead. I was more interested in getting the documentary off the ground than the drama, but I could never get permission to film a group of painters because these guys break all the safety regulations. In the end, I got bored with waiting – and I was unemployed – so I started writing it as a drama. It struck me that you could do anything with a drama.

Draw inspiration from a girlfriend's climbing accident, say.

That's right. She was in a spinal-injuries ward after falling off a cliff, and I would go up to Sheffield to see her. I always start with a visual or a thematic aspect, and the ideas for both *Among Giants* and *The Full Monty* came from wandering around Sheffield in the rain waiting for visiting hours.

Watching lots of other men wandering around in the rain.

That's what occurred to me. It was a reversal of all your expectations: the women were working and the men weren't.

The women had fairly crap jobs, but at least they were earning money and had a disposable income – and were doing something with that disposable income, which normally involved going out on a Friday night – whereas the men had expected to be apprenticed in the steel industry like their fathers and grandfathers, and were unsurprisingly not prepared to work in supermarkets. It was a very odd place to be at that time, Sheffield; it's very different now.

What inspired your interest in pylon-painters?

I've always been fascinated by landscape and architecture, and how they affect and reflect the character of the people living in their midst. I was born and brought up in Keighley, and as a kid my mum used to take me down to Hebden Bridge, which was the industrial equivalent of the Valley of the Kings. The whole area was full of derelict warehouses and abandoned machinery, and you could wander from one empty woollen mill to another in a long line all the way down the river. There was something very beautiful and grand and sad about it all, not just the mills but the mill chimneys and the gasometers and the cooling towers – a magnificent dereliction. My mum is an environmentalist so she's always seen pylons as an encroachment of man on the countryside, but I have a much more ambivalent attitude towards them because they're very beautiful structures to me. We were able to film on them because only one side of the power lines was being used: Sheffield isn't an industrial town any more so it doesn't need all that power. It only needs power to light the Meadowhall Shopping Centre, which was built where the steel mills used to be.

Would you say that your central theme was very much to do with place?

That's what inspired me to write a film rather than a stage play or anything else – how people are dwarfed by a gigantic industrial landscape – but the greater theme was how people can crush what they want most by trying to pin it down. This guy falls in love with a free spirit and the first thing he wants to do is marry her, which is a completely natural and understandable impulse but would take away all her freedom of spirit. The idea of a woman among a group of men also interested me. Groups of men have always interested me: how they operate together and how they operate when an outsider comes in.

Were the painters meant to resemble a bunch of cowboys?

Yeah. The campfire scene, the whiskey-drinking scene and the wagon train of vans were specifically Western references, because I felt that these pylon-painters were like frontiersmen: a group of people forced together for long periods of time in the middle of nowhere who finally hit town and create havoc. That's exactly what these guys did. They earned really good money but had nowhere to spend it until Friday night when they headed for the nearest place with a pub, usually some village in the middle of the moors. So it was very much like a Western, although with elements of a social drama and a love story. It made the film hard to market, because audiences are conditioned to go and see a love story or an action movie, and if you cross genres they apparently get confused – or, more likely, the reviewers get confused.

Did you find it difficult to get to grips with writing dialogue?

No, I find dialogue the easiest thing to write. It's also the most enjoyable thing, apart from waking up with the initial idea. You have a millisecond of pleasurable inspiration, then you have two years of boredom and frustration and angst – except when you get some dialogue to do, which is when your characters come to life. I've written two films which are really about the male psyche, because I've spent a lot of time among big groups of men, listening to them talk and wondering why I always felt like an outsider. I got a sixth-form scholarship to an all-boys school, which was formative in me being a screenwriter because I read a lot of plays and did a lot of acting, but I didn't have the same home life as everyone else, financially speaking. I played rugby for many years, and I've been on various hugely male climbing expeditions, and I never fitted in there either. Most of the characters in *The Full Monty* came from a summer I spent cleaning machine tools in a factory, and I felt like a naturalist sitting there and examining this gang of blokes. I ended up being able to write very easily about men, because I spent so long thinking about how they were different from me. Most writers don't fit in.

How long did it take you to write *Among Giants*?

It went through endless drafts over a period of about six years, during which time I learnt the 'craft' of screenwriting. It just came out as a long splurge, not particularly good technically but with a lot of life, then people tried unsuccessfully to fit it into a three-act structure. The thing is, *Among Giants* was never *going* to fit into a three-act structure. It still doesn't, really. It feels like an uncomfortable mix of an original story which I was interested in telling and a screenplay written by someone who wished he had never heard the words 'three-act structure'. The first draft was about 180 pages because I didn't even know how long screenplays were.

Did you think about reading other screenplays to see how it was done?

I was too frightened to. I'm very suspicious of becoming good at writing screenplays – and by 'good', I mean technically competent. I try to see as few films and read as few screenplays as possible. You start trying to find the key to why a film works, and then you start writing films in the same way. I can never go and see films when I'm writing because I start writing like the film I've just seen. You write all day and think, 'This is going well!' then you re-read it and think, 'This is the tone of the film I saw last night, not the tone of the film I'm supposed to be writing.' It gets in my blood really quickly.

Presumably the same applies to screenwriting manuals?

I keep being sent these screenwriting magazines from the States, and I find them absolutely blood-curdling: 'How to start your script! Ten ways to end Act One!' They use a load of jargon which I've never heard of, and it makes me think I know nothing about screenwriting. I have to put them in the bin, take a step back and say, 'I write screenplays! That's what I do!' If someone asked me how you can ensure that your secondary characters move into the main part of the screenplay at the defining moment of Act Two, I'd say, 'I don't know! Just trust the natural rhythm of the story!' I find the idea that there is *a way* of writing a film really scary.

Do you think the script was actually made weaker by the rewrites?

It just became a different beast, a hybrid. Most of the films I write are hybrids. I come up with a vague theme, then I find my characters and then I start writing. The idea of breaking down the story into three acts doesn't come up until some script executive turns around and says to me, 'I'm a little confused about where Act One ends and Act Two begins.' I know how to do that but it doesn't interest me at all, which is why our company has just done a digital film, and why I did an interactive film on the Web: to get away from this hidebound notion that there is only one way of telling a story. Everyone says that three-act structure is Aristotelian; it's not – unless they simply mean a beginning, a middle and an end. In fact, it was invented by the studios as a way of fitting stories into three little boxes which they could conveniently talk about. Life isn't that straightforward.

Did you have to pitch the script?

I've never had to pitch, which is lucky because I'd be rubbish at it. Any idea which you can encapsulate on the back of an envelope is not very interesting to me. I don't know anybody who *has* had to pitch, really. It's a myth that you can just storm into the BBC and say, 'Here's my idea', and they'll go, 'Here's the cash.' People are much more careful than that about commissioning ideas, certainly in this country. It doesn't matter if you're a brilliant pitcher; they want to know if you can write. That's the bottom line. Most writers have a long journey of endless meetings, and by the time you come up with an idea which people like, everyone knows you can write. It's a slower, more organic process than tripping up there with a cool pitch, then opening a bottle of champagne and going, 'The movie's in the bag!'

In that case, how did you set about placing it?

I sent it to a couple of producers, and one of them, Stephen Garrett, was quite taken with it. He was rather amused by such a massive tome, but he was very gentle about whittling it down. I was telling ten different stories, because each character went on their own particular journey, so we focussed on three main stories, one of which got lost in the edit. All the characters in *The Full Monty* go on their own journey, but the script is more succinct – better written, in craft terms – so you can squeeze more in.

You seem to be torn between finding notions of craft a help and a hindrance.

You're right. It's a deathly tension, in a way. I'm basically suspicious of craft because when misused, as it is so often in commercial cinema, it gives films a plastic veneer, anaesthetises the audience and is disrespectful to the whole storytelling process.

You can smell that kind of three-act Steven Spielberg storytelling a mile off: 'Make them cry now! Here comes the music!'

Yet people roll up in droves to see those kind of stories.

Absolutely. But it's not my job to make people roll up in droves. Everyone thinks it's my job because *The Full Monty* made a lot of money. That was just an accident; I was just trying to write a good film. But when Miramax come along and make *Blow Dry*, they think they can do the same thing all over again: squeeze different ingredients into the boxes marked Acts One to Three, and get *The Full Monty 2*. It's calculated and cynical, which is why I never wrote a sequel to *The Full Monty* despite being offered *vast* sums of money. The best thing about *The Full Monty* is its *lack* of cynicism. It was written, produced, directed and acted by people who simply wanted to make a good film. We had no idea that it would be a hit. In fact, we were fairly convinced that it wouldn't be.

I think everyone expected *Among Giants* to be a retread of *The Full Monty*.

I tried to warn people about this. 'A gang of blokes painting pylons. It's a retread of *The Full Monty*.' To me, it's a love story with jokes. Until quite late in the day, *The Full Monty* was a political story with jokes. Then, in the editing, it turned into a comedy with some politics. The politics, with a small 'p', is still there – the disenfranchisement of men since work ceased to be the mainstay of their existence – but the film was cut very short, it was cut for the gags and a lot of music was put underneath to lighten it up. I don't mourn the other cuts, because they weren't really working, but the film just leaped into a different genre. It's the one film I've written which does slot into a genre, and in some ways it's the least interesting because of it. To me, anyway.

So your other work suffers from being 'by the writer of *The Full Monty*'?

All the time. We had to fight to keep that off the poster for *The Darkest Light*. People would have been walking out if they had expected it to be like *The Full Monty*. *Among Giants* was inevitably compared with *The Full Monty* because it was marketed as a comedy, and the comparison was inevitably unfavourable because it was actually a love story. That kind of marketing is really damaging – and really stupid.

Among Giants also verges on magic realism, whereas *The Full Monty* is closer to social realism.

As long as it's emotionally believable, I like to push things a bit further than plain reality. But only a bit. It's not quite social realism, even though I was brought up on the *Wednesday Play* and *Play for Today* and come from a documentary background. And it's not quite magic realism, because nothing in *Among Giants* or *The Darkest Light* hasn't really happened to people. It's somewhere in between. Everyone remembers the dole-queue scene in *The Full Monty*, but it was nearly cut so many times because we all said, 'This isn't real. This wouldn't happen.' We got away with it because the scene comes fairly late in the film, when you're on a wave of generosity towards the characters, but it steps further outside the boundaries of social realism than I or the director or anyone else was comfortable with.

Did the scene stay in because preview audiences liked it?

I don't know why it stayed in. The problem was that we knew it was wrong but we loved it anyway. It was also one of the first scenes I came up with. I remember thinking, 'This isn't me at all. I don't want to do a tacky, voyeuristic film about male strippers.' But Uberto had read *Among Giants* and said I could do exactly what I wanted, so I thought, 'I will do a film about male strippers if I can really write about unemployment. How can I tie together unemployment and stripping?' And a bunch of blokes dancing in a dole queue seemed to say it all. I always like to have scenes like that in my work, which encapsulate what I'm trying to say in a single image, and they usually turn out to be the first ones I write.

The cooling-tower scene in *Among Giants*, for instance?

I had a sort of industrial-Eden scene in my mind, and I came up with the cooling towers when I realised that they were full of running water. It's unexpected, and very beautiful, to find running water at the bottom of these 200-foot-high concrete structures, and you rarely get close enough to see it – you just see the steam coming out of them. But that was very early on in my writing, and those scenes are visually strong but they don't quite knit together with the rest of the film. Similarly, there was originally a subplot in which the young guy involved in the love triangle is caught fiddling dole cheques and dies trying to escape from the police, but in the film there are only a couple of references to that because come the edit the thinking was, 'This slows the story down. This is another story altogether.' I would now know how to embed that subplot into the main plot so it wouldn't be cut out, which I suppose is good because it saves you filming unnecessary scenes. But I also know that there are certain things which won't work in a three-act structure, so I immediately feel censored by having learned a lot about the craft. What scares me is the danger of using so much 'craft' that you end up telling a more anodyne story. I don't want to know how to tell a story before I start; finding out how is the most important part of the writing journey.

The Full Monty is a very mainstream screenplay, though.

You cannot set out to make a hit film – just look at *Blow Dry*, which was a disaster – but we did sit down and say, 'Let's see if we can make a film about working-class people which working-class people will actually want to watch.' Uberto Pasolini is a very sharp producer, and he saw that the way to do this was to make it funny. Ken Loach's work has got funnier and funnier over the years, because I think he's realised that comedy is a way of pulling in audiences who might not otherwise go and see stories about unemployment and the disenfranchisement of men. It's a way of sugaring the pill – and sadly you now have to use more and more sugar.

Do you think you ended up with too much sugar on *The Full Monty*?

It's hard for me to say. It clearly didn't work in the way we envisaged, and it really does work in its current guise, so it would be a bit ridiculous to say, 'I wish it was the unsuccessful film I always wanted to make.' In fact, it became such a phenomenon that I can't say any more, hand on heart, that it *isn't* the film I wanted to make. I didn't *think* I'd written a feelgood comedy, but everyone else thinks I did so perhaps I did. But in some ways I am rather embarrassed that it was such a massive hit, because I don't usually write those kind of films. I write films like *Among Giants* and *The Darkest Light*, which have a much smaller, arthouse audience.

Did you change the ending of *Among Giants* before the film was shot?

Yeah. There was a certain amount of pressure writing *Among Giants* because people thought that the ending was too 'down', whereas we had a great deal of trouble editing *The Full Monty* because we all thought that the ending was too 'up'. I actually wrote a couple of scenes about what happens the next day, but the ending was such a showstopper that you couldn't really stick anything after it.

The fact remains that these guys will still be on the dole the next day.

That's absolutely right. They're only going to earn a few hundred quid from doing this. It might be a life-changing event in terms of self-respect, but not in terms of how much money they've got in their pockets at the end of each week. It was interesting showing the film in Sheffield, because people there had a much more serious response to it. By the end they were laughing as much as anyone, but for the first twenty minutes no one laughed at all. They were just sitting there going, 'This is what things are like.' I'm pleased when people say that they saw it at the cinema and thought it was a hoot, but saw it again on video and thought it was very sad – because there is a very sad thesis underlying the film if you want to see it.

That was ignored by Tony Blair: he cited the film as an example of 'Cool Britannia'.

He just wanted to associate himself with every major cultural event that was going on, which I thought was pretty hypocritical given that there were loads of theatres closing at the time. The film was about people whose lives were so desperate that they had to take their clothes off to earn a bit of cash – and I hardly see that as a fabulous advert for Britain. But I think there was a sort of optimism around just after the election, and unemployment was perceived as a problem of the past which you could now laugh at. If the film had come out in the middle of the Thatcher years, I wonder whether it would have done as well.

Were you trying to show that unemployment reduces men to a childlike state?

That's right. If you're unemployed you're bored, so you go and play on the swings and smoke cigarettes, or sit on a hillside and gaze into the distance. I also wanted to give the men a naive quality, because the film was meant to have a fairytale element about it. *The Full Monty* is like the fairytale version of *Among Giants*. The characters in *Among Giants* are more complex and have a nastier side, but I kept them quite simple in *The Full Monty* because I wanted to tell a very simple tale. It was important that you should really want these people to succeed.

How did the directors, Peter Cattaneo and Sam Miller, differ in their approach?

We had quite a loose approach to *Among Giants*. Sam let the actors improvise, which I completely agreed with because I thought it was right for that particular film. *The Full Monty* is pretty much what I wrote word for word. Peter cut out a lot of the jokes at the script-editing stage, but Uberto basically likes the script to be ready before he hands it over to a director. I now know how unusual that is, but at the time I simply thought, 'That's the way it should be.' I've almost had my career in reverse: I started off with very positive experiences and a massive hit, then went on to desperate experiences and commercial oblivion.

Were the jokes cut for the same reason that you nearly lost the dole-queue scene?

Yeah. Peter was very keen not to turn the characters into two-dimensional vehicles for funny lines and situations, but to make them three-dimensional so that you would be moved by them as well as finding them funny. That was my instinct as well, but I think he was braver than I was: it takes a lot of balls to look at a comedy and say, 'It's got too many jokes. Let's cut some out.'

What did the executives at Fox Searchlight make of decisions like that?

Fox Searchlight weren't that interested in it. It's hard to remind people now that this was a film which no one particularly wanted to make. We managed to get FilmFour to commission a second draft, but they weren't at all convinced. They'd already made a film set in Yorkshire, *Brassed Off*, and apparently you only go up north every once in a while. We sent it to the BBC, and they didn't even reply. It sat on a desk at British Screen. It was actually with Miramax for a short time, but Uberto pulled out of that. Fox Searchlight, the arthouse end of Fox, only stuck the money in because they were desperate: a couple more films which didn't work and the word on the street was that they were for the chop. Lindsay Law had made a film with Uberto before, and trusted him to get on with it. They didn't change the title, even though no one really knew what it meant. They didn't tidy up the vernacular for American audiences, because I don't think they thought it would get to America. They didn't force any stars on us, but just said, 'Cast who you like.' When Peter said, 'I'd like to cast this guy called Robert Carlyle', Fox said, 'Is he any good?' and Peter said, 'Yeah', and that was the end of the discussion. But it seems to be a revolutionary suggestion that if you leave the film-makers alone to make the film then it might actually be quite good. Instead of doing the same as Fox Searchlight, all the other studios go, 'How can we make something even more *Full Monty*-ish than *The Full Monty*? Let's change the title. Let's tinker with the script so as many people as possible can understand it. Let's bring some big stars in.' And what you get is *Blow Dry* – a film which ended up having few merits.

Did it come as a surprise when *The Full Monty* received an Oscar nomination for Best Original Screenplay?

Yeah, it did. We all thought the film was OK, but I don't think any of us thought it was more than OK. Peter sat down after he'd finished it and said, 'Perhaps it'll be one of those films which people stick on the video when they come back from the pub on a Friday night.' That was his ambition for it at the time, and I agreed. I thought it would be nice to make a film which people warmed to and were fond of. The idea of it cleaning up all over the world wasn't in our heads for one moment, so Oscar nominations were equally unreal.

When it did clean up all over the world, Hollywood must have come calling.

I went for a run once, and when I came back there were twenty-six messages on the answerphone. It wasn't even a marathon; it was only five miles. I found it very stressful, because I thought I had to ring them all back and politely say, 'No, thank you', rather than ignore them, which is what I do now. I naively assumed that people would think, 'This is a guy who writes about particular things. I wonder if we can find an interesting project for him?' Instead of which, they slung any old treatment at me in the hope that what Peter calls 'Monty Dust' might settle on it and the film would magically become a hit. Dino De Laurentiis rang me up and said, 'We want to make another *Conan the Barbarian* type of film. Do you want to write it?' I thought, 'Have you *seen The Full Monty*? Do I *seem* like the kind of person who would want to write another *Conan the Barbarian*?'

You were offered nothing of interest at all?

Not a single project – otherwise I would have done it. I don't dislike American cinema *per se*. I had an American agent for a while, but I got rid of them because they kept sending me garbage through the post. I would patiently say, 'I write stories about working-class people. Please don't send me any more scripts set in space', and they'd say, 'We completely understand.' Then they would ring back and say, 'They've added a nought', and I'd say, 'We discussed this. It's not about the money. It's about the integrity of the project.' It's hilarious, looking back, and wonderfully naive on my part. I tried to explain that I don't write big commercial movies. I even sent them a list of my favourite films, stuff like *Days of Heaven* and the work of Alan Clarke. I thought that they would listen when I told them these sort of things, but they thought that when I said no it was because I wasn't being offered enough money.

Were you ever tempted to do one for the studios and then one for yourself?

I don't understand that approach; you are what you write. All you've got is your body of work and your reputation as a writer. If a film is shit, I'm a shit writer. That's the reason why *Blow Dry* is so infuriating. My script wasn't the best script ever, but it wasn't a bad script, and now it *looks* like a bad script – even though the credit is 'based on the screenplay *Never Better* by Simon Beaufoy'. Ironically, I got stuffed by taking on a small British project in a similar vein to my other projects.

Who originally commissioned the script?

A company called West Eleven Films, which was just two people. I was happy to write a script for two people. Then Intermedia got involved, and it suddenly became a much bigger concern. Then Miramax got involved, and it went totally out of control. I was writing for a committee of producers. There were seven different producers, including Harvey Weinstein and Sydney Pollack, and I was getting seven different sets of script notes – all of which contradicted each other. I actually have it written into my contract now that script notes have to come from one source. Miramax hadn't even read it by the time they piled in. They thought that a script about competition hairdressing would be hilarious, little realising that I was writing about cancer and lesbianism. I stayed on board as long as possible to try and keep it on track, because the last thing a writer wants is to walk away from their own work, but in the end it became unbearable. The mainstay of what I write about is emotional complexity, and, as far as I could see, Miramax will allow all the emotional complexity of a Labrador puppy in their films: you're either happy or sad, and they'll go with one or the other – preferably happy.

I notice that no other writer is credited. Was the script rewritten after you left?

They brought in another writer. He wasn't even a bad writer, but by that stage it was a mess. They went the opposite way to *The Full Monty*. It should have been a $3 million film featuring a cast of unknowns, but it became a $10 million film starring American teen idols as people from Yorkshire – so even on a cynical level Miramax didn't do the thing very well. I kept using the word 'authenticity', and they'd simply stare at me as if I was talking Tibetan. They didn't understand that the authenticity of the characters was absolutely key to the film working.

What did you learn from this experience?

It made me even surer of the road I want to go down, in the sense that I will never do anything like that again. I'd rather stop writing screenplays. That's why I jointly formed Footprint Films in 1995: to work with people I know well and trust implicitly. I didn't have a bad relationship with the director of *Blow Dry* – we were just walked all over – but I've been working with Bille Eltringham since film school. She co-directed *The Darkest Light* with me, she directed our last film, *This is Not a Love Song*, and she'll direct our next one, *Waterloo Sunset*. Some companies have a massive slate of films and hope that one of them comes off, but we have a tiny slate and make them one at a time. We always said that we weren't going to do commercials and we weren't going to do promos, just drama and shorts. For ages we worked out of our bedrooms, and occasionally we've had to shut the office down because we can't afford to keep it going, but we believe passionately in the work we develop – which keeps us going in the bad times.

Did you write *The Darkest Light* before or after the success of *The Full Monty*?

I certainly wrote *The Darkest Light* before *The Full Monty* came out, maybe before we started shooting. I can't remember. I do remember making a conscious decision that it would be my next film, even though it was everybody's least favourite option. The big agents and the major studios would say, 'Have you got anything else?' and I'd say, 'Yes', and they'd say, 'Fantastic! Does anyone own it?' and I'd say, 'No', and they'd say, 'Wow! Can we have a look at it?' and I'd say, 'Yes', and this thing would come across their desks, and you could see them thinking, 'We've got it! It's ours!' Then they'd read it and go, 'What *is* this?'

If you deliberately sat down to write a script which would horrify the money men, you could hardly do better than leukaemia, foot-and-mouth disease and religious visions.

There's always that temptation, isn't there? Just to be really awkward. But, after some time, Pathé very bravely put the money up. And the Lottery helped because we got a lot of Arts Council funding. There was also licence-fee money from the BBC – as there was in *Among Giants* – which is a good way of getting the last bit of finance for a film.

Did the success of *The Fully Monty* help at all in setting up *The Darkest Light*?

Pathé, reading that script, cannot possibly have thought, 'There's a stripping scene hidden in here somewhere. We're going to clean up.' They're no fools. They're putting millions of quid in and they don't do that lightly. But it obviously helped in terms of my profile. And, because no one in the film industry knows anything, there might just have been some magic Monty Dust in there to make audiences turn out in droves to see a film about leukaemia, foot-and-mouth disease and religious visions. Which, sadly, was not the case.

Although foot-and-mouth disease may be old news by the time the film is aired on TV, it was actually quite a prescient script.

It should be screened now, really. It's not that different from a lot of the news footage. I think they use white suits rather than yellow, but it was pretty accurate in terms of the way they deal with the disease: spraying everything with disinfectant. We had to film *This is Not a Love Song* in Scotland because of it, but when we were shooting *The Darkest Light* everyone was saying, 'Is this a period piece?' because it was about foot-and-mouth instead of BSE. There was a lot of discussion about 'Why not BSE?'

Why *not* BSE?

Because foot-and-mouth is much more insidious. It's an air-borne virus; it doesn't just infect one type of animal, it infects all cloven-footed animals; and it has the potential to cross over into humans – which at one stage of the writing was very important, although it subsequently got written out. I used leukaemia as the human equivalent because you don't really know where it comes from, in the same way that they know foot-and-mouth started at a pig farm but they don't know how it got into the country. When I was researching it, all the vets were absolutely convinced that there was going to be an outbreak, and they were telling me about these warehouses in Cumbria stacked with disinfectant and coal and railway sleepers which had been mothballed since the last outbreak in 1966. They said, 'It's all sitting there waiting. It's only a matter of time.'

The theme of the film seems to be that when people are failed by the state and the church, they need to believe in something else – anything else.

Absolutely. That sums it up. I wanted to write about a beautiful landscape poisoned under the surface by men and governments, and how that chimes thematically with faith as something unseen and no longer to be trusted. I grew up in the prettiest part of Yorkshire – the Dales – but it never seemed very pretty to me. I couldn't square James Herriot's Yorkshire, all fluffy sheep and fluffy clouds and Farmer Giles walking his cows to milking, with my Yorkshire, full of dead animals in streams and depressed people on drugs and kids speeding around in stolen cars. It was a Yorkshire which I hadn't seen on film, because everyone had overdosed on the chocolate-box picture of the Dales and how lovely it is to be a farmer. All the time I was going to school there were rabbits with mixomatosis; radioactive sheep in parts of Cumbria – ten years after Chernobyl; leukaemia clusters around Windscale – now known as Sellafield; and army firing-ranges up by Penrith – fantastic to play on but littered with dangerous stuff.

And in the midst of all this – in the film, at least – people no longer go to church.

It's really interesting, what's happening to those spaces. People go to church to have community meetings not to pray, and some have been turned into climbing walls because the buildings are very tall. A climber falling into frame in front of a stained-glass window is quite a symbolic shot, and very un-British in terms of cinema. I was trying to take on every theme in the book – although, in the end, it's actually a simple story about a girl who thinks she can cure her brother by a sheer act of will.

Did you ever consider being more explicit about the 'vision' which the two girls see on the firing range?

We wanted to keep it ambiguous, because if you've answered the question, 'What is faith?' then in lots of ways there's no film. It's also an unanswerable question! Every day I had this eleven-year-old actor saying, 'What did she see?' and I'd say, 'What do *you* think she saw?' and she'd say, 'But what *did* she see?' You could have done a big special effect, but as I say those words I immediately think, 'That would be awful!' A special effect of what? The Virgin Mary? The idea is that it's probably a plane going over, which is how I got the idea for the whole film. I went walking in the fells, and was sitting having my lunch when a fighter plane came out of nowhere and nearly took my head off. It almost gave me a heart attack. You think you've had your shock, then the sound comes afterwards and knocks you over. That's something else you never see on film: the endless fighter planes going over the Dales.

One of the girls is Indian. Was that a way of exploring different faiths?

Having an Indian family there helped provide an outsider's view of this strange event, but it was also another part of my de-Herriotisation of Yorkshire. Every Yorkshire town, and most Yorkshire villages of any size, have Indian takeaways. I just wanted to move on from the cultural stereotype of what living in a farming community is like.

Whether or not you saw it as being a religious experience, the vision highlights the cultural differences between the two girls.

I saw it as being a bit like thunder: some children hide under the table and others go out and play in the rain. They're watching the same thing, but they have completely different interpretations of it. But it's not really about how the two girls interpret it; it's about how the people around them put interpretations on what the two girls saw. It was essentially a non-verbal experience which they had, but when somebody says, 'What did you see?' they have to start describing it, and they can only use the image system they've been given – and Catherine's is a Catholic one and Uma's is a Hindu one. The only words Catherine's got are, 'We saw something religious', which means she's immediately trapped, but in some ways it's very useful since she can then say, 'That means my brother's going to get better', because in her children's Bible that's the way God works.

Catherine believes the vision is a good omen but her brother dies of leukaemia; Uma believes it was a bad omen but at the same time her sister is born healthy. Were you trying to suggest something even more un-British: reincarnation?

I wasn't really saying that, but it's certainly been interpreted like that. I was trying to say that miracles do happen, but probably when everyone is looking somewhere else. Catherine wants the miracle to happen over here, but it happens on the other side of the hospital. The baby actually died in the first draft, and everybody went, 'For God's sake! Would you lighten up a bit?' I conceded that unremitting gloom is not helpful, and the fact that the child now lives reinforces the message that the only faith which a lot of people have left is faith in family and the continuity of life – which in itself is a kind of miracle. It also fits in better with the system of reversals which I often use in my writing to undermine expectations. You expect the community to pull together, but the nature of foot-and-mouth means people are scared to say hello to their neighbours. You expect the vision to be a good thing, but all it does is make visitors walk this contagious disease all over the fells. You expect the father to comfort his sick son, but instead he shaves all his hair off and then gets his son to do the same to him. If you do exactly the opposite of what people expect, it often bears fruit in quite odd ways.

Why did you decide to tell the story from the point of view of the two girls?

Adults ask too many questions. They sit and talk about things, and rationalise their way out of them. Children have a greater acceptance. They don't have the experience or the vocabulary to rationalise events, so they make more imaginative use of them. Catherine shamelessly manipulates this strange event, not out of cynicism but out of desperation that her brother is dying.

The children also allowed you a few moments of humour. Do you think humour is important in such a serious film?

I wish there was more humour in it, actually. It's packed with big themes. Life isn't simply all dark or all funny. *The Full Monty* is only as funny as it is because it's as sad as it is. The two things counterpoint each other. The humour in *The Darkest Light* is understated, but it's very important that it's there. I should have written more.

Why did you want to co-direct *The Darkest Light* – and who did what?

It depends on the project. *The Darkest Light* had a specific emotional landscape which I wanted to have a hand in creating, but there are other things which interest me as a writer and not a director. Bille is writing a feature on her own at the moment because it's a story very personal to her, but we have another feature which we're writing together because it felt right for the pair of us to do that. We don't know who'll direct that one. Could be her. Could be me. Could be both of us. If both of us direct, we do everything together in pre-production and post-production, then on the set we separate and one deals with the cast and the other deals with the crew. On this occasion, Bille dealt with the cast and I dealt with the crew.

In terms of your writing, did you learn anything from directing a feature which you hadn't learned from directing the earlier short films?

It's an endless learning exercise. I've just watched a cut of *This is Not a Love Song*, and I've realised for the millionth time that scenes which read well may not always film well. I basically started the story four times, with one carefully shaped scene after another, and each of them slows the film down. In the script you just flick from page to page, but on the screen you keep getting this enervating deceleration. You'd think that having directed I'd learn those kind of things, but I don't seem to.

What role does your producer, Mark Blaney, play in relation to you and Bille?

He's the business head. He steers things creatively and keeps the pair of us moving in the same direction. He's incredibly supportive, but he always reckons that with two co-writer/ directors working on the script a third person isn't going to be very useful. He gets the films made and keeps the company running while we bicker in the corner.

The film did get made and the company is still running, but some of the finance for *This is Not a Love Song* came out of your own pocket. Is that anything to do with the fact that *The Darkest Light* failed to make its money back theatrically?

I'm a complete believer in films which make their money back, especially if it's other people's money. *This is Not a Love Song* was going to be a 'difficult' film, so I thought I should put my money where my mouth was. *The Darkest Light* was also 'difficult' but we thought it would get its money back if it was marketed in the right way and shown to the right audiences. It will eventually make its money back from international sales, but it came out at a time when those sort of $3 to 5 million films weren't taking off – and subsequently most British films haven't taken off. They're not necessarily bad films. It's just that they don't suit the merciless ethos of the largely American distribution system: 'Let's look at the receipts after the first weekend, and if they're not brilliant we'll pull the film.' But how *can* you get big box-office returns over the first weekend with a film like *The Darkest Light*? It's just not that kind of film.

Why did you make the film as a cinema feature rather than a television drama, which would have instantly guaranteed you a much bigger audience?

That's a good question. You're right that it would be seen by a lot of people on TV, but I've always aimed for people to see my films in a cinema. I write with landscape and images in mind, and cinema is the place for those. And, to be honest, *The Darkest Light* wouldn't have been commissioned for TV in the present climate. Those single dramas don't exist any more, really, or if they do they're usually pretty dumbed-down.

Do you already have a distribution deal for *This is Not a Love Song*?

No, we deliberately made it without a distributor on board so we could retain as much creative control as possible. The Film Council put in a chunk of money, I put in a chunk of money and all of us deferred our fees: writer, director, producer and the production fee for Footprint Films. In return for that, we became joint investors with the Film Council. The lovely thing is that it was made very fast with a great deal of energy, instead of being three years in pre-production like most films. We actually shot it in twelve days for £250,000, with me and the producer doing the catering.

Why is the film so commercially difficult that you need to make it with some of your own money on such a low budget?

It's only 'difficult' in such an unadventurous market. It's got a beginning, a middle and an end – in that order. If it really is 'difficult' it's because it crosses genres: an action film which is also a love story. Between two men. Who are not gay. It's a sort of modern version of an old John Buchan story about two people who go to ground on the moors. They've shot somebody and a community gets together to find them, keeping the police out of it. It's quite scary having two main characters instead of a big ensemble in terms of keeping the audience interested for ninety minutes, but in many ways it was very liberating in that you have a lot of time to develop their relationship. I wrote it in a very different way as well. We had a four-page story outline and cast the leads from that, then I workshopped it with them and wrote characters tailor-made for those actors. It was another way of tricking myself out of the craft. The first cut looks really powerful, but the editor is going up the wall because the tone is so strange. It's a tense thriller, but it has an oddly humorous feel. It's about people being hunted down, but it has the lyricism of a love story – which works against the action genre.

What if the tone is so strange that you can't actually cut the film together?

That's exactly what I'm trying to do. How else will you discover new ways of making films except by pushing things as far as they can go? Not pushing them until you can't actually cut the film, but pushing them until you're forced to cut it in a completely different way. With ninety-nine per cent of films I know what will happen within five minutes of sitting down, because the manuals teach you to set everything up in the first scene and make sure everyone has an inkling of the story which is about to unfold. And that's boring. I won't do it. I *can* do it. I know *how* to do it. But it *worries* me that I know how to do it. Film-making isn't evolving, in fact it's going backwards – and I would rather not write films at all than write films which hark back to a way of film-making which was invented sixty years ago. *Waterloo Sunset*, which we're hoping to make next year, is probably as conventional as I get.

In a way, you are doing one for you and then one for them, in the shape of a difficult film followed by a more conventional film?

I'd never do something just for the money, but the only way you can keep on making films like *This is Not a Love Song* is by doing bigger-budget films which pay a bit better. *Waterloo Sunset* centres around a builder and his family, but a lot of it is about the transport system collapsing, so some scenes are set in Waterloo Station, which is very expensive to shoot in. It's just the size of film which isn't working at the moment.

Too expensive to keep control of but not expensive enough for people to see.

In a nutshell. People are making compromised films which please neither audiences nor themselves – and a film which pleases nobody is such a pointless exercise. I don't want to play that game. I've never written anything which didn't please me. Even with *Blow Dry*, the original script pleased me.

Waterloo Sunset is your first screenplay which doesn't take place in Yorkshire. Have you finished mining that landscape?

When you move away from a place, it becomes clearer in your head for a while and then it starts to fade. I've lived in London on and off for ten years, so I don't really know Yorkshire now. I did know the Yorkshire of *Among Giants*, but that landscape doesn't exist any more. Those abandoned mills have all been done up, and the mill chimneys have either gone or been turned into arts cafes.

You still seem to be merging the personal and the political, though.

I don't know how you can write a story which isn't political, with a big or a small 'p'. Everything's political. I couldn't care about a story which didn't impact on people in a fundamental way, whether it be gender politics or the politics of trying to live in a poisoned landscape. I was commissioned by FilmFour to write a film about Laurel and Hardy, and sure as hell that will turn into a story about Communism and the Red Peril.

In its own way, a film about Laurel and Hardy is as much of a departure for you as *This is Not a Love Song*.

It's a very big departure. I don't know why I'm doing it, really, except I thought that I couldn't. But when you think about it, I've been writing about dysfunctional men all my career, and

Laurel and Hardy are about as dysfunctional as they come. The brief was a biopic, but I said I wouldn't write one of those because it's impossible for me to stay faithful to the life of a real human being and make a good film. Those two dynamics work against each other. So I'm writing about their doubles, people who looked exactly like them and did a lot of their stunts and went to film premières instead of them, but who had none of the fame and the money and the glamour. And because Laurel and Hardy are quintessentially popular, I'm not scared of this particular film being quite high-concept and people casting ridiculous stars. Whoever they are they still have to be Laurel and Hardy, so it's sort of star-proof.

So you do sometimes think about how people will respond to what you write?

I always think about how people will respond, but I never think about *how many* people will respond – which, of course, is all that studio executives *do* think about. I'm not aiming for a Friday-night audience in Leicester Square; I'm aiming for an audience made up of people like me.

But in this case it would be rather wilful if you wrote an unpopular story about popular entertainers.

It would be very bloody-minded. It would also be doing them a terrible disservice if the script wasn't funny. But I'm having trouble getting my head around it, because the characters I've written until now have all been amalgams of people I've met, whereas I never met Laurel and Hardy, so I'm having to research everything and none of it is coming out of me. I've always said that I would never write characters if I didn't know exactly how they talked, which means I've got to find that out before I write anything. I've never done that before. I do minimal research, on the whole. The emotional truth is what's important to me.

You must sympathise with Laurel's studio battles for artistic control.

It's the oldest battle there is. There have been film-makers trying to do something new, and financiers trying to stop them, since celluloid was first turned through a camera. My films hopefully reflect the complexity of things – which, of course, spells box-office doom. If you say to executives, 'I want my films to reflect the complexity of things', they say, 'Thank you very much', and padlock the door.

Do you wonder from time to time whether you're actually working in the wrong industry?

Not from time to time; most days. Uberto Pasolini once said, 'Film-making is not for grown-ups', and I think he's right. Films are becoming more and more childish, more and more simplistic. The last film I saw, Tim Burton's *Planet of the Apes*, didn't seem to work on any level. The ending doesn't even make logical sense, and if nonsense is now accepted as valid then I *am* in the wrong industry. *This is Not a Love Song* is a calculated experiment to see if we can get away with making films we believe in which push the boundaries of cinema just a tiny bit, and if it doesn't work then perhaps there isn't room in the marketplace for my kind of writing. You can't make people distribute your films if audiences don't want to watch them – although I think audiences *do* want to watch them but aren't being given the chance. Everyone who saw *The Darkest Light* found the film very moving, but hardly anyone did see it. It was only in cinemas for two weeks and that was it: three years of work just gone. I won't keep doing that. It's a waste of time and creativity. I'd rather go off and be a potter instead.

Index

A NOTE ON THE EDITOR

Alistair Owen is the editor of *Smoking in Bed: Conversations with Bruce Robinson*, also published by Bloomsbury, and is currently working on a book of interviews with playwright, screenwriter and director Christopher Hampton, for Faber.

A NOTE ON THE TYPE

The text of this book is set in Linotype Sabon, named after the type founder, Jacques Sabon. It was designed by Jan Tschichold and jointly developed by Linotype, Monotype and Stempel, in response to a need for a typeface to be available in identical form for mechanical hot metal composition and hand composition using foundry type.

Tschichold based his design for Sabon roman on a fount engraved by Garamond, and Sabon italic on a fount by Granjon. It was first used in 1966 and has proved an enduring modern classic.